# PSYCHIATRIC JUSTICE

Other books by Thomas Szasz

PAIN AND PLEASURE

THE MYTH OF MENTAL ILLNESS

LAW, LIBERTY, AND PSYCHIATRY

THE ETHICS OF PSYCHOANALYSIS

THE MANUFACTURE OF MADNESS

IDEOLOGY AND INSANITY

THE AGE OF MADNESS (Ed.)

THE SECOND SIN

CEREMONIAL CHEMISTRY

HERESIES

KARL KRAUS AND THE SOUL-DOCTORS

SCHIZOPHRENIA

THE THEOLOGY OF MEDICINE

PSYCHIATRIC SLAVERY

THE MYTH OF PSYCHOTHERAPY

SEX BY PRESCRIPTION

THE THERAPEUTIC STATE

INSANITY

# PSYCHIATRIC JUSTICE

Thomas Szasz

SYRACUSE UNIVERSITY PRESS

Syracuse University Press Edition 1988

97 96 95 94 93 92 91 90 89 88   6 5 4 3 2 1

The paper used in this publication meets the
minimum requirements of American National
Standard for Information Sciences—Permanence of
Paper for Printed Library Materials, ANSI Z39.48-
1984. ∞™

**Library of Congress Cataloging-in-Publication-Data**

Szasz, Thomas Stephen, 1920–
  Psychiatric justice.

  Reprint, with new afterword. Originally published:
New York: Macmillan, 1965.
  Includes index.
    1. Insanity—Jurisprudence—United States.
  2. Competency to stand trial—United States.
  3. Forensic psychiatry—United States.
  4. Criminal liability—United States.   I. Title.
KF9242.S94   1988                    345.73'04      88-31859
ISBN 0-8156-0231-6 (alk. paper)      347.3054

Manufactured in the United States of America

¶ For the simpler among us the evil of our times can be defined by its effects rather than by its causes. The evil is the State, whether a police state or a bureaucratic state.*

¶ [The rebel] humiliates no one. The freedom he claims, he claims for all; the freedom he refuses, he forbids everyone to enjoy. He is not only the slave against the master, but also the man against the world of master and slave. Therefore, thanks to rebellion, there is something more in history than the relation between mastery and servitude.†

¶ [T]he man of today . . . needs a society based on reason and not on the anarchy into which he has been plunged by his own pride and the excessive powers of the State.‡

---

* Albert Camus, "Why Spain?" (1948), in *Resistance, Rebellion, Death*, translated from the French, and with an Introduction by Justin O'Brien (New York: Alfred A. Knopf, 1961), p. 78.

† Albert Camus, *The Rebel: An Essay on Man in Revolt* (1951), translated by Anthony Bower (New York: Vintage Books, 1956), p. 284.

‡ Albert Camus, "Reflections on the Guillotine" (1957), in *Resistance, Rebellion, Death*, p. 231.

# CONTENTS

# PREFACE TO THE FIRST EDITION

"In all criminal prosecutions the accused shall enjoy the right to a speedy and public trial, by an impartial jury of the State and district wherein the crime shall have been committed. . . ." So begins the Sixth Amendment to the Constitution of the United States of America.

Is this right unconditional, like the right to "life, liberty and the pursuit of happiness . . ." or is it conditional, a privilege, like the opportunity to practice medicine or law?

Framed this way, the question may seem foolish; nearly everyone will say that the right to trial is more elementary than the right to be a barber or a professor. Yet, as the material assembled in this book shows, there is a widespread and increasing tendency in the United States to regard standing trial for a crime as a complex social performance, not unlike an occupation. Only some persons are considered capable of doing so; many others are deemed unfit. Who are these people? And on what grounds are they disqualified? Briefly stated, they are those termed "mentally ill," barred on the grounds of psychiatric criteria. But this is no real answer; it is rather a series of words strung together to look like a sentence. The question is: How do we determine who is fit to stand trial and who is not? And what happens to those declared unfit? These are some of the questions I try to answer in this book.

Are these questions important? Does this subject deserve the attention of the general public, or is it a special problem that concerns only the district attorneys, judges, and forensic psychiatrists who must implement the law? The answer we give reflects the image of the social order we envisage: It may be one in which informed public opinion plays a decisive role—or in which all significant judgments are formed by experts. With the steady expansion of population and the increasing complexity of our artificial environment, democracy may easily become technocracy. Moreover, if the technocrats are benevolent or can convince the people that they are, why should anyone complain?

The vision of the perfect society, governed by a wise philosopher-king, is as fresh today as the day Plato first dreamed of it. I reject this dream—of the self-restrained, virtuous leader—as a nightmare. Instead, I cast my vote with the English and American political tradition which places its trust in the checks and balances of a constitutional, representative government.

While at first glance my subject may seem limited to forensic psychiatry, it is in fact nearly as broad as our daily life. There are many ways for the individual to come into conflict with the state: today, one of the most common is through some aspect of mental-health legislation. In the United States, growing numbers of people are constrained by psychiatric sanctions—not only from standing trial but also from driving cars, getting jobs, and in general, managing their own lives. It seems that as fast as we gain personal freedom through improved economic opportunities and lessening racial and religious discrimination, we lose it through stiffening psychiatric-social controls. Deprivation of the right to trial on the ground of alleged mental incompetence is a case in point.

Viewed in perspective, the problem discussed in this book must be considered a part of the larger problem of social controls in a modern mass society. Regardless of their moral or political outlook, most men today agree that the modern state is the most awesome repository of power the world has ever known. Through its numerous and vast bureaucracies, such a state has the power to influence the life of the individual as never before. Is this good or bad? It is not easy to tell.

In the United States there are two general views on this question. The Liberal holds that only through the modern state can many men, not just a few, attain economic and political freedom; he therefore regards the state as his friend. The Conservative holds that only through the modern state can many men, not just a few, be reduced to abject slavery; he therefore regards the state as his enemy.

In my view, both are right. As I read the lessons of recent history, the modern state has been responsible for both unparalleled good and unparalleled evil in the twentieth century.

Of one thing we can be certain: Communist or capitalist, the state will not wither away. The individual might. This is why the individual always needed, and still needs, more protection than the state.

Like almost everything in the world, psychiatry may be used for various purposes. In this book, I discuss certain uses of psychiatry by the state. My aim is to demonstrate how the modern state may use psychiatry as a weapon against the individual citizen. The involuntary pretrial psychiatric examination of persons accused of crime is such a weapon. The individual subjected to such an examination is imprisoned first and tried later, if at all. To be sure, as we might expect in this age of humanitarian inhumanism, we do not refer to this procedure in plain English as imprisonment without trial. We call it psychiatric hospitalization because of unfitness to stand trial.

Such "hospitalization" is not hospitalization but imprisonment. Usually, it is actuated not by the defendant's unfitness to stand trial but by his social deviance and helplessness. I contend that this practice is a travesty on justice and healing, and ought to be repudiated by both the legal and the medical professions.

THOMAS S. SZASZ, M.D.

Syracuse, New York
March 15, 1965

# ACKNOWLEDGMENTS

I wish to thank Professor George J. Alexander and Dr. Kenneth Barney for reading various drafts of the manuscript and offering many helpful suggestions; the Foundations' Fund for Research in Psychiatry for a grant which partially supported this work; the staff of the Library of the State University of New York, Upstate Medical Center in Syracuse, and Mrs. Evalena Dunn, Assistant Librarian, College of Law Library, Syracuse University, for unstinting aid in obtaining references; the authors, editors, and publishers of the works from which I have quoted for permission to reproduce copyrighted material (the sources are fully identified in the footnote references); Mrs. Arthur Ecker for conscientious editorial assistance; and, once again, my secretary, Mrs. Margaret Bassett, for devoted and inestimable help in connection with all phases of preparing and writing this book.

# PSYCHIATRIC JUSTICE

# 1 INCOMPETENCE TO STAND TRIAL: DIAGNOSIS OR STRATEGY?

¶ The welfare of the people in particular has always been the alibi of tyrants, and it provides the further advantage of giving the servants of tyranny a good conscience.*

## THE NEED FOR THE CONCEPT OF COMPETENCE TO STAND TRIAL

The criminal law of England and of the United States regards law enforcement as a contest or game. The individual accused of breaking the law is pitted against society charged with enforcing it. The relationship between accuser and accused is, however, carefully regulated by rules equally binding on each.

This is essentially a sportsmanlike view of the judicial process. As hunting deer with a machine gun would be slaughter, not sport—so hunting down a person accused of crime with physical and mental torture would be persecution, not law enforcement. As fairness is indispensable to games, so due process is indispensable to the criminal law of a free society. Thus denial of due process has been defined as "the failure to observe that fundamental fairness essential to the very concept of justice."†

The reasons for this emphasis on fairness and due process are easy to understand. A game played unfairly is, in a sense, not a game at all. For a contest to be a fair en-

---

*—Albert Camus, "Homage to an Exile" (1955), in *Resistance, Rebellion, Death,* p. 101.
† *People* v. *Leyra,* 98 N.E. 2d 553, 559 (1951).

counter, there must be an element of uncertainty about the outcome: both contestants must have a chance to win —and to lose.

The idea of competence to stand trial or the lack of it arises from this view of the judicial process. It happens sometimes that a person accused of crime cannot participate effectively in his defense. For example, he may have been shot in a hold-up and be recovering from his wounds in a hospital; or, he may be disabled by an acute attack of lobar pneumonia or a recent myocardial infarction. It would clearly be unfair for the prosecution and the court to schedule and hold a trial in such cases. Therefore, if a defendant so disabled requests postponement of his trial on the ground that he is physically unfit to defend himself properly, a delay will be granted until he recovers.

Inevitably the notion that there are diseases not only of the body but also of the mind led to efforts to extend this principle to so-called mental illnesses as well.* The purpose of this book is to describe some of the results of these efforts.

Our first task must be to clarify the concept of mental (or psychiatric) competence to stand trial. It is tempting to conceive of mental competence on the analogy of physical competence. Up to a point, the analogy is useful. For example, it is likely that a businessman charged with income tax evasion, whose wife and children were killed in an accident a week before his trial, would, if he asked for it, be granted a postponement of his trial, on the ground that he was too upset to participate effectively in his defense. In this respect, a physical condition like pneumonia and a mental condition like depression are comparable disabilities. Were this all there was to the problem

---

* See Thomas S. Szasz, *The Myth of Mental Illness: Foundations of a Theory of Personal Conduct* (New York: Hoeber-Harper, 1961) and *Law, Liberty, and Psychiatry: An Inquiry Into the Social Uses of Mental Health Practices* (New York: Macmillan, 1963).

of mental competence to stand trial, the problems described in this book could never arise.

The differences between what is generally understood by the terms "bodily illness" and "mental illness" are so great that procedures built on similarities between them are bound to suffer. This has indeed happened, and here is how.

In the case of a defendant suffering from a medical illness—for example, some type of heart disease—the question of whether he is capable of standing trial is a problem for himself, his defense counsel, and his personal physician. Standing trial may be a dangerous strain for him, but a postponement may be an equally great, or even greater, strain. Clearly, the defendant, with his agents, must decide whether or not to request a postponement on the ground of disability. This is obvious; who else could do so? It would be absurd for the prosecutor to ask the court for this postponement. That is not his business.

This is not so for mental illness. It is unusual for a defendant to plead mental incompetence to stand trial, and for good reason: doing so would be more likely to harm him than help him. (The reasons for this will become clear later on.) I shall therefore not discuss this situation.

In the vast majority of these cases, it is not the defendant or his agents who raise this issue, but the prosecution or the court. This is justified on two basically different grounds.

The first argument of those who support the present practice—of allowing the prosecution to question the defendant's mental competence to stand trial and to instigate the court to order a pretrial psychiatric examination of him—is based on their view of the nature of "mental illness." Though medically ill individuals usually realize the nature of their condition and seek help for it, mentally sick persons, because of the very character of their sickness, are unaware of it and do not seek help for it. Hence others must act in their behalf. In this way the district attorney assumes a dual role: to prosecute the accused for the offenses with which he is charged, and to protect him from the mental illness from which he is suspected to suffer. A defendant may be able to protect himself from a district attorney who is his enemy, but not from one who claims to be his friend and whose claim is honored by the courts. (To be sure, in Anglo-American law the prosecutor is not—or is not supposed to be— simply the defendant's antagonist. In addition to prosecuting persons accused of crime, the district attorney is also expected to protect the integrity of the judicial process, and hence the interests of the defendant.)

The second argument justifying this practice is based on the premise that there are two kinds of criminal acts: normal and abnormal. (This is a variant of the notion that there are two types of offender: mentally healthy and mentally sick.) Thus, going through a red light or speeding would be considered normal offenses; sexual exhibitionism or murdering a member of one's family would be considered abnormal offenses. According to this view, only persons accused of ordinary offenses should be tried before a lay jury; those accused of "peculiar" offenses cannot be properly judged by laymen in a courtroom and, instead, should be examined and judged by psychiatrists in a mental hospital.

My purpose in this book is to examine the common practice—well accepted by jurists, psychiatrists, and the public—of allowing the prosecution and the court to question the mental competence of a defendant. They are permitted to do this, moreover, not only against the objections of the defendant himself, but also against the objections of his relatives, defense lawyers, and personal psychiatrists. As a result a person accused of crime may be declared mentally unfit to stand trial and committed to a mental institution until he recovers his competence to stand trial. Such commitment is for an indefinite period. It is often, in effect, a life sentence.

The law, of course, regards mentally ill persons unfit to determine their own best interests. Hence they must not be permitted to act on their own behalf, but instead must be provided with "guardians" to protect them. This view is often false, and often also wicked, but at least it is clear and understandable.

But who is the proper guardian of the mentally ill? This question receives a curious answer in those cases in which the person alleged to be mentally ill is also charged with crime. Here the suspicions of the law about mental competence are extended to all those the accused himself considers his agents or friends. Thus, the prosecution and its psychiatrists are allowed to overrule not only the defendant's wish to stand trial, but also the wishes of his relatives, defense attorneys, and personal psychiatrists. In effect, the law regards the district attorney as a better guardian of the defendant-patient's interests than the defense attorney. The reason for this is not clear. But the consequences for the defendant are painfully obvious.

## DEFINITIONS OF INCOMPETENCE TO STAND TRIAL

It is possible to take any idea and give it a purely semantic definition. However, when words are rich in meaning—like *love* or *democracy*—such definitions are useless. Instead, we must examine the actual uses of such concepts.

The verbal definition of competence to stand trial is simple. A person accused of crime is mentally fit to stand trial only if he understands the charges against him, the nature and object of the proceedings, and can assist counsel in his defense. In New York state, for example, the accused is considered incompetent to stand trial if he is "in such a state of insanity that he is incapable of understanding the charge or proceeding or of making his defense."*

Much of what follows in this book may be regarded as an effort to replace this purely semantic, and rather worthless, definition of incompetence to stand trial with one based on actual usage.

The idea of competence (or incompetence) to stand trial may be used in two basically different modes. The abuse of this concept and the resulting confusion are caused by failure—sometimes deliberate, sometimes unwitting—to distinguish between these two linguistic modes.

In other words, the assertion that a man cannot stand trial—or cannot play the fiddle—may have two meanings. It can be a statement of fact: Bill may not know how to play the fiddle. Or it may be a recommendation: Bill may know how to play the fiddle—perhaps not very well—and we may be telling Bob, who needs a violinist for his orchestra, not to hire Bill.

*Factual assertions* are either true or false. *Strategic recommendations* are either fair or unfair, justifiable or unjustifiable. They are also helpful to some, harmful to others.

Let us now examine the concept of incompetence to stand trial, first as factual assertion, then as strategic move in the game of law enforcement.†

* *Mental Illness and Due Process,* Report and Recommendations on Admission to Mental Hospitals under New York Law, by the Special Committee to Study Commitment Procedures of the Association of the Bar of the City of New York, in cooperation with The Cornell Law School, (Ithaca, N.Y.: Cornell University Press, 1962), pp. 222-23.

† See Thomas S. Szasz, "Criminal Insanity: Fact or Strategy," *The New Republic,* November 21, 1964, pp. 19-22.

*Incompetence to Stand Trial:*
*A Judgment of Inability to Perform*

In every social situation the participants must possess certain kinds of knowledge and skills. This enables the "player" to engage in the particular "game" he is called upon to play.

Ordinarily, we take many kinds of competence for granted. However, we must note that to engage even in such simple acts as buying a theater ticket, taking care of one's automobile, or paying the gas bill, a person needs certain kinds of information and social skills. More complicated performances—such as laying bricks, playing tennis, or composing music—require more sophisticated skills.

Similarly, standing trial for a crime calls for a certain kind of performance: The accused must defend himself against the charges brought against him (if this is what he wants to do). It is reasonable to ask, therefore, whether a particular defendant has, or has not, the ability to stand trial. Logically, this question can mean only one thing: Can the accused perform the role required of him as defendant?

Let us carry this line of reasoning one step further. Not the defendant only, but everyone participating in a criminal trial has a role to play. The district attorney must prosecute; the jury must listen to evidence, weigh it, and reach a verdict; the judge must conduct the trial and pass sentence; and so forth. If, as a matter of principle, we do not take it for granted that the accused is capable of standing trial (even though he chooses to), why do we assume that the prosecutor, the judge, the jury, and the witnesses are capable of performing their roles adequately? This "discrimination" against the defendant seems especially illogical and arbitrary since his role is probably easier than that of most of the other participants. As our criminal laws are now written, they not only allow but actually encourage the casting of doubt upon the defendant's sanity and hence his competence to stand trial; at the same time, they do not allow the defendant to question the sanity of the prosecutor or the judge and hence their competence to participate in the same proceedings.

Nevertheless, as an abstract concept, the notion of competence to stand trial makes sense. Furthermore, it is reasonable to assert, without bothering to prove, that the ability to defend oneself in a court of law, like the ability to do anything else, must vary considerably among individuals. One would expect that a practicing lawyer or a professor of political science could defend himself against a criminal charge much better than a farmer or a laborer. The problem of assigning clear meaning to the abstract notion of competence to stand trial thus presents no special difficulties. As a concrete, practical question, however, it is an exceedingly vexing problem.

In theory it is easy to discriminate among various levels of competence, whether to stand trial, speak a foreign language, or conduct an orchestra. We can do this because "we"—as jurists, teachers, or music critics—set our own standards (or select the standards we wish to use) and judge whomever we wish (or those seeking to be judged).

In practice the task is far more difficult. This is not because we—as attorneys, psychiatrists, or judges—do not know how to judge competence. We do. But we are confronted by others, with aims and aspirations often antagonistic to ours, who base their judgments on different criteria. Thus, as a practical matter, the problem of competence to stand trial requires not logical and semantic analysis of concepts but functional analysis of social situations. We must ask such questions as: What is the standard used for judging competence to stand trial? Who has devised it? Who is implementing it? Who decides whose

competence may be called into question? What are the
consequences of declaring a defendant incompetent to
stand trial? In this book I have tried to answer these
questions, and many others as well.

There are reasonably clear criteria for judging competence in such matters as pitching baseball, removing a
brain tumor, or preparing a fine meal. Nor, as a rule, is
there doubt in these performances about who judges
whom, and why. When it comes to judging ability to stand
trial, however, we seem to be at sea, with no compass to
guide us. This is due largely to the introduction of psychiatric methods and criteria into areas where they are not
needed and do not belong. It is necessary that we understand this clearly.

The difficulty is not simply that there are no standards
for establishing whether or not a person is fit to stand
trial—although judging by the way such determinations
are made, it may well seem that such is the case. There is
a standard: A person is fit to stand trial only if he understands the charges against him, the nature of the proceedings, and can assist counsel in his defense. To be sure, this
is a purely verbal definition—but so are most definitions.
The difficulty in this case is that we have no rational,
generally accepted method for translating a legal standard
into a social act.

The law, as we have seen, provides a standard for determining competence to stand trial. On the face of it, moreover, it is a reasonable standard. The questions that now
arise are: Who will interpret the standard and how? Who
will implement it and how?

The criminal trial is, so to speak, the judge's "ball
game." Since he is the umpire, he certainly ought to know
who can and cannot play the game. If competence to stand
trial means competence to play the role of defendant—as
indeed the legal standard specifies—why cannot the judge
determine if the defendant is competent to stand trial? If

this is what the judge wishes to ascertain, why does he not try to do so in the two most direct and simplest ways possible: either by talking to the defendant or by proceeding with the trial and observing the defendant's conduct in the courtroom?

Actually, the judge does neither. Instead he delegates the task of assessing what kind of game-player the defendant is to psychiatrists. But this means that, merely because of a "suspicion" about the defendant's mental state, he is removed from the category of an ordinary human being, with whom judges can *converse*—and is placed in the category of the insane, who, having been demoted from person to patient, must be *examined* by psychiatrists. In this way, and at a single stroke, the whole procedure of determining competence to stand trial is rendered irrational, is debased morally, and is transformed into an instrument of violence against the defendant.

Furthermore, the idea that a person should have to prove to a psychiatrist that he is competent to stand trial is inconsistent with certain basic assumptions underlying morality and law in a popular democracy. While there is, perhaps, no such thing as a completely unconditional right—in a free society many rights are or ought to be very nearly unconditional. In the United States, social life is based on the fundamental premise that every adult is capable of performing a repertoire of basic social acts. This assumption is incorporated into our laws and legal system and is illustrated by the maxim "ignorance of the law is no excuse." (Whether this assumption is well founded need not concern us here. Actually, it is generally well founded, but occasionally not.)

Indeed, as a moral and legal system, our "American way of life" is characterized by the automatic acquisition of certain privileges and obligations when a person comes of age. In other words, young adults "inherit" certain rights and duties, liberties and responsibilities—without prior proof of their competence to perform their new social roles. Young men and women are free to marry and to suffer the consequences. Reaching a certain age is the sole requirement for "competence to marry." (Having to submit to a blood test before marriage and the fee for the license are not intended as tests of marital competence, nor do they perform that function.) Similarly, adults, single or married, are free to procreate; again, they, and their children, must suffer the consequences. The right to have children is not contingent upon proving competence to be a parent. (The privilege to adopt a child is, significantly, conditional upon proving precisely this ability.) The right to purchase and consume alcoholic beverages is likewise not contingent upon proving competence to avoid intoxication.

The concept of competence to stand trial must be viewed against this background. Accordingly, this idea points to a *human condition,* shared by all adults in a democratic community, rather than to an esoteric problem, the understanding of which requires legal and psychiatric sophistication. The fact that some people are more competent to stand trial than others need neither surprise nor distract us. People differ in all their abilities.

We are concerned here, first, with *social expectations:* the community expects children to be raised so that, as adults, they will be able to perform certain acts; and second, with *"unconditional" rights:* adults expect society to let them exercise certain rights. What is "the right to a speedy and public trial," guaranteed by the Sixth Amendment to the Constitution, if not a promise of such a privilege? Whether a citizen has or has not the ability to use this right, like his ability to get along with his wife or to live within his means, is his business, not the government's.

This does not imply that the government must turn a deaf ear to a disabled citizen's plight. If a person feels that he is incompetent to stand trial—or to get along with his wife, or earn a living, or perform any of a myriad of social acts necessary for human survival in a complex society—he should be able to bring his problem to the attention of appropriate authorities. And I see no reason why an enlightened people should not empower their government to provide certain kinds of assistance to people in such quandaries. But these remedial efforts would have to be clearly labeled and understood for what they were: educational and paraeducational enterprises to help people overcome interpersonal "stupidities" and acquire social skills in living. Such a definition of "help" would of course preclude the government's snooping into a citizen's private affairs and would nullify its privilege to designate certain people as needing—and hence being fit subjects for receiving, under duress if necessary—this type of assistance.

Nor does this view imply that the court must try every defendant who wants to stand trial. In principle, the judge, and perhaps even the prosecutor, may question the defendant's ability to stand trial. In practice, however, we must make certain that by so doing they benefit the defendant, not themselves. Otherwise we are likely to create a game which a contestant can win simply by getting his opponent declared incapable of playing. This is just what we have done by means of our present practices. (In Chapter 8, I offer some practical suggestions for ascertaining competence to stand trial and protecting the defendant from the abuses of our current practices.)

### Incompetence to Stand Trial: A Legal-Psychiatric Strategy

The description of men and their conduct often requires us to distinguish between two different types of communication: factual identification and strategic maneuver. The distinction between an assertion and a request expresses the same sort of difference.

For example, the sentence *The door is ajar* is an assertion; the sentence *It is drafty, please shut the door* is a request. There would be no need to dwell on this were it not possible to make a statement do the work of a request. This can be accomplished either by punctuating the message with a certain kind of vocal tone and with certain facial expressions or by placing it in a certain kind of social context.

Identification may likewise serve double duty: one factual—to identify or communicate information, the other strategic—to convince or promote action.

For example, a passport photograph serves to identify the bearer of the document. When a photograph of the same person appears on a poster pinned to the wall at a post office with the legend WANTED printed on it in large letters, it serves to bring about the man's arrest. The difference between these two modes of communication is clear.

A more difficult situation is presented when a seemingly factual identification is used for strategic communication. This can usually be inferred from the context of the message. For example, an applicant for life insurance may be asked if he has ever suffered from tuberculosis. Ostensibly the question requires a factual answer; actually its purpose is to uncover whether the applicant has had tuberculosis and, if he has, to alert the insurance company to this fact. Similarly, an applicant for a driver's license is asked his name, address, age—and whether he has ever been in a mental hospital; though these questions resemble one another in grammatical form, they differ in strategic import.

The most complicated situation is one in which factual identification is consciously and deliberately used for a strategic purpose but where this use is explicitly denied. When a person in authority employs this tactic against an inferior (in the sense of less powerful) person, he places his victim in a very unhappy position. It has been suggested that this type of communicational tactic, employed by a parent against his child, drives the child crazy—that is, makes him behave in a schizophrenic way.*

No doubt this is hardly a friendly way to relate to another person. As a matter of fact, it is much like attacking a man at gunpoint, claiming to be saving his life. This example is too simple, however. It is difficult to disguise the use of dangerous weapons and to obscure the harmful consequences of such acts. In contrast, communications are often subtle acts. Ostensibly helpful communications can easily be used destructively. Psychiatric practice abounds with such occurrences. The particular act which forms the main subject of this book is an example. A person accused of crime wants to stand trial but the district attorney, charged with prosecuting him, declares that he is too "sick" to do so and should therefore be "saved" from this ordeal; instead, he ought to go to a psychiatric "hospital" for "diagnosis" and "treatment" so that, at a later date, he will be better able to stand trial. This complex communication and the social acts based upon it cannot be understood except as the strategic use (to discredit and destroy) of a seemingly factual assertion (that the defendant is incompetent to stand trial).

Vainly then do we search for "objective" or "rational" psychiatric criteria of competence to stand trial. In doing so, we merely obscure the issues and befuddle ourselves. The assertion that a defendant is mentally unfit to stand trial is *always* a strategic ploy. (This does not mean that it may not also be a true, factual statement.)

If the defendant makes this claim, it is a strategic move on his part, designed to place him in a better position than if he were tried.

If the prosecutor (or the court) makes this claim, it is a

* Gregory Bateson and others, "Toward a Theory of Schizophrenia," *Behavioral Science, 1:* 251–264, 1956.

strategic move on his part, designed to place him in a better position than if the defendant were tried.

As in all legal contests, power plays a crucial role in this kind of communicational ploy. Indeed, because it has long been recognized that in a criminal trial the government is far more powerful than the accused, the defendant must be protected from this handicap lest he always lose, irrespective of the merits of his case. English and American legal tradition and practice reflect a consistent effort to right this power imbalance, so that what the defendant lacks in power is made up in a kind of preferential treatment by the rules of the game (the law). Thus, a person may be tried only once for any particular crime. If the prosecution cannot obtain a conviction on the first trial (excluding a mistrial), it has lost the "game." The convicted defendant, on the other hand, can appeal his conviction not just once, but many times. Also, the jury must find that the defendant is guilty "beyond a reasonable doubt"; uncertainty must be resolved in favor of the defendant. These and other provisions of our criminal law reflect and uphold a deeply felt conviction about "fair play": since the contest between the government and the citizen is uneven, the individual must be provided certain advantages to achieve a better balance between the players.

Because psychiatric-legal strategies are not considered destructive for the defendant, and because there is no long-established legal tradition for their use, they lack such safeguards for the individual confronted by the state. The government can thus move, not once but many times, to have the defendant incriminated as mentally incompetent to stand trial. And if there is doubt about the accused person's mental status, it is resolved in favor of the government, not the individual: the "patient" is declared unfit to stand trial and is committed to a mental hospital.*

* See Thomas S. Szasz, *Law, Liberty, and Psychiatry*, especially pp. 59–66 and 162–68.

## THE PSYCHIATRIST'S JUDGMENT OF THE DEFENDANT'S ABILITY TO STAND TRIAL: FACTUAL OR STRATEGIC?

Those who look with favor on the psychiatrist's participation in the criminal trial hold that his judgment is, in
general, scientific and professional—in a word, *factual*.
Those who disapprove of such practices hold that the psychiatrist's judgment is, in these situations, moral and partisan—in a word, *strategic*. Which of these views is closer
to the truth? The information and reasoning presented in
this book are offered to enable the reader to answer this
question for himself.

It should suffice here to summarize the thesis of this
chapter. The jurists, psychiatrists, and others who favor
the psychiatric screening of defendants suspected of being
mentally sick, to determine whether they are mentally
competent to stand trial, make a number of assumptions
(which I consider invalid):

1. Mental illness, or at least some types of mental illness, deprives the patient of his "fitness" to stand trial.

2. Only those "mentally fit" should be allowed to stand
trial.

3. Mental hospitalization—even involuntary hospitalization in an institution in which no specific "treatment"
is available for the inmates—is likely to restore patients to
mental health or at least to improved capacity to stand
trial.

The proponents of this view compare defendants awaiting trial with sick persons awaiting surgery. It is a fact that
often people are so sick—dehydrated, anemic, and so forth
—that they are unfit to undergo a surgical operation; were
they operated upon in such a condition, their chances of
survival would be slim. The proper procedure is to pre-
scribe a course of preoperative therapy for them, to in-

crease their resistance to the stress of surgery; after receiving intravenous fluids, blood, and perhaps other medicinal agents, the physician may declare the patient ready for surgery.

Those who wish to apply psychiatry to the law regard the defendant suspected of mental disorder in the same way. If the accused is considered "mentally sick" he is declared unfit for the trauma of standing trial. Just as the very sick patient is given preoperative treatment, such a defendant is subjected to "psychiatric therapy" (usually consisting of involuntary mental hospitalization), so that, at a later date, he will be able to stand trial.

The opponents of involuntary pretrial psychiatric examination of defendants also make a number of assumptions (which I consider valid):

1. Competence to stand trial varies among people.

2. The relation between so-called mental illness and competence to stand trial is uncertain and generally irrelevant to the fundamental aims of the criminal law.

3. The right to trial is not and should not be contingent on meeting certain criteria of mental health; it is essentially absolute or unconditional.

4. The criminal trial is an adversary proceeding in which the prosecutor is the defendant's antagonist, not his therapist.

Our present practice of allowing the district attorney to coerce unwilling defendants to submit to pretrial psychiatric examinations resembles the plight of the Negro resident of Mississippi who desires to vote, rather than the problem of the debilitated preoperative patient who requires surgical treatment. To undergo an operation is not a right; to do so, one must obtain the cooperation of a surgeon, who will always set conditions for his participation (these may include not only building up the patient's health but also being paid for his services). However, to vote is a right. Or is it?

In Mississippi, voting is not an unconditional right: residents of the state must register and pass a "test" which determines whether or not they are competent to vote. Surely here is a better analogy to determining competence to stand trial. In Mississippi, the standards of voting competence are poorly defined and capriciously interpreted. Most whites qualify; most Negroes do not. Thus the situation of a Mississippi Negro wishing to vote and being found unfit to do so is truly comparable to that of a defendant wishing to stand trial and being found unfit to do so. Both are tested and judged by their adversaries.

Opposition to the currently well-established practice of allowing the prosecution (or the court) to raise the question of the defendant's competence to stand trial rests on a repudiation of the analogy between the courtroom and the hospital; the defendant is not a "patient," the prosecutor and his psychiatrists are not his "doctors." The relationship between the defendant and the state (and its representatives) is antagonistic, not cooperative. The attempt to make it appear cooperative—such as forcing the defendant to submit to psychiatric examination by agents of the state—is simply a strategic maneuver by the government to render its opponent impotent. It is a symptom of despotism—of the worst kind.

# 2 LAWS PERTAINING TO THE MENTAL COMPETENCE OF THE DEFENDANT

¶ Every ambiguity, every misunderstanding, leads to death; clear language and simple words are the only salvation from this death. It is worth noting that the language peculiar to totalitarian doctrines is always a scholastic or administrative language.*

Earlier I spoke of the double incrimination of a person as criminal and as mental patient. This is effected whenever an accused person is considered mentally unfit to stand trial and is ordered by the court, against his will, to submit to pretrial psychiatric examination (usually while confined in a mental hospital). Most jurisdictions in the United States countenance such double incrimination. I shall present the relevant statutes for three: New York state, the District of Columbia, and the federal courts.

## IN THE STATE OF NEW YORK

There are several statutes in this state pertinent to the issue of a defendant's sanity, some in the Code of Criminal Procedure, others in the Mental Hygiene Law.

### Orders for Examination

Chapter V of the Code of Criminal Procedure is entitled "Inquiry into the Insanity of the Defendant, Before

* Albert Camus, *The Rebel*, p. 283.

37

or During the Trial, or After Conviction." Section 658 states:

> *Court order for examination as to sanity of defendant*—If at any time before final judgment it shall appear to the court having jurisdiction of the person of a defendant indicted for a felony or a misdemeanor that there is reasonable ground for believing that such defendant is in such a state of idiocy, imbecility or insanity that he is incapable of understanding the charge, indictment or proceedings or of making his defense, or if the defendant makes a plea of insanity to the indictment, instead of proceeding with the trial, the court, upon its own motion, or that of the district attorney or the defendant, may in its discretion order such defendant to be examined to determine the question of his sanity.

Section 870 further states:

> *Order for examination as to sanity of a defendant*—If at any time it shall appear to a court or magistrate having jurisdiction of a defendant charged with a felony or misdemeanor but not under indictment therefor, or charged with an offense which is not a crime, or in the city of New York charged with a misdemeanor in a case where an information has not been filed by the district attorney, that there is reasonable ground to believe that such defendant is in such a state of idiocy, imbecility or insanity that he is incapable of understanding the charge or proceeding or of making his defense, the court or magistrate upon his own motion or that of the district attorney or of the defendant may in his discretion order such defendant to be examined to determine the question of his sanity.

These laws are buttressed by statutes that eliminate the need for classifying certain alleged offenders as "defendants." Instead they may be treated as suspected mental patients and subjected to confinement on this ground alone.

Where there are receiving hospitals for psychiatric patients, a person may be sent to one of these institutions for sixty days under Sections 81 (a) and 81 (5) of the Mental Hygiene Law. All that is necessary to effect such an admission is the judgment of the hospital's director that the suspected patient is "in immediate need of care and treatment or observation." For example, the police may bring a person to such a hospital on their own initiative, or they may be ordered to do so by a district attorney or magistrate. The patient cannot resist such psychiatric detention. Once incarcerated, he may try to obtain the services of an attorney who may attempt to secure the patient's release on a writ of habeas corpus. Such effort, however, is likely to prove fruitless.

Persons may also be detained in receiving hospitals in New York City and in Erie County under Section 81 (5) of the Mental Hygiene Law. This states that "Any person, apparently mentally ill, and conducting himself in a manner which in a sane person would be disorderly, may be arrested by any peace officer and confined in some safe and comfortable place until the question of his sanity be determined."

What actually happens under the provisions of this section is that information is laid before a magistrate alleging that a person appears to be mentally ill. "The magistrate must then issue a warrant directed to a peace officer commanding the officer to arrest the patient and bring him before the magistrate's court which issued the warrant. If, upon arraignment, the person appears to the magistrate to be mentally ill, the magistrate must certify him to the care and custody of a receiving hospital for not more than sixty days, until the question of such person's mental illness is determined. . . . A peace officer in New York City or in Erie County often has discretion on whether or not to seek a warrant authorized by this section. Instead he may, as in other parts of the state, simply arrest a person appearing to be mentally ill and behaving in a disorderly manner and arraign him for disorderly conduct. The magistrate then has power to commit him to a receiving hospital for observation under Section 870 of the Code of Criminal Procedure (criminal order) or under Section 81 (2) of the Mental Hygiene Law (civil order). The criminal order procedure is often used in New York City."*

Minor offenses or disorderly conduct (a notoriously ill-defined offense) may thus be used as a pretext for the involuntary mental hospitalization of a person for a sixty-day period. This is in effect a sixty-day sentence to a mental hospital, authorized by a *criminal order,* but without trial. The impression that such an order is a kind of sentence—although one carried out without even legal formalism, much less legal substance—is confirmed by what happens if, after the sixty-day observation, the accused is certified for indefinite commitment to a state hospital. In such a case, if the complaint charges an offense or a misdemeanor, "such commitment is deemed a final disposition of the offense charged."†

*The Pretrial Psychiatric Examination*

If the defendant is charged with an offense more serious than a misdemeanor, and if the court or the district attorney also suspect that he is mentally incapable of standing trial, his fate varies, depending on the part of the state in which he is apprehended. In New York City, such a defendant must be examined by two psychiatrists designated by the director of the Division of Psychiatry of the city's Department of Hospitals. These psychiatrists must

* *Mental Illness and Due Process,* Report and Recommendations on Admission to Mental Hospitals under New York Law, by the Special Committee to Study Commitment Procedures of the Association of the Bar of the City of New York, in cooperation with The Cornell Law School (Ithaca, N.Y.: Cornell University Press, 1962), p. 96.
† *Ibid.,* p. 221.

be members of the staff of the above-named Division. Outside New York City, this examination must be made by two psychiatrists qualified as specialists in psychiatry by the state Department of Mental Hygiene and designated by the superintendent of any public mental hospital.

Examinations may be made in the jail in which the defendant is detained or, if the hospital director so recommends, the court may send the defendant to a mental hospital designated by the director for not more than sixty days "for the observation and examination" (Code of Criminal Procedure, Section 660). In New York City, the examination is usually conducted in the prison wards of Bellevue, Kings County, or Elmhurst hospitals. Outside New York City, it is usually conducted in the security wards of the state hospital nearest the court of jurisdiction.

## Confinement of Defendants Found Unable to Stand Trial

If the psychiatrists appointed by the court conclude that the defendant is incapable of standing trial, and if the court agrees, the court's disposition of the defendant will depend on the place where the court sits, the nature of the charge, and the status of the criminal action at the time of the examination.

1. When the charge is an offense or a nonindictable misdemeanor (that is, lawbreaking of a minor type), the defendant is committed by civil proceeding under Section 174 of the Mental Hygiene Law. Thus the defendant, now called patient, will be sent to a civil mental hospital of the Department of Mental Hygiene. This certification for an indefinite period of mental hospitalization and treatment is considered the final disposition of the criminal charge against the patient.

2. When the charge is an indictable crime in which no indictment has been returned, or, in New York City, when it is a charge of a misdemeanor on which no information

has been filed, the court handling the certification "may commit the defendant to any appropriate state institution of the Department of Correction or the Department of Mental Hygiene" (Code of Criminal Procedure, Section 872). Such a defendant may be committed either to a civil mental hospital or to a hospital for the criminally insane such as Matteawan State Hospital (which is under the jurisdiction and control of the Department of Correction). It is to be noted that such a person, starting with his role as innocent citizen, may be placed successively in the roles of defendant accused of crime and mental illness, suspected mental patient undergoing psychiatric examination, and finally, inmate in a facility of the state Department of Correction—all against his will and without benefit of trial. A sanity hearing before a judge is deemed sufficient guarantee of the defendant's civil liberties. The courts (in New York State) have held specifically that a jury trial is not a constitutional requirement in determining the issue of insanity rendering a person incapable of standing trial.[*]

Inasmuch as the court has discretion whether to commit such a defendant to a civil mental hospital or to a hospital for the criminally insane, the question arises as to what determines its judgment. According to the Cornell study, the court's decision is based not on the need to guard the defendant's civil rights, nor on the desire to provide him with the best psychiatric care available, but rather on the wish to save money for the county:

When a defendant is certified to a civil hospital his maintenance, care, and treatment while confined in the hospital must be paid for by the county from which he was committed. The county incurs no such expense when a defendant is committed to Matteawan. Several district attorneys told our staff that they make very sure, in all cases involving an indictable crime, that the defendant will be committed to Matteawan in

[*] *Ibid.*, p. 228.

order to avoid this expense to their county. One prosecutor remarked that the requirement of payment for care of a defendant in a civil hospital puts an unfair burden on a county.*

We must remember, however, that this disposition is applied to persons who have never been tried and hence are, in our system of jurisprudence, presumed innocent. To confine them in a facility of the Department of Correction is therefore to inflict harm on them and to stigmatize them even more than if they had been committed to a civil hospital. In addition, incarceration at Matteawan creates the impression that the inmate is dangerous, more dangerous than if he were confined in a state hospital. It is clear that mental patients become identified by the place of confinement and the length of time spent there. Hence, their commitment to Matteawan rather than to a civil hospital is likely to result not only in harsher treatment, but in longer punishment (confinement) as well.

3. When the charge is an indictable crime for which an indictment has been returned, or, in New York City, when it is a misdemeanor on which an information has been filed, the court handling the commitment *must* certify the defendant to Matteawan (Code of Criminal Procedure, Section 785 [3]). Thus, despite possible extenuating circumstances or therapeutic indications, the court in which the indictment or information is pending has no discretion to order certification to a civil hospital. In practice, this harsh and inflexible rule is often mitigated. The staff of the Cornell study found that "when a defendant is informed against in the Court of Special Sessions for a misdemeanor and he is found too ill to stand trial, the district attorney will invariably discharge the defendant on his own recognizance so that the Supreme Court may acquire jurisdiction to certify him to a civil hospital."†

* *Ibid.*, pp. 231–32.
† *Ibid.*, p. 233.

## IN THE DISTRICT OF COLUMBIA

Chapter 3 of the District of Columbia Code is entitled "Insane Criminals." Section 24-301 states:

*Commitment of persons of unsound mind to the District of Columbia General Hospital—Certification to the Court— Acquittal by jury on grounds of insanity—Confinement in a mental institution—Conditions for release after confinement —Conditional release—Expenses—Writ of habeas corpus— Inconsistent provisions of Federal Statutes superseded.*

(a) Whenever a person is arrested, indicted, charged by information, or is charged in the juvenile court of the District of Columbia, for or with an offense and, prior to the expiration of any period of probation, it shall appear to the court from the court's own observations, or from prima facie evidence submitted to the court, that the accused is of unsound mind or is mentally incompetent so as to be unable to understand the proceedings against him or properly to assist in his own defense, the court may order the accused committed to the District of Columbia General Hospital or other mental hospital designated by the court, for such reasonable period as the court may determine for examination and observation and for care and treatment if such is necessary by the psychiatric staff of said hospital. If, after such examination and observation, the superintendent of the hospital, in the case of a mental hospital, or the chief psychiatrist of the District of Columbia General Hospital, in the case of District of Columbia General Hospital, shall report that in his opinion the accused is of unsound mind or mentally incompetent, such report shall be sufficient to authorize the court to commit by order the accused to a hospital for the mentally ill unless the accused or the Government objects, in which event, the court, after hearing without a jury, shall make a judicial determination of the competency of the accused to stand trial. If the court shall find the accused to be then of unsound mind or mentally incompetent to stand trial, the court shall order the accused confined to a hospital for the mentally ill. . . .

(b) ....

(c) When any person tried upon an indictment or information for an offense, or tried in the juvenile court of the District of Columbia for an offense, is acquitted solely on the ground that he was insane at the time of its commission, that fact shall be set forth by the jury in their verdict.

(d) If any person tried upon an indictment or information for an offense, or tried in the juvenile court of the District of Columbia for an offense, is acquitted solely on the ground that he was insane at the time of its commission, the court shall order such person to be confined in a hospital for the mentally ill. . . .

It must be noted that these laws operate in a jurisdiction where the Durham Rule governs. According to this rule, enunciated in 1954, "an accused is not criminally responsible if his unlawful act was the product of mental disease or mental defect." Since this decision resulted in an immediate and steadily growing increase in the number of persons acquitted by reason of insanity in the District of Columbia (see pp. 51–54), Congress passed a law in 1955 requiring the mandatory commitment of such defendants (Section 24:301 [d]).

In sum, there are four interrelated psychiatric-legal provisions and tactics which interfere with the defendant's right to a fair and speedy trial in the District of Columbia. They are:

1. The Durham Rule governing the relation between "mental illness" and criminal responsibility.

2. The automatic commitment clause of Section 24:301.

3. The criminal court's power to commit, rather than try, an individual brought before it, even though the defendant has not been declared mentally incompetent to stand trial. (In *Williams* v. *Overholser*,* the U.S. Court of Appeals for the District of Columbia Circuit declared this maneuver improper. The Appeals Court held that

* *Williams* v. *Overholser*, 259 F. 2d 175 (1958).

the criminal commitment power of the trial court was limited to cases involving lack of competency to stand trial.)

4. The option of the prosecution to foist a plea of "not guilty by reason of insanity" on an unwilling defendant, and so secure his commitment to St. Elizabeths Hospital. (In *Lynch* v. *Overholser,** the Supreme Court struck down this abridgment of the defendant's right to choose his own defense strategy. See Chapter 7.)

These interferences are additional to the practice common in the District of Columbia, the federal courts, the New York state courts, and the courts of many other jurisdictions—the right of the court and of the prosecution to raise the question of the defendant's mental competence to stand trial and through this means to deny him the right to trial and effect his psychiatric incarceration for an indeterminate period.

## IN THE FEDERAL COURTS

Chapter 313 of the United States Code is entitled "Mental Defectives." Section 4244 states:

*Mental Incompetence After Arrest and Before Trial.*
Whenever after arrest and prior to the imposition of sentence or prior to the expiration of any period of probation the United States Attorney has reasonable cause to believe that a person charged with an offense against the United States may be presently insane or otherwise so mentally incompetent as to be unable to understand the proceedings against him or properly to assist in his own defense, he shall file a motion for a judicial determination of such mental competency of the accused, setting forth the ground for such belief with the trial court in which proceedings are pending. Upon such a motion or upon a similar motion in behalf of the accused, or upon its

* *Lynch* v. *Overholser,* 369 U.S. 705 (1962).

own motion, the court shall cause the accused, whether or not previously admitted to bail, to be examined as to his mental condition by at least one qualified psychiatrist, who shall report to the court. For the purpose of the examination the court may order the accused committed for such reasonable period as the court may determine to a suitable hospital or other facility to be designated by the court. If the report of the psychiatrist indicates a state of present insanity or such mental incompetency in the accused, the court shall hold a hearing, upon due notice, at which evidence as to the mental condition of the accused may be submitted, including that of the reporting psychiatrist, and make a finding with respect thereto. No statement made by the accused in the court of any examination into his sanity or mental competency provided for by this section, whether the examination shall be with or without the consent of the accused, shall be admitted in evidence against the accused on the issue of guilt in any criminal proceeding. A finding by the judge that the accused is mentally competent to stand trial shall in no way prejudice the accused in a plea of insanity as a defense to the crime charged; such finding shall not be introduced in evidence on that issue nor otherwise be brought to the notice of the jury.

The fate of the defendant found mentally unfit to stand trial is governed by Section 4246, which states:

*Procedure upon finding of mental incompetency.*
Whenever the trial court shall determine in accordance with Sections 4244 and 4245 of this title that an accused is or was mentally incompetent, the court may commit the accused to the custody of the Attorney General or his authorized representative, until the accused shall be mentally competent to stand trial or until the pending charges against him are disposed of according to law. . . .

As a rule, when a defendant arraigned in a federal court is suspected of being mentally ill and unfit to stand trial, he is committed—usually for a period no longer than two months—to the Medical Center of the United States Bureau of Prisons, in Springfield, Missouri, or to St. Elizabeths Hospital, in Washington, D.C. Following their examination of the accused, the psychiatrists employed by these institutions report their findings and recommendations to the court. Except when the defendant is wealthy and well-educated (which, of course, is only rarely the case), the determination made by the government psychiatrists—who are agents of the defendant's adversary—remains uncontested. Hence it tends to carry undue weight with the judge.

If the accused is adjudged mentally incompetent to stand trial, he is committed to the Medical Center at Springfield or to St. Elizabeths Hospital until he is certified mentally fit to stand trial or until the charges against him are dismissed. The noted American poet Ezra Pound, having been charged with treason but declared unfit to stand trial, was confined to St. Elizabeths Hospital for more than thirteen years. He was finally released in 1958, after the hospital authorities certified him as "incurably insane, but not dangerous," and after the government dismissed the charges against him.

## FREQUENCY OF DENIAL OF RIGHT TO TRIAL BECAUSE OF MENTAL INCOMPETENCE

What is the practical significance of these laws pertaining to the mental competence of defendants to stand trial? Are they "dead letter" statutes, like so many laws on the books? Are they rarely enforced and therefore affect but a handful of people? Or are these laws in daily use and hence of utmost importance for tens of thousands of Americans?

In other words, how often is the issue of the defendant's mental incapacity to stand trial raised by the prosecution or the court? How many individuals suspected of crime who wish to stand trial—to be exonerated or sentenced to punishment set by law—are deprived of this constitutional right?

It is often argued—rightly—that the loss of even one person's liberty without due process of law is a serious injury, not only to the individual affected but also to the society in which he lives. Still, the more often such violations of basic human rights occur and the more widely they are accepted by society—as occurred, for example, in Nazi Germany and in our own Southern states—the more grievous the offense both against the persons injured and the society in which they live.

Unfortunately, I do not possess exact information on the frequency of denial to defendants of the right to trial. Nor do I believe that such information exists. Perhaps the research now being conducted by the American Bar Foundation will supply it. The evidence available at present (summarized below) and the case material cited in Part Two make clear that this is not a rare phenomenon. Just the contrary.

## IN NEW YORK STATE

In New York state, the majority of the defendants found mentally unfit to stand trial are confined at the Matteawan State Hospital for the Criminally Insane pending further disposition of their cases. Thus, the number of defendants confined there while awaiting trial gives us an approximate idea of how many are placed in this category. At the same time, we must remember that this figure is smaller than the total number so disposed of in the courts, for some persons accused of both crime and insanity are not indicted and are committed to civil hospitals. Nor can we tell from the figures I shall cite in how many of these cases the defendant had agreed to a psychiatric disposition of his case and in how many he had not. It is safe to assume, however, that in the majority of the cases such disposition was effected against the defendant's wishes or without his knowledge and consent. This is likely to be the case in all instances of minor lawbreaking, where the penal sanction would be less than the psychiatric.

The total capacity of the Matteawan State Hospital is approximately 2000 patients. Well over half of them are confined on the ground of inability to stand trial. Here are the precise figures as of November 5, 1962, provided by the Superintendent of the hospital, W. C. Johnston, M.D.*

The total number of resident patients on that date was 2142. Of this number 1167, or 54.5 per cent, had been admitted in accordance with Section 662 (b) of the Code of Criminal Procedure. This statute specifies that if, following pretrial psychiatric examination of the defendant (Section 658 *et seq.*), "the court is of the opinion that the defendant is in such a state of idiocy, imbecility, or insanity as to be incapable of understanding the charges against him, or the proceedings, or of making his defense . . . the court shall commit the defendant to an appropriate institution of the Department of Correction."

An additional 239 patients, or 11 per cent, had been admitted in accordance with Section 872 of the Code of Criminal Procedure. This statute is similar to Section 662 (b) except that, as noted before, it applies to persons not yet indicted or against whom information has not yet been filed; if deemed incapable of standing trial, the court may commit them "to any appropriate state institution"— either to a civil state hospital or to Matteawan.

We can see how large this category of inmates is by comparing it with those confined at Matteawan after having been found "not guilty by reason of insanity": the

* I wish to thank Dr. Johnston for providing this information.

latter group constitute only one-half of one per cent of the hospital population.* In other words, for every patient found "not guilty by reason of insanity" and confined at Matteawan, there are more than one hundred confined because of mental incompetence to stand trial.

If, in a single state, there are this many defendants declared incompetent to stand trial, the total number of persons deprived of the right to trial in the country as a whole must be considerable. That this is so is borne out by comparable figures for Michigan. There, at the Ionia State Hospital, of a total patient population of 1484 in August 1960, 705 had been committed as incompetent to stand trial.†

## IN THE DISTRICT OF COLUMBIA

I do not have precise information on the frequency of denying trial to persons charged with offenses in the District of Columbia because the prosecution or the court raises the issue of the defendant's incompetence to stand trial. However, a reading of Washington newspapers gives one the impression that hardly a week passes without such an instance being reported. The assumption that this is a common occurrence is consistent with the data on the frequency of imposing the insanity defense on unwilling defendants.

Discussing this problem at the Senate Hearing on the Constitutional Rights of the Mentally Ill, A. Kenneth

* "Psychiatrists and Jurists Discuss Problems of Law and Psychiatry." *Bulletin of the New York State District Branches, American Psychiatric Association*, 6: 10 (December) 1963.

† John H. Hess and Herbert E. Thomas, "Incompetency to Stand Trial: Procedures, Results, and Problems." *American Journal of Psychiatry, 119:* 713–720 (Feb.) 1963. It is of interest to note that these authors have estimated, on the basis of past records, that "well over one-half of the individuals committed as incompetent to stand trial will spend the rest of their lives confined to the hospital" (pp. 717–18).

Pye, Professor of Law at Georgetown University Law Center in Washington, made these trenchant comments:

"Most insanity cases in the district court involve serious offenses and the assertion of the defense of insanity by a defendant which is opposed by the Government. In the Municipal Court for the District of Columbia, the situation is quite different. The maximum punishment which may be imposed for each offense is 1 year. The usual sentences are comparatively light. In this situation the Government is inclined to attempt to obtain a verdict of not guilty by reason of insanity which may result in detaining the defendant in the custody of the Government for a longer period than he could have been detained after a conviction.

"In informal interviews with the U.S. Attorney's office within the Municipal Court, it has been indicated that there have been seven cases since the first of the year [between January 1, 1961, and May 5, 1961] in which insanity defense has been foisted on an unwilling defendant. During the same period of time there have been no cases in which a defendant has asserted a defense of insanity where it has been opposed by the Government. The cases where the defendant asserts the defense of insanity are cases where the Government does not oppose it. The Government, presumably, is just as happy if he goes to St. Elizabeths for an indefinite period of time as if he is sentenced to 30 days in the District of Columbia jail."*

One case, probably included among the seven mentioned by Professor Pye, was briefly mentioned. The defendant, a young man named Jeffrey, had committed larceny and pleaded guilty. The presentence investigation

* *Constitutional Rights of the Mentally Ill;* Hearings before the Subcommittee on Constitutional Rights of the Committee of the Judiciary, United States Senate, Eighty-seventh Congress, First Session; Part 2— Criminal Aspects, May 2, 4, and 5, 1961 (Washington, D.C.: U.S. Government Printing Office, 1961), p. 709.

uncovered the fact that Jeffrey had been discharged from the Army with a diagnosis of schizophrenia. As a result, even though Jeffrey's family was willing to make restitution and even though the defendant, represented by counsel, objected, the judge committed Jeffrey for ninety days' observation to determine if he was mentally competent to stand trial. Thus he received what was in effect a ninety-day sentence, and perhaps one that would last even longer. Had he been allowed to plead guilty, he would most likely have received a brief suspended sentence and would have remained free on probation.

Since the Durham decision there has been a tremendous increase in the number of persons acquitted by reason of insanity in the District of Columbia. We may assume that in some of these cases the insanity defense was not freely chosen by the defendant. If so, in a certain proportion of these cases—exactly what proportion we do not know— the defendant was denied the right to trial.

What are the figures on the incidence of acquittals by reason of insanity in the District of Columbia? Prior to Durham (that is, to 1954), the number of persons found "not guilty by reason of insanity" in any given year was about 1 per cent of the number of cases tried in the U.S. District Court.* Sometimes it was even less than that. In 1951, for example, there were 1936 defendants, and not a single one was acquitted by reason of insanity. In 1953, 2103 persons were indicted, and only three were found not guilty by reason of insanity.†

The Durham decision, and especially the mandatory commitment law, changed this radically. In fiscal year 1957, 1.5 per cent of those tried were found "not guilty by reason of insanity"; by fiscal year 1959 the proportion had risen to 6.7 per cent; in fiscal year 1960 to 8.5 per cent; in the first half of fiscal year 1961 the proportion reached

* *Ibid.*, p. 585.
† *Ibid.*, p. 622.

14.2 per cent; and in February 1961 it rose to 25 per cent. Thus one person in four charged with crime in the District of Columbia, and tried, is punished for it by means of psychiatric, rather than penal, sanctions. An unknown proportion of these defendants—that is, those forced to plead "not guilty by reason of insanity"—would probably have received a lesser punishment had they been allowed to plead guilty.

## IN THE FEDERAL COURTS

The medical director of the Bureau of Prisons, U.S. Department of Justice, Charles E. Smith, M.D., reported recently on the implementation of U.S. Code 4244 *et seq.* (the statute pertaining to the mental competence of defendants to stand trial): "Our experience with these provisions has shown that defendants should have a determination of their mental competency whenever there is a history of mental illness or prior hospitalization; when there are unique and unusual circumstances, facts, or deviations surrounding the commission of the offense; or when there is some unusual or bizarre behavior observed while in detention, awaiting trial, or during appearance in court. Generally, it is also desirable to consider the mental competency of defendants charged with sex offenses, and with offenses against persons such as assault, threatened assault, or the mailing of the obscene and threatening letters."*

It is clear from the wording of these "psychiatric indications" that the defendant's own wishes in the matter play no role and that, generally speaking, coerced pretrial psychiatric examination is the rule rather than the exception.

* Charles E. Smith, "Psychiatry in Corrections." *American Journal of Psychiatry, 120*: 1045–1049 (May) 1964.

While Dr. Smith gave no figures on how often pretrial psychiatric examinations are requested against the wishes of the defendant, he did state how many of those examined were barred from standing trial: "An analysis of our experience with the first 200 defendants examined under these provisions showed that one-third were found to be incompetent. A substantial portion of this group were placed in State or Veterans Administration hospitals following dismissal of the charges pending against them. This action was taken after it was determined that the individual was suffering with a severe chronic mental illness which would delay his trial indefinitely."

As if to reassure the reader, Dr. Smith explained that "We have reached the point now where the average intelligent person is able to recognize mental illness when he sees it. Many of those who work in law enforcement and corrections receive special training which makes them especially adept at recognizing mental aberrations."

After all this legalistic and mentalistic justification of depriving people of their right to stand trial, let us stand back and look at the basic issue. The Sixth Amendment to the Constitution of the United States provides that "In all criminal prosecutions, the accused shall enjoy the right to a speedy and public trial . . ." The Constitution does not say that this right is contingent on the ability of the accused to prove his sanity to the satisfaction of adversary psychiatrists.

# 3 THE PSYCHIATRIST AS ADVERSARY

¶ Our society must now defend herself not so much against the individual as against the State.*

## SOCIAL CONTEXT AND THE PSYCHIATRIST'S ROLE

It is comfortable to hold the simple view that physicians always try to help people, or at least never deliberately try to harm them. Unfortunately this is not so. It cannot be so. Modern society is a complex web of social relationships in which individuals and groups are in constant conflict. When physicians become entangled in such conflicts, they are bound to help some and harm others. I do not deplore the existence of this fact, but only its denial—especially when such denial serves strategic aims in an antagonistic relationship.

My thesis is simple. I hold that in a medical situation it is not enough to note who is the doctor and who the recipient of his medical attention. The latter is not necessarily a "patient" nor the former a "physician"—at least not in the usual sense of these terms. Whenever the physician is employed by someone other than the patient, his loyalty and responsibility to his employer must be frankly recognized. In some cases such loyalty to third parties does not interfere with the physician's conscientious care of the sick person. In others it interferes only slightly. In still others, it requires that the "patient" be harmed rather than helped. In this chapter I shall be concerned with

* Albert Camus, "Reflections on the Guillotine" (1957), in *Resistance, Rebellion, Death*, p. 227.

those social situations in which psychiatrists are hired by representatives of public bodies—for example, prosecutors or judges—to oppose, not support, the best interests of an individual. (In the case of adults, I consider that an individual's "best interests" are whatever he himself says they are.)

Instances of physicians doing harm—not by accident, but by design—are numerous and familiar. We like to think, however, that these are exceptional occurrences— the basic pattern of the physician-patient relationship being one of cooperation and helpfulness. This is wishful thinking. The hard fact is that as society becomes more complex and more collectivized, the proportion of situations in which the doctor has an antagonistic rather than a cooperative relationship with his "patient" is increasing. As a result the profession of medicine—and especially psychiatry—may come to resemble the profession of law. Attorneys traditionally play dual roles—they support some persons (their clients), and oppose others (their antagonists). To the extent that they help the former, they harm the latter. The district attorney, who prosecutes and obtains a conviction, helps the community but harms the defendant. The defense attorney, who represents the accused and gains an acquittal, helps the client, but harms the prosecutor. More often than we realize, physicians play similar roles.

We may start with the most extreme example: the Nazi "doctors of infamy."* These physicians acted as torturers and executioners. They were, to be sure, in the employ of the Nazi state; their clients were not "patients," but "victims." Certainly nothing quite like this exists in democratic countries. However, I submit that what was unusual about the Nazi physicians was not that they were employed

* Alexander Mitscherlich and Fred Mielke, *Doctors of Infamy: The Story of the Nazi Medical Crimes,* translated by Heinz Norden, with Statements by Andrew C. Ivy, Telford Taylor, and Leo Alexander (New York: Henry Schuman, 1949).

by the state to harm individuals but that they were asked and agreed to commit enormous brutalities. Injuries of a lesser kind and on a smaller scale are inflicted against some persons by physicians in all countries. Because of the nature of their work this is inevitable. We must frankly recognize this aspect of medical practice. Only then can we properly guard against its dangers.

What, then, are some of the commonly occurring and widely accepted situations in our society in which physicians harm certain persons?

The role of the physician employed to examine and pronounce dead the bodies of convicts executed in the gas chamber or electric chair resembles the role of the physician employed in the concentration camp. Such a doctor helps agents of the state—the prison officials—to implement the law. Where there is a death penalty, there must be persons who kill convicts, and physicians who assist such persons in their work. I do not question here the moral legitimacy of the death penalty. While I personally lean toward the view that this penalty ought to be abolished, it cannot be denied that some reasonable arguments can be advanced in its defense.* My point is to call attention to the social role of the physician assisting in executions: the convict to be put to death is not his "patient," whom he helps, but his antagonist, whom he harms.

And what of the psychiatrist called upon to pronounce on the sanity of persons sentenced to death? The law generally exempts "insane" prisoners from execution, this "ultimate" penalty being reserved for those "mentally competent" to be put to death. This is no absurdity—however much it may seem so—but the law governing the implementation of the death penalty. The psychiatrist who agrees to participate in the determination of a con-

* See, for example, Jacques Barzun, "In Favor of Capital Punishment," *The American Scholar, 31:* 182–191 (Spring) 1962.

vict's competence to be executed cannot help but harm someone. If he declares his client competent—he places him, in effect, in the electric chair; if he declares him incompetent—he harms society (by circumventing its laws) and other convicts declared sane (by giving preferential treatment to those declared insane).

These situations may seem unusual. Let us therefore look at an ordinary case, such as that of the physician employed by a life insurance company. In this situation, the doctor's task is to serve the company, not to care for the person he examines. Thus the physician may be called upon to examine a young man suffering from rheumatic mitral stenosis, as a result of which he has a greatly enlarged heart. If he reports this finding to his company, the applicant will be unable to obtain life insurance or will be able to do so only by paying a premium much higher than that of a normal person of his age. By protecting the interests of the life insurance company, the physician injures the interests of some applicants for life insurance. Conversely, by deliberately or unwittingly overlooking the physical handicaps of some applicants, the physician injures the interests of the company.

Another example, drawn from a different context, is the psychiatric testimony used in the famous Hiss trial. One of the government's chief witnesses against Alger Hiss was Whittaker Chambers. A prominent American psychiatrist, retained by Hiss' counsel, testified that Chambers was a psychopathic liar whose testimony was untrustworthy. This physician could help Hiss only to the extent that he could injure Chambers. As it happened, this defense strategy was unsuccessful. The psychiatrist failed to injure Chambers and failed to help Hiss.

The dilemma of commitment (involuntary mental hospitalization) is another example of the physician being cast in a role where he must injure some to help others. Consider the case of an elderly and somewhat senile grandfather living in his married daughter's home. As he becomes more of a burden to his daughter and her family, the possibility of committing him to a state hospital may arise. The doctor is here drawn into a conflict of interests between the old man, who would prefer to live out his days with his daughter, and the young woman and her family, who would prefer to have others care for him. If the doctor recommends commitment, he helps the daughter but harms the father, and vice versa.

To summarize: Whenever people wish to pursue a goal and are frustrated in doing so by medical—and especially by psychiatric—opinion concerning their fitness to do what they want, the medical expert is foe, not friend. Baldly stated, this proposition may seem absurdly obvious. However, in our age of Orwellian "newspeak" and psychiatric pseudo-sophistication, plain facts are frequently denied or considered unbelievable; in their place, fancy interpretations are asserted as "reality" and widely accepted as "truth."

When the Negro wants to vote and is denied the right to do so, we are told that this is not a fascist maneuver by white supremacists but a democratic protection against giving the vote to those incapable of reasoned choice. Voter registration and testing, according to this argument, serve the best interests of the oppressed Negro just as much as they do those of the oppressing white.

When a person accused of crime wants to stand trial and is denied the right to do so, we are told that this is not a deliberate strategy by the prosecution, but that it is a democratic safeguard against subjecting mentally ill persons to the trauma of standing trial. Pretrial psychiatric testing, according to this argument, serves the best interests of the powerless defendant as much as of the powerful state.

This blunting of the edge of what is in fact an antagonistic relationship renders the oppressed utterly helpless.

In at least two situations the psychiatrist is clearly the adversary of the person he examines and "treats": one, when his subject is a person accused of crime who wishes to stand trial but whom the prosecution or court suspects of mental illness; the other, when his subject is a person, not accused of crime, who wishes to be left alone but whom others, usually members of his family, suspect of being mentally ill. From the case histories in the second part of this book the reader may draw his own conclusions about this view of some types of psychiatrist-patient relationship. Here I wish to cite data from the literature to substantiate this opinion.

## REVIEW OF THE LITERATURE

Because most relationships consist of a mixture of antagonism and cooperation, it is always possible, by exaggerating one or another of these aspects, to misrepresent a situation. Thus a largely antagonistic relationship may be portrayed as essentially cooperative, and a largely cooperative relationship as essentially antagonistic. The relocation of Japanese Americans during the second world war is a case in point.

### "Social Psychiatry" in Time of War

In the spring of 1942, the United States government removed from the Pacific coastal regions all of the Japanese (approximately 110,000) who had formerly lived there. Since the majority of these people were American citizens who had committed no offense, the government made sincere efforts to mitigate their hardship. Nevertheless, the evacuees suffered. This situation is instructive. I cite it because it was studied both by a psychiatrist and a political scientist. Addressing themselves to the same phenomena, the psychiatrist saw a wartorn nation whose government engaged in a necessary act and tried as best it could to help the evacuees; the political scientist saw a government misled into a faulty political decision, motivated partly by economic antagonism against the Japanese Americans, which led to unjustifiable suffering by the evacuees. According to the first view, the relationship between the American government and the Japanese American evacuees was basically cooperative; according to the latter it was basically antagonistic.

Alexander Leighton, who later became a prominent figure in social psychiatry, stated that "the Government adopted a policy of protecting [the evacuees'] welfare, developing self-government within the Relocation Centers, and reestablishing economic independence."*

This was no mean task, in view of the many facts which belied such purely therapeutic intent on the part of the government. Leighton, however, seemed to have accepted the official thesis, emphasizing cooperation between keeper and kept, and de-emphasizing antagonism between them. In one of the camps the temperature in the summer reached 124 degrees in the shade, the inmates had to work in mud, which they considered degrading, and received twelve dollars a month in wages. In view of such unpleasant facts, Leighton was forced to recognize that "To talk about democracy and making Poston [one of the camps] a democratic community was particularly resented by the Niseis who looked on their evacuation and their detention in the camp as a violation of their citizen rights indistinguishable from Fascism."†

Were these incarcerated men right or wrong? Were they or were they not deprived of their constitutional rights as American citizens? (In Leighton's whole book, which runs

---

* Alexander H. Leighton, *The Governing of Men: General Principles and Recommendations Based on Experience at a Japanese Relocation Camp* (Princeton, N.J.: Princeton University Press, 1945), p. vii.

† *Ibid.*, p. 104.

to 367 pages, there is not a single reference to the Constitution or to civil rights or liberties—save for the above-mentioned strangely stilted use of the term *citizen rights*.) Leighton is not concerned with these questions. Instead, he forgives the complainants by "understanding" them: "To speak to people in their position about democratic principles seemed a mockery as they were too close to their misery and anger to have any perspective concerning it."*

Here we have the psychiatric-therapeutic view of man deployed as a strategic device: the focus is shifted from the *rights* of citizens to the *problems* of patients. The result is total victory for the powerful. The aggressor in this way succeeds in debasing and dehumanizing his opponent. For choosing to "understand" the suffering of displaced Japanese Americans is itself a strategic maneuver on the part of the psychiatrist: by so doing, he not only enhances his own position from that of ordinary citizen to sympathetic therapist, but also succeeds in denying his own participation in and responsibility for the situation.

My point is not so much that the social psychiatrist plays a particularly immoral or evil role in this type of situation; it is rather that his role is partisan: he is his government's agent and his subject's adversary. Indeed, Leighton was serving as a medical officer in the Navy while at the relocation centers. The aim of his project, in his own words, was: "first, advising the administrative officers concerning current situations in the Center; and second, making observations and analyses that would have bearing on general problems of administration and government in occupied areas."†

Bluntly stated, then, the first aim was to spy on the camp's inmates; the second, to help the government improve its control of occupied populations. The use of psychiatrists for the promotion of such aims may be con-

* *Loc. cit.*
† *Ibid.,* pp. vii–viii.

sidered comparable to the use of soldiers in wartime and hence judged morally acceptable; or it may be considered comparable to the use of doctors in concentration camps and hence judged morally unacceptable. This choice need not concern us here. Our task is to clarify what such doctors do: whom they help and whom they harm.

The type of "research" produced by Leighton throws no light on the question: Which did the Japanese Americans in relocation camps need more—understanding psychiatrists or defenders of their constitutional rights?

Jacques Barzun saw this issue clearly when he pointed out that "Washington in 1774 was not willful, stupid, greedy, or afraid; he simply preferred independence and was a 'problem' to the British. He did not need to be cured or saved, but satisfied—like his opponents. How could behavioral science have helped—and on which side?"*

Just so the Japanese Americans on the Pacific Coast in 1942: They were not indigent, unemployed, mentally ill, or security risks; they simply preferred to live as the free Americans they were, and hence were a "problem" to our government at war with Imperial Japan. The Japanese Americans needed not government support, make-work, or therapy, but satisfaction—which, in this instance, would have meant being treated like other Americans.

This is the conclusion which Morton Grodzins, a prominent political scientist, reached in his study of the Japanese evacuation: "The decision in favor of evacuation was in error, fundamentally at odds with the spirit of democracy and unnecessary as a war measure."†

The American Civil Liberties Union has called the Japanese evacuation "the worst single wholesale violation

---

* Jacques Barzun, *Science: The Glorious Entertainment* (New York: Harper & Row, 1964), p. 186.

† Morton Grodzins, *Americans Betrayed: Politics and the Japanese Evacuation* (Chicago: The University of Chicago Press, 1949), p. xi.

of civil rights of American citizens in our history."* If so, those who actively participated in and supported the relocation were, to say the least, the evacuees' adversaries, not their friends.

Grodzins considered the treatment of the relocated Japanese Americans an act of oppression: "[T]he history of the evacuation policy could be an episode from the totalitarian handbook. The resident Japanese minority became the scapegoat of military defeat in Hawaii. Racial prejudices, economic cupidity, and political fortune-hunting became intertwined with patriotic endeavor. In the face of exact knowledge to the contrary, military officials propounded the theory that race determined allegiance. Civil administrators and the national legislature were content to rubber-stamp the military fiat."†

How then shall we categorize the social roles of physicians, including psychiatrists, who assisted the government in setting up and administering the relocation camps?

### "Social Psychiatry" in Time of Peace

The social uses of psychiatric practices—or what has rather misleadingly become known as "social psychiatry" —are evidently not without dangers of their own. One would expect social scientists to be especially aware of these risks. In general, such has not been the case. On the contrary, many social scientists have quite uncritically embraced psychiatry. Harold Lasswell, a leading figure in law and political science, is an example. His views on psychiatry and society are pertinent to the question of the right to trial and the psychiatrist's role vis-à-vis defendants who may be their involuntary clients.

The gist of Lasswell's thesis is that "man's great enemy is man; or, speaking more precisely, human destructive-

* *Ibid.*, pp. 373–74.
† *Ibid.*, p. 373.

ness."* This is not a particularly new idea. What is novel is that Lasswell makes a phobia of destructiveness into a virtue. A fear of "destructive impulses and destructive practices" leads Lasswell first to a condemnation of disagreement and ultimately to an outright denial of antagonism in human relationships.

"Our conception of democracy," he writes, "is that of a network of congenial and creative interpersonal relations. Whatever deviates from this pattern is both antidemocratic and destructive."†

This is a curious definition of democracy; it emphasizes harmony in human relations and neglects the regulation of interpersonal antagonisms. Traditionally, democracy is not what Lasswell says it is, but rather a form of government in which, directly or indirectly, the people (the majority) rule; in a liberal democracy, moreover, although the majority rules, the rights of the minorities are guaranteed and respected. Thus, while Lasswell emphasizes interpersonal harmony, the standard concept of democracy stresses the basic purposes and limitations of governmental power. The former denies antagonism in human affairs; the latter seeks to regulate it.

Lasswell pleads for a utopian society "free of destructiveness": "Men would not knowingly kill one another, whether in war, revolution, uprising, criminal violence or criminal repression. Men would not kill themselves. Human beings would not mutilate or chastise one another. If these glaring specimens of destructiveness are brought to the vanishing point, a profound transformation will have occurred in the major cultures of the globe."‡

Fortunately, the realization of this ideal society is not imminent. But what is one to say to such rhetoric? Lass-

* Harold D. Lasswell, *Power and Personality* (New York: W. W. Norton, 1948), p. 111.
† *Ibid.,* p. 110.
‡ *Ibid.,* p. 111.

well places "criminal violence" and "criminal repression"
—aggression and self-defense—in the same category and
calls them both "destructiveness"; similarly, he places war
and suicide in the same class and calls them both "destructiveness." But if self-defense and suicide are eliminated from the repertoire of human action, in what sense
is man free? Is suicide necessarily a manifestation of destructiveness? Was Socrates destructive? Or the European
Jews during the Nazi holocaust who preferred suicide to
the gas chambers?

Lasswell is intolerant of all antagonism and disharmony
in human relations. To justify this position, he naturally
finds the modern psychiatric perspective congenial. Thus
he does not hesitate to state that "We can speak of human
practices and impulses as pathological when we discover
that they destroy or threaten to culminate in the destruc-
tion of creativeness and congeniality in interpersonal relations. It begins to appear, therefore, that the leader-élite-
destructiveness problem is closely equivalent to the
problem of disease and health, seen in the perspective of
mankind as a whole."*

Although no evidence is presented for this view, it is
stated as if it were a conclusion—"It begins to appear,
therefore, that. . . ." Actually, the notion that antagonism
is bad or pathological is Lasswell's basic premise, his fundamental moral position. The following passage supports
this interpretation: "The banker who makes a commercial
loan in the ordinary course of business, the board of direc-
tors that retains a monopolistic advantage for the company, the trade union that condones restrictions of
production, the pressure group or trade association that
sustains a trade barrier may unwittingly contribute to a
wave of happenings that spell collective inflation and
collapse. A social practice is destructive which provokes
intense concentration of destructive impulse, although

* *Ibid.,* p. 112.

most of the process occurs under circumstances in which the participants neither see nor seek these results."*

No doubt actions such as those listed by Lasswell may produce unhappy results for some people, but not for everyone. The issue, again, is conflict in human relations. The severity of such conflicts can be mitigated by the rules of conduct of a civilized society; but the conflicts themselves can never be eliminated save at the cost of relinquishing individual liberty. So long as men are free they will pursue, at least some of the time, selfish or self-seeking goals; they will thus come into conflict with their fellow men engaged in the same type of pursuit. However, such simple, everyday problems need not disturb the grand planners of social strategy. For salvation is at hand; it lies in "social psychiatry."

Rather than bothering to explain exactly what social psychiatry *is*, or what its individual practitioners *do*, Lasswell offers a modest definition of the discipline: "[A] social psychiatry of society . . . is in fact the social psychiatry of democracy. It becomes one of, if not coterminous with, the developing sciences of democracy, the sciences that are slowly being evolved in the interest of democratic policy."†

This should quiet any and all arguments; social psychiatry is *defined* as serving the interests of democracy. Hence, social psychiatry cannot serve the interests of fascism or communism.

Having defined social psychiatry as a "policy science," Lasswell compares it to law. The main function of the law is to regulate human relations, especially when cooperation breaks down and overt antagonism erupts. But even in the face of this, Lasswell refrains from acknowledging the role of antagonism in human affairs and the position of social psychiatry as perhaps a peace-making enterprise

* *Ibid.*, p. 111.
† *Ibid.*, p. 119.

(that cannot possibly please everyone equally). No. Instead, he defines the social psychiatrist as a "policy scientist" and bewails the fact that "At present, our civilization is not equipped with a public image of the practitioner of the sciences of democracy."*

Lasswell's advocacy of social psychiatry—as a panacea that can do no harm, but can do endless good—is unrestrained: "[T]he problem of democratic leadership and éliteship is equivalent to the development of social health rather than disease. This appears to be the program of social psychiatry, in particular, among the medical sciences. Hence social psychiatry becomes equivalent in scope to the policy sciences of democracy, the sciences which discover the factors that condition the democratic equilibrium."†

How should social psychiatry maintain the "democratic equilibrium?" By screening persons for all sorts of occupations and positions. Thus, what some consider psychiatric invasions of privacy, Lasswell considers indispensable safeguards for democracy: "It is an axiom of democratic polity that rational opinion depends upon access to pertinent facts and interpretations. Surely no facts are more pertinent than those pertaining to the character structure of candidates for leadership."‡

Note that Lasswell speaks of "character structure," not of "character." What is the difference? The "character" of a candidate for public office is something the voters may be expected to judge, partly at least on the basis of what the candidate has stood for in the past. But his "character structure" is something only an expert in psychiatry can judge; and this judgment must rest not on public data but on personal secrets the psychiatrist is expected to worm out of his subject.

* *Ibid.*, p. 132.
† *Ibid.*, p. 146.
‡ *Ibid.*, p. 187.

Lasswell does not discuss the pretrial psychiatric examination of defendants. But no doubt he would approve the practice, for he advocates an even wider scope for psychiatric interference with personal aspiration. America, as the proverb has it, is the land of unlimited opportunity: here every boy can grow up to be President. Not if Lasswell and his brand of social psychiatry can help it; candidacy for that office would be contingent not on being a WASP (white Anglo-Saxon Protestant), as used to be the case, but on meeting certain standards of "democratic mental health." In Lasswell's own words: "What is needed is a *National Personnel Assessment Board* set up by citizens of unimpeachable integrity which will select and supervise the work of competent experts in the description of democratic and antidemocratic personality. The Assessment Board can maintain continuing inquiry into the most useful tests and provide direct services or certifications of testers. When this institution has been developed it will slowly gather prestige and acceptance. Sooner or later candidates for elective office will have enough sense of responsibility to submit voluntarily to an investigation by the board, which would say only that the candidate has, or has not, met certain defined minimum standards. Gradually the practice of basic personality disclosure can spread throughout all spheres of life, including not only local, state, national or international government personnel, but political parties, trade unions, trade associations, churches and other voluntary associations."*

But who would set the standards for this board? And what mechanism would there be in society to prevent the testers from becoming the pawns of this or that group holding power?

To me, this proposal is a complete repudiation of the values which a constitutional democracy such as the United States is expected to foster. In such a society, indi-

* *Loc. cit.*

vidual liberty and personal responsibility are supreme values. Accordingly, destructiveness—as judged by a psychiatrist—is not punished; only lawbreaking—as judged by a jury—is.

For this system, which admits the reality of conflict in human affairs and tries to control it humanely and justly, Lasswell would substitute a system which denies antagonism by invidious labeling and covert coercion.

Clearly, the trouble with frankly recognizing that a situation is adversary in character is that it helps the weaker party—the accused, the mentally ill, the socially oppressed —to defend himself. Thus, if what is wanted is an adversary proceeding better suited for repressing "deviants"— whoever they might be—the thing to do is to have an adversary proceeding that is *not* an adversary proceeding. It is the best kind. Here is an example of it.

## When an Adversary Proceeding is Not an Adversary Proceeding

If a person committed to a state mental hospital wishes to leave but the staff psychiatrists refuse to discharge him, what can he do? He can petition the court for a habeas corpus hearing. Here, one would think, is a situation that is undeniably adversary in character: the psychiatrist is the "patient's" opponent, and vice versa. But no. "Basically, this is not an adversary situation," says the director of a New York state hospital.

The problem of mental hospital patients petitioning for release was described briefly in a 1964 newspaper article.* "At the head of the table sits a black-robed Supreme Court judge. On one side wait a battery of doctors and an assistant state attorney general. Opposite them are men and women come to ask for their freedom. The petitioners are not prisoners, but patients. . . . Should the patient who

* Abraham Rabinovich, "Patients Stand Alone in Quest for Freedom," *Newsday* (Garden City, N.Y.) July 16, 1964, p. 2.

can't afford it—and that includes most—have legal counsel and his own psychiatrist at these sessions? Or are such cases too complicated for this to be practical?"

Edwin S. Clare, a former Legal Aid Society lawyer, is quoted as holding that "The judicial process is an adversary system. Each side presents before the court his view. This concept is being ignored here. The state is represented by an assistant attorney general and staff doctors. Who represents the patient?"

Hospital psychiatrists see the situation differently. They hold that, even in such circumstances, the psychiatrist is not the patient's adversary but his representative. "The relationship between patient and physician in mental hospitals is like that of a physician with any other patient," said Dr. Henry Brill, director of Pilgrim State Hospital. "Basically, this is not an adversary situation."

The confusion about this matter is perhaps heightened by the fact that such hearings are often held at the state hospital, not in the courtroom. For patients confined in four mental hospitals in Suffolk County (Long Island), they are held in a meeting room at the Pilgrim State Hospital. Since patients are not usually confined against their will in medical hospitals, it is difficult to see how the relationship between a state hospital psychiatrist and an involuntary patient is similar to that between a medical hospital doctor and a voluntary patient.

## The Role of the Committing Psychiatrist

The psychiatrist tends to function as the involuntary "patient's" adversary not only when the latter seeks release from a hospital but at every point in their encounter. This is illustrated by the fate of persons who, suspected of mental illness, are forced to submit to examination by court-appointed psychiatrists to determine whether or not they should be committed.

Kutner,* describing commitment procedures in Chicago in 1962, reports that "Certificates are signed as a matter of course by staff physicians after little or no examination . . . the doctors recommend confinement in 77% of the cases. It appears in practice that the alleged-mentally-ill is presumed to be insane and bears the burden of proving his sanity in the few minutes allowed to him." (This view is fully supported by the case histories cited in Part Two.)

Scheff,† who studied commitment proceedings in a Midwestern state, came to a similar conclusion. He noted that "it is a fairly general understanding among mental health workers that state mental hospitals in the U.S. accept all comers" and cited the results of a study of two large mental hospitals in California where ". . . the investigator never observed a case where the psychiatrist advised the patient that he did not need treatment."

"The data presented here," writes Scheff, summarizing his findings, "indicate that, in the face of uncertainty, there is a strong presumption of illness by the court and the court psychiatrist." To substantiate this view, Scheff cites observations like these: in one of the courts, twenty-two judicial hearings were observed, "all of which were conducted perfunctorily and with lightning rapidity. (The mean time of these hearings was 1.6 minutes.)"

The court psychiatrists dispatch their cases with similar rapidity. Scheff and his staff observed the examinations of one such physician, whose work appeared typical, and they reported that he "actually spent 8, 10, 5, 8, 8, 7, 17, and 11 minutes with the patients, or an average of 9.2 minutes."

Moreover, even when there is no "evidence" of mental illness, the examiner usually recommends commitment.

* Luis Kutner, "The Illusion of Due Process in Commitment Proceedings," *Northwestern University Law Review*, 57: 383–399 (Sept.) 1962.
† Thomas J. Scheff, "The Societal Reaction to Deviance: Ascriptive Elements in the Psychiatric Screening of Mental Patients in a Midwestern State," *Social Problems*, *11*: 401–413 (Spring) 1964.

One physician stated that he "thought the patient was suspicious and distrustful because he had asked about the possibility of being represented by counsel at the judicial hearing." Another stated that he "had recommended 30-day observation for a patient whom he had thought *not* mentally ill, on the ground that the patient, a young man, could not get along with his parents, and 'might get into trouble.' This examiner went on to say: 'We always take the conservative side. (Commitment or observation.) Suppose the patient should commit suicide. . . . I had rather play it safe. There is no harm in doing it that way.' "

Finally, Scheff notes that the jargon of the committing doctors is a rhetoric justifying psychiatric detention. "The language used by these physicians tends to intimate that mental illness was found, even when reporting the opposite. Thus in one case the recommendation stated: 'No gross evidence of delusions or hallucinations.' This statement is misleading, since not only was there no gross evidence, there was not any evidence, not even the slightest suggestion of delusions or hallucinations, brought out by the interview."

Still another physician stated that in so-called petition cases—in which the patient's family initiated the request for hospitalization and which comprised the majority of the cases—commitment is "automatic": "If the patient's own family wants to get rid of him you know there is something wrong."

It is clear, then, that in all of these instances the physician acts as the so-called patient's adversary. Sometimes he represents the family; sometimes the court; but never the individual suspected of mental illness.

## The Role of the Prosecuting Psychiatrist

One of the few empirical studies of psychiatric determinations of competence to stand trial is contained in a short paper by Hess and Thomas.* They found that many persons declared unfit to stand trial were so categorized to punish them. But they failed to state this plainly, and instead obscured the problem and their own findings by needlessly complicated formulations couched in psychiatric jargon.

Hess and Thomas found that:

1. "In many cases nothing in the record indicated . . . that the defendant appeared 'to be insane,' nor, in most records, was there anything to suggest that it might be 'claimed that such a person became insane after the commission of the felony with which he is charged.' "

2. "The records studied at Ionia [Michigan] State Hospital revealed that frequently the psychiatrist assumed the role of judicial expert. In the case of P.F., the psychiatrist's report read, 'This man is a chronic alcoholic. He is impulsive and extremely dangerous. He is not treatable and should be sent to the hospital for a good long time, if not for life.' "

3. "The majority of the psychiatrists' reports were empty and meaningless, and yet were accepted and acted upon by the courts as if they contained information which could be construed as evidence and, as such, decided upon."

4. "[Sometimes] the courts . . . grant permission for parole which can allow the 'incompetent individual' to function in society for as long as three years before any final conclusion to the legal process."

5. "[T]he majority of individuals committed as incompetent could be readied for trial within a matter of weeks or months."

6. "[T]he [hospital] staff apparently bypassed entirely the legal intent behind the incompetency principle and

* John H. Hess and Herbert E. Thomas, "Incompetency to Stand Trial: Procedures, Results, and Problems," *American Journal of Psychiatry*, *119*: 713–720 (Feb.) 1963.

sought to perceive and manage the incompetent patient as they would patients committed to them for other reasons."

7. "[W]ell over one-half of the individuals committed as incompetent will spend the rest of their lives confined to the hospital." (At the time of this study, the patient population at Ionia State Hospital was 1484, of whom 705 were those committed as incompetent to stand trial.)

8. "[M]any of the patients committed as incompetent to Ionia State Hospital do not consider it a hospital but rather a prison, and an extremely undesirable prison at that."

Hess and Thomas concluded that:

1. "This remarkable confusion of designations [in the Michigan statutes governing the determination of competence to stand trial] not only suggests the bewilderment of those who wrote the statute, but has had a powerful influence on what actually happens to persons committed as incompetent to stand trial."

Why does this suggest confusion? Why not the intent to impose severe penalties upon some persons considered dangerous to the public peace and welfare and to disguise such harm as therapy?

2. "[T]he issue of the defendant's competence to be tried was most frequently raised not on the basis of the defendant's mental status but rather was employed as a means of handling situations and solving problems for which there seemed to be no other recourse under the law."

Why contend that there was no other recourse? Why could these men not be put on trial, sent to jail if guilty, or set free if innocent? Is that too old-fashioned?

3. "[W]e found that almost without exception the psychiatrist's role was grossly distorted."

Distorted from what to what? Why do the authors shirk the conclusion that the psychiatrist's role was what they found it to be: to impose harsh punishments on people, and then act as their prison guards?

4. "[T]he psychiatrist took it upon himself to make moral and judicial decisions."

Moral decisions, yes; judicial, no.

Perhaps it was inevitable that Hess and Thomas should have tried to avoid seeing what was staring them in the eye: the psychiatrist as the "patient's" adversary. They expressly disallowed this possibility when they set out on their investigation: "In undertaking the research to be described, it was our hypothesis that both the individual and society have become the victims of a principle designed for their mutual protection." Herein lies the crux of the problem: Two psychiatrists set out to study a delicate subject such as incompetence to stand trial and begin with the assumption that in this drama there are no villains, only victims. I do not subscribe to any simplistic conspiratorial theories of human conduct or social relations. But I think it is absurd to categorize in advance everyone involved in a procedure such as this as a hapless victim of circumstances. No one forces psychiatrists to participate in such pseudo-psychiatric determinations; they are free to eschew such activities—and, indeed, many psychiatrists do just that. Why then consider those who do not avoid such work as "victims" rather than as persons who have more or less freely chosen to earn a living by depriving some men of the right to be tried?

The second half of Hess and Thomas' "hypothesis" deserves also to be scrutinized: the proposition that involuntary pretrial psychiatric examination of defendants is "a principle designed for [the] mutual protection" of defendant and society cannot be a premise; it is precisely what must be demonstrated. In any case, it is difficult to be sure what legislators intend; but it is easy to ascertain what they accomplish. I am skeptical that those drafting repressive psychiatric-legal statutes are animated by benevolent intentions. But even if such had been their motives in the past, surely, in the light of what has now been obvious for several decades, a hypothesis of malevolent rather than of benevolent intentions would seem more plausible.

An article by LaPlante,* a professor of law, not a psychiatrist, contains a more forthright criticism of the forensic psychiatrist as the defendant's covert adversary.

LaPlante's article deals with the legal ramifications of the case of Benjamin Reid, a nineteen-year old Negro who was arrested by the New Haven police on January 16, 1957, for the murder of Mrs. Florine McCluney. He was not told that he had a right to have counsel but was instead interrogated by the police. Reid admitted the killing. On January 17 he was booked for murder. The next day, still without having been given an opportunity to consult with a lawyer, Reid was examined by a psychiatrist at the request of the State's Attorney. "At this examination the doctor asked Reid to relate the circumstances connected with the crime. Reid complied and made incriminating statements. . . . The doctor's report, containing not only the medical conclusion that Reid was legally sane but also the incriminating statements, was submitted to the State's Attorney." Not until March 7, seven weeks after his arrest, when Reid appeared before the grand jury, did he have an opportunity to talk with an attorney, the Public Defender for Hartford County. In due time Reid was tried, found guilty, and sentenced to death. The death sentence, however, was commuted to life imprisonment.

What interests us here is the role of the psychiatrist in this type of situation. As we have noted, within thirty-six hours after his arrest Reid was examined at the county jail by a psychiatrist. Why was he examined? "[F]or the

* Joseph A. LaPlante, "Connecticut Criminal Law: Deficiencies Disclosed in the Reid Case," *Connecticut Bar Journal,* 37: 17–51 (March) 1963.

purpose, according to the doctor [who performed the examination], of determining whether he [Reid] was sane under Connecticut law." However, "At the trial the State made use of the report in cross-examining Reid." To make matters worse, LaPlante points out that "There is no statutory authority under Connecticut law for an examination of the type conducted." In other words, the prosecutor cannot order this type of examination; only the judge can. Indeed, ten days before the trial, a pretrial psychiatric examination, ordered by the judge, was conducted by two court-appointed psychiatrists.

It is clear, then, that in the examination conducted at the behest of the prosecutor, the psychiatrist acted as the defendant's adversary. Commented LaPlante: "Even if we agree that a prosecuting official has the inherent power to order, without permission of the court, an examination to determine the mental condition of an accused, there can be no question but that the psychiatrist's action in asking the accused questions about the crime and then making a full report to the prosecutor of everything the accused said will create doubt as to the true purpose of the examination. The alleged purpose of Reid's examination—to determine whether he was sane—may not seem convincing to some in the light of the circumstances surrounding the examination: (1) it was made at an exceedingly early stage; (2) it was not made pursuant to a court order; (3) a report, including Reid's incriminating statements, was given to the State's Attorney."

The Reid case is not an isolated instance.* LaPlante reports that in "the case of *State* v. *Taborsky* the same psychiatrist who examined Reid conducted several examinations of the State's principal witness, the brother and accomplice of defendant Taborsky. The psychiatrist testi-

* See, for example, the attempt by psychiatrists to incriminate Major General Edwin A. Walker as mentally ill on the basis of his Army medical records, pp. 188–218.

fied that he submitted reports of these several *ex parte* examinations, containing details of the crime, to the State's Attorney's office."

This physician had examined still another defendant, named Culombe, for the prosecutor. In Culombe's trial, this psychiatrist was questioned about the nature of his practice, and testified as follows: "*A*. Well, for over thirty years I have been examining for the Hartford City Police Court and I have examined persons accused of crimes in New Haven County, Windham County, Tolland County, and Hartford County. *Q*. Have you for some years been requested by the State's Attorney's office to examine psychiatrically accused that are charged with crime? *A*. I have."

This method of obtaining evidence is not uncommon. The leading case is that of *People* v. *Leyra*. "In that New York murder case a psychiatrist was called in by the District Attorney for the purpose of questioning a suspect. The questioning took place in privacy, but the psychiatrist was aware that the room was wired and that the police could overhear what was being said. By playing on the suspect's fears, hopes, and feelings of guilt, the doctor induced the accused to make incriminating statements. Immediately following the interview, the suspect made several full confessions to the police."

Leyra appealed and his conviction was reversed. He was retried and was again convicted. His conviction was appealed all the way to the United States Supreme Court, where it was reversed.

Leyra's first conviction was set aside in the Court of Appeals in New York.* The court set forth some of the details concerning Leyra's psychiatric interrogation which show us clearly the psychiatrist in his role as the defendant's adversary—as a kind of assistant prosecutor.

The police captain charged with investigating the mur-

* *People* v. *Leyra*, 98 N.E., 2nd, 553 (1951).

ders of which Leyra was suspected "introduced defendant to a physician who is also a specialist in neurology and psychiatry . . . and one who uses the technique of psychoanalysis in his practice. This doctor . . . had been called to the police station by the District Attorney, who outlined the case to him." The doctor then talked to Leyra in a room which he knew was wired by the police department.

The decision handed down by the court noted that "A transcript of the recorded interview shows that he [the psychiatrist] told the defendant at the outset: 'I'll tell you what the purpose of my talk to you is. I want to see if I can help you.' To this the defendant answered: 'Yes, Doctor.' The doctor asked him about his sinus condition and the treatment he had had, and in the course of the interview said: 'I'm your doctor.' The transcript further discloses that on at least forty occasions the doctor in one way or another promised to help the defendant. . . ."

The court reversed Leyra's conviction, arguing that we must bear in mind "the undisputed setting in which the interview was arranged and recorded . . . ; the psychiatrist calling himself the defendant's doctor . . . ; informing defendant that he was not morally responsible; making deceptive offers of friendship and numerous promises, express and implied; giving assurance in a pseudo-confidential atmosphere of physician and patient; and all the attendant circumstances taken together—this interview was a subtle intrusion upon the rights of defendant and was tantamount to a form of mental coercion which . . . we may not countenance here."

LaPlante cites three other decisions. In one, the court found "no error to have allowed testimony of psychiatrist of defendant's statements about the killing"; in another, the court ruled that it was "not error to have jury hear tape recording of defendant's confession obtained by attending physician at state mental hospital from defendant-patient"; and in a third, the court stated that it is "not error to allow two psychiatrists' testimony of defendant's incriminating statements where defendant had been given following warning: 'We were sent here by District Attorney of Nassau. We were asked to make an examination of you. You need not say one word if you don't want to speak to us. That is your right. We may be called to testify in your case. If you decide to speak to us, if you decide to tell us about this crime, I trust that you will tell us the truth.' "*

This shocking state of affairs prompted LaPlante to ask: "How do we citizens, who condemn police brutality being used to obtain evidence, react to the State in effect making use of a psychiatrist as one of its evidence-gathering representatives?"

How do we, indeed? The answer is not reassuring. Most people are indifferent; many knowledgeable persons applaud the practice and advocate its wider use; only a few condemn it.

* LaPlante, *op. cit.*, p. 45.

# PART II

# 4 THE CASE OF MR. LOUIS PERRONI

¶ There is, in fact, nothing in common between a master and a slave; it is impossible to speak and communicate with a person who has been reduced to servitude. Instead of the implicit and untrammeled dialogue through which we come to recognize our similarity and consecrate our destiny, servitude gives sway to the most terrible of silences.*

## I

Until May 5, 1955, Mr. Louis Perroni† operated a filling station in Glenview, a Syracuse suburb. On that day his world fell apart.

The events that led up to this fateful day, though rather trivial, are typical of the Kafkaesque webs in which the small man gets caught in a big bureaucracy; and how, once caught, the more he struggles, the more firmly he is held.

Early in 1955, Perroni was informed that the lease on his filling station, which was to expire on July 1, was not going to be renewed. The station he had operated for approximately ten years was in an area that was to be razed in preparation for a new shopping center.

During the winter, Perroni was approached by agents of the real estate developer with a request that he vacate his premises early, preferably no later than May 1. Although offered compensation, Perroni refused.

As Mr. Perroni tells it, the real estate developer went

* Albert Camus, *The Rebel*, p. 283.
† The dates and the names of persons, places, and institutions (except mine, the Onondaga County Court's, and the Matteawan State Hospital's) are fictitious; otherwise, the account is factual.

to court and obtained permission to take possession of Perroni's filling station on May 1. Perroni was the last occupant on the property, and therefore the only obstacle in the way of proceeding with the building of the new shopping center. After urging Mr. Perroni to move and offering him bonuses for doing so, the agents of the real estate developer allegedly threatened him with court action. He, on the other hand, began to feel that he was being "pushed around," and resolved not to give an inch from what he considered his "legal rights."

On May 2, 1955, representatives of the real estate developer erected a sign on what Mr. Perroni considered his gas station. He remonstrated with them and removed the sign. At last, when two men appeared on May 5 and proceeded to erect another sign, Mr. Perroni took a rifle from his station and fired a warning shot into the air. The men departed. Soon Mr. Perroni was arrested by the police.

This was Perroni's first brush with the law. Nor had he had any previous contact with psychiatry. During the second world war, Perroni had served for nearly five years in the Army as a mechanic and received an honorable discharge. Until his arrest, when he was forty years old, he was a responsible, self-supporting citizen.

Mr. Perroni was arraigned but was not indicted. Instead, at the request of the district attorney, the Onondaga County Court judge before whom he appeared ordered him to undergo pretrial psychiatric examination to determine his fitness to stand trial. He was examined by two court-appointed psychiatrists, found incapable of standing trial, and committed to the Matteawan State Hospital.

Aided by his brothers, Perroni tried by every means possible, including an appeal to the United States Supreme Court, to secure his right to be tried. At long last, in June 1961—six years after Perroni was committed to the Matteawan State Hospital—a writ of habeas corpus was heard and sustained by the State Supreme Court judge in Dutchess County (where the hospital is located). Perroni was ordered to be tried or discharged. Nevertheless he was not immediately released. "The wheels of justice moved slowly," reported the Syracuse *Post-Standard,* "and only when officials of Matteawan State Hospital were faced with contempt charges did they send Perroni back to Onondaga County."

Perroni was returned to Syracuse on Thursday, August 31, and held incommunicado in the county jail. "His relatives," according to the newspaper, "have not been allowed to visit him." Perroni was to be arraigned in County Court, Tuesday, September 3. His arraignment was adjourned to the following day. On September 4, however, he was neither indicted nor released. Instead, he was ordered to submit to a fresh pretrial psychiatric examination.

A month later, on October 1, 1961, the Syracuse *Herald-Journal* reported that the court issued a new order for "mental tests" on Perroni. "For the fourth time since his arrest—and the second in less than a month—Louis Perroni, 46, former operator of a Glenview gasoline station, has been ordered to a hospital for mental tests. Perroni, who has been in and out of County Court more than a half a dozen times since his arrest in 1955, was in court again yesterday. And again, County Judge Francis T. Kirby ordered mental tests."

In due course, Perroni was committed to the Oakville State Hospital near Syracuse to determine once more whether he was competent to stand trial.

In anticipation of the hearing to be held in Onondaga County Court concerning Mr. Perroni's fitness to stand trial, the defendant's family and his attorney, Mr. Jerome Gross, sought my help. They requested that I furnish psychiatric testimony to support the claim—shared by the defendant, his family, and his attorney—that Mr. Louis Perroni was mentally competent to stand trial. It must be noted that in the course of the past seven years, while Mr. Perroni tried to gain his freedom, he had never had the help·of a psychiatrist retained by himself and his attorney. Thus no psychiatric testimony favorable to him was ever presented in court.

After conferring with Mr. Perroni's relatives and his attorney, I interviewed the defendant at the Cedar Street Jail in Syracuse. I considered him competent and agreed to testify on his behalf.

The hearing was held on April 12, 1962, in Onondaga County Court before a judge and without a jury. It lasted for two full days. The following excerpts from the hearing are taken from the official records of the court stenographer. Much of the testimony was, of course, repetitious and trivial, and, for the sake of readability, I have omitted the larger part of it. I have tried to retain only enough to convey the atmosphere of the proceedings and the sorts of information elicited from the witnesses.

## II

PROCEEDINGS BEFORE HONORABLE FRANCIS T. KIRBY, COUNTY COURT HOUSE, ON APRIL 12, 1962, AT 10 A.M.

APPEARANCES:

FOR THE PEOPLE: Robert Jordan, Esq., Assistant District Attorney

FOR THE DEFENDANT: Jerome Gross, Esq.

[Defendant and both attorneys present in Court]

    THE COURT: This is the time set for a hearing to controvert the findings of the psychiatrists in the matter of The People of the State of New York versus Louis Perroni. Is the defendant ready, Mr. Gross?

    MR. GROSS: The defendant is ready, Your Honor.

    MR. JORDAN: The People are ready, Your Honor.

    THE COURT: You may proceed, Mr. Jordan.

JAMES B. ROSCOE, having been called and duly sworn, testified as follows:

*Direct Examination*
*by* MR. JORDAN

Q   Dr. Roscoe, can you tell us where you live, please?

A   I live at Oakville State Hospital, Oakville, New York.

Q   And what is your present employment, sir?

A   I am Assistant Director, Clinical, of Oakville State Hospital.

Q   And in what field are you engaged in at Oakville State Hospital?

A   I am engaged in the practice of psychiatry.

Q   And for how long, sir, have you been a psychiatrist?

A   I have been a psychiatrist for fifteen years.

Q   Now, Doctor, during the course of your career as a psychiatrist have you had occasion either in your employment or with any mentally ill person to be in contact with the alleged criminal insane?

A   On very many occasions I have examined cases under the Code of Criminal Procedure.

Q   Now, would you tell the Court and the defense, please, approximately how many people you have seen pertaining to the criminal insane and according to the Code of Criminal Procedure?

A   I have examined approximately 200 individuals under the Code of Criminal Procedure.

Q   Doctor, let me ask you, have you ever had occasion to talk or meet an individual by the name of Louis Perroni?

A   Yes, I have.

Q   Now, if you can recall, when was the first time you examined Mr. Perroni?

A   I examined Mr. Perroni on February 24, 1962.

Q   Now, can you tell us what your examination consisted of?

A   It consisted of an interview of an hour and a half's duration, proceeding in the usual form of a psychiatric interview in order to ascertain the individual's mental state. I determined his attitude and general behavior. I determined his stream of mental activity, his emotional reaction, his content of thought, and his sensorium.

Q   Now, Doctor, as a result of your examinations of Mr. Perroni were you able to form an opinion whether this patient was in such a state of idiocy, imbecility, or insanity as to be able to understand the nature of the charge against him and to make his defense?

A   Yes.

Q   What is that opinion, Doctor?

A   It is my opinion that Mr. Perroni is in such a state of idiocy, imbecility, or insanity as to be unable to understand the charges against him, the procedures, or of aiding in his defense.

. . .

Q   Did you at any time, Dr. Roscoe, inquire or discuss with the patient the charges against him?

A   I attempted to talk with him about the charges against him.

Q   Can you tell us the conversation about that, sir?

A   He refused to discuss the charges against him. As I recall, he maintained that under the Fifth Amendment he did not have to discuss the nature of the charges against him.

Q   And did you ask him anything further pertaining to the charges against him?

A   I asked him whether he felt he had been dealt with fairly under the laws dealing with these charges.

Q   And let me ask you, Doctor, was the fact that he didn't discuss the charges against him, was that decisive in determining whether this man was in such a state of idiocy, insanity, or imbecility as not to be able to understand the charges against him?

A   It was not.

Q   Then you say this was part of the interview, but it wasn't decisive, is that correct?

**A**   It was not decisive.

. . .

MR. JORDAN: You may inquire, Mr. Gross.

*Cross-examination*
*by* MR. GROSS

. . .

**Q**   Dr. Roscoe, can you tell us what Mr. Perroni is charged with—what the charge is?

**A**   I believe it is a charge under the Penal Law having to do with carrying a gun.

**Q**   Do you know whether or not he is charged with assault?

**A**   That I do not know.

**Q**   I see. And is he charged with anything else, Doctor?

**A**   To my knowledge, no.

**Q**   And do you know, Doctor, whether carrying a gun is a violation of law?

**A**   I do not know. I'm not a lawyer.

**Q**   I see. Doctor, in order to defend against a charge of carrying a gun what does a defendant have to know in order to aid his attorney in the trial of the case?

MR. JORDAN: I will object to that, if Your Honor please.

THE COURT: No, overruled.

MR. GROSS: It is the meat of the case, Your Honor. It is the very basis of it.

THE COURT: The witness may answer.

MR. JORDAN: I don't know if a proper foundation has been laid for the witness to be qualified to answer.

THE COURT: He may so state if he is not.

MR. GROSS: I will withdraw that question, Your Honor.

THE COURT: All right.

**Q**   Doctor, you have stated as a conclusion and as the result of your examination of this defendant Perroni under Court order, you have come to the conclusion that

Perroni is not able to understand the charges or to assist with his defense. Now, Doctor, is it not true that in order to come to that conclusion, whether you be a psychiatrist or a man on the street, that it is first necessary to know what a defendant has to know in order to understand the charges against him and to aid his attorney? Is it not necessary first to know what capacity he must have in order to cooperate with his attorney?

A I would say that he had to be capable of judgment, capable of sufficient thinking capacity to be able to co-operate.

Q Is it not true, Doctor, that the defense of different charges would require different capacities for the purpose of defense?

A I am not a lawyer. I don't believe I can answer that question.

Q Doctor, I do not mean from a legal standpoint, but I mean from a layman's standpoint and a psychiatrist's standpoint.

A From a psychiatric standpoint again a person must have demonstration of judgment, intelligence, contact with reality to be able to cooperate in defending any charge.

Q Any charge? Would there be a different capacity required between defending a murder charge and a speeding charge?

A From a psychiatric point of view, no.

Q No difference at all? In other words, the simplicity of the charge and the simplicity of the defense makes absolutely no difference?

A That would be my opinion.

Q And is that a psychiatric conclusion, Doctor?

A Yes.

. . .

Q All right. Now, when you first examined Mr. Perroni—that was, you say, on February the twenty-fourth?—

did you have any reason to believe that he was abnormal at that time?

A   I did.

Q   Why was that, Doctor?

A   Because of the attitude the patient had, the inappropriateness of his emotional affect, the evasive manner in which he discussed things—nondirect way—

Q   (Interrupting) Excuse me, Doctor. I want to cut off your answer for this reason. I don't think you understand my question. When he first came in for the interview on February twenty-fourth, as you started that interview did you have any conclusion of his normalcy or abnormalcy?

A   I had none.

Q   What you are testifying to now is what your conclusion was at the conclusion of that first interview; is that right?

A   Yes.

Q   Now, you say he was evasive, Doctor. Is that what you said?

A   Yes.

Q   In what way? Can you give us some specifics, Doctor; how was he evasive?

A   To my questions he answered with a response "That is a good question."

Q   Well, which question was it? Give us one question he answered that to.

A   I do not recall specifically.

Q   Well, Doctor, February twenty-fourth isn't long gone. It is just two months. Can't you remember a single solitary question that he so responded to with "That is a good question"?

A   I do not. There were a number of them on that occasion.

Q   But you cannot remember a single solitary question?

A   I cannot specifically remember a question.

Q You didn't make a single note of any question you asked him?

A I did not write up the results of this interview on a question-and-answer basis.

Q And is there anything abnormal, Doctor, for any person to respond "That is a good question"—anything abnormal about that?

A When this is a response to a number of different questions it has significance psychiatrically.

Q How many times did he repeat that phrase, Doctor? How many times on February twenty-fourth did he use that phrase "That is a good question"?

A At least half a dozen.

Q At least half a dozen times in an hour and a half, is that right?

A Yes.

Q By your standards and your judgment you think the phrase "That is a good question" during an hour-and-a-half interrogation, that indicates in some fashion to you, does it, Doctor, that that is an abnormality?

A It does.

Q Do you remember, Doctor, to what type of question he so responded?

A To certain questions relative to his marriage, to certain questions relative to his confinement, and to other questions which I don't clearly recall.

Q Isn't it true, Doctor, that those responses "That is a good question" were to questions in the area only of his marriage and of the circumstances that happened on the day he was arrested, isn't that true?

A No, that is not true.

Q What other area did he refuse to answer in?

A I cannot recall specifically, but there definitely were other areas.

Q But you don't remember a single one of them?

A    I don't remember.

. . .

Q    Now, Doctor, I understand you to say this man was untidy?

A    Yes.

Q    Can you describe in detail for me what that untidiness was?

A    On every occasion that I examined Mr. Perroni the upper button or two of his shirt was unbuttoned, his sleeves were not buttoned, and his shoelaces were untied.

. . .

Q    Have you brought with you in Court, Doctor, the records of Oakville State Hospital pertaining to Louis Perroni?

A    Yes.

Q    And those records go back how far as far as Oakville is concerned?

A    They go back to his first admission in Oakville State Hospital, which I believe was in September of 1961.

Q    Have you ever examined those records, Doctor?

A    I have.

Q    Part of those records are clinical notes, are they not, Doctor?

A    What do you mean by clinical notes?

Q    What are clinical notes? You are a doctor.

A    I am asking your definition. It may be different.

Q    Do you have a form in your hospital that is printed and marked "Clinical Notes"?

A    I believe you refer to what we commonly call nurses' notes.

Q    Is there not in your hospital—Oakville State Hospital—where you say you have been a doctor for fifteen years, a printed form called "Clinical Notes"? You answer that question. Tell me if you have such a form?

A    I believe there is.

Q    You believe or you know, Doctor?

MR. JORDAN: Just a moment. I believe the witness answered the question.

MR. GROSS: This is cross-examination.

THE COURT: Overruled, Mr. Jordan. Proceed. (To witness) You may answer the question.

Q   Do you have such a form in your hospital printed in black type—bold black type "Clinical Notes"?

A   Yes.

. . .

Q   Now, taking the very first clinical note that you have, will you tell us the first entry—the date of the first entry?

A   September 3, 1961. 9:30 P.M.

Q   All right. Tell us what that clinical note is.

A   Middle-aged, white male admitted to ward by Mrs. Mason. Quiet and cooperative to admission care. Nutrition good. Cleanliness good. Vermin, none noted. Patient states he has been in the State Prison and does not want to talk about it. Small round scar upper left leg. Pimple on right hip. No skin diseases noted. Vaccination left arm. Temperature 100. Pulse 80. Respiration 20.

Q   Read the date and the next clinical note.

A   The next clinical note is on the same date at 10 P.M. Quiet and cooperative.

Q   Is that all?

A   That's all.

Q   What is the next date and the next note?

A   The next note is the same date. Twelve midnight. Sleeping.

Q   Will you continue on, Doctor, reading the dates and the clinical notes? Give the date and then give the note opposite.

A   September Fourth. Twelve midnight. Asleep all night. Cooperative. Quiet. Urine specimen to lab.

Q   I want you to keep going, Doctor. Read the dates. Give the date on each occasion and give the clinical note.

A   Twelve noon. Temperature 98.6. Pulse 84. Respiration 20. Regular diet. This patient remains quiet and cooperative. Ate well. Offers no complaints. Reads. Watches TV. Patient seems uninterested in ward routine.

. . .

Q   Will you go on with your clinical notes?

A   Five P.M. September 5, 1961. Regular diet. Appetite good. Quiet. Cooperative. Watching TV. Twelve. Sleeping. Another note, the time not given. Patient sleeps well at night. Quiet. Cooperative. Ate good breakfast in the morning. This is on September Sixth.

Q   Keep going.

A   Again September Sixth. Eight A.M. Regular diet. Patient quiet, cooperative. Ate good dinner. Four P.M. Patient reads. Watches TV. Is somewhat seclusive. Offers no complaints.

Q   Doctor, what do you mean by somewhat seclusive? What does that mean?

A   I didn't make that note.

Q   I see. But it is an official record of your hospital?

A   Yes.

Q   You wouldn't know what that meant?

A   I know what the term seclusive means in psychiatry.

Q   What does it mean, Doctor?

A   It means the patient stays by himself and aloof from others.

Q   Is that a significant indication in schizophrenia?

A   It is one of the symptoms that is frequently found in schizophrenia.

. . .

Q   You mean he doesn't socialize with other people?

A   He does not socialize or mingle.

Q   Tell us, how is he supposed to mingle? What is a normal person supposed to do when he is in an institution?

A   There are no normal people in institutions.

Q   There are no normal people in institutions? I see. Doctor, as a matter of psychiatry, when a person comes to you to be examined does he bring a presumption with him —and I mean a presumption in regards to his normalcy?

A   Many patients come to the hospital of their own volition desiring help.

Q   That is not my question. Please try to understand it. I will repeat it. When a person comes to you for a psychiatric examination, is there any presumption on your part as to his sanity or lack of sanity?

A   Not at the time he comes in.

Q   Does a person psychiatrically carry a presumption of normalcy?

A   When a patient comes to the hospital it is a matter of their coming for examination and treatment—a determination of whether they are normal or mentally sick is made after they have had this examination.

Q   That is not my question, Doctor. I am asking about a presumption. Is there in psychiatry a presumption whether a person is normal or not normal?

A   Yes, people would be classified generally as either normal or ill.

. . .

Q   Now, let me make the question just a little more specific. A person off the street, whom you have never seen before, who has absolutely no history that you know of, is that person—does that person have with him a presumption of sanity?

A   Yes.

Q   So that, Doctor, when you took the oath to determine for the Court whether Perroni was normal or not normal, you at that time knew that he had been at Oakville before, and did that in your mind—in your own mind carry a strike against Perroni? By that I mean was there already a presumption in your mind that this man was not normal?

A There was not. This did not occur.

Q Did you not a moment ago tell me that if a person came from another institution transferred to your institution, that there was a presumption of abnormality?

A Mr. Perroni came to us from jail.

Q But he had been at Oakville State Hospital and you knew that he had been at Oakville in September and again on a separate commitment in October, is that true?

A That's true.

Q So that knowing that he had been in your institution twice before, did that in your own mind, Doctor, carry a presumption of mental illness?

A It did not.

Q And why, Doctor, was there an exception in this case to the rule that you stated a moment ago, that when a patient with a history of prior illness or prior confinement, that they carry a presumption of insanity?

A I said if the individual is transferred directly from another mental hospital to us.

Q But if a patient had been in your own hospital before, the rule would be different?

A Not necessarily. The situation would be that there could be a change from the time that Mr. Perroni had been in Oakville State Hospital before.

Q But Doctor, that is not what I am asking you at all. I am asking you whether when a patient comes from another hospital transferred directly to you—you said that there was a presumption of abnormality, right? Isn't that what you said?

A I did.

Q All right. I am asking you did Perroni, having been at Oakville in September and October of 1961, and the records at your hospital so showing, and you knowing that these were the records, did that in your own mind carry any presumption?

A It did not carry a presumption.

Q   Why the exception to the rule that you stated a moment ago—that when a person is transferred directly from another institution he is presumed to be abnormal?

A   As I explained a moment ago, Mr. Perroni was away from the hospital for a period of time in jail.

Q   Are you talking about remission, Doctor?

A   No.

Q   When a patient is out of a hospital for three months or six months, is it possible that he is improved?

A   It could be possible, yes.

. . .

Q   Doctor, I want you at this point, please, to go on reading your clinical notes.

A   Eight o'clock on the sixth of September. Temperature 99. Pulse 78. Respiration is 18. Regular diet. Quiet and cooperative. Appetite good. No complaints. September Eighth. Asleep all night. Cooperative. Appetite good. Eight in the morning. Ambulatory. Quiet and cooperative. Shaved this morning.

Q   Go ahead.

A   At noon. Temperature 98.4. Pulse 86. Respiration is 20. Regular diet. Ate well. Regular diet. Appetite good. Quiet. Cooperative. Watching TV. Twelve. Sleeping.

Q   Keep going.

A   September Ninth—8 A.M. Ambulatory. Quiet and cooperative. Regular diet. Ate well. Noon. Temperature was 98. Pulse 92. Respiration was 20. Watched TV this afternoon.

Q   Doctor, instead of pulse and temperature and that, will you read only what is on the extreme right-hand side of the page—those notes—rather than the physical status of the patient?

A   No complaints. Sleeping.

Q   Give us the dates and what is on the extreme right hand.

A   Twelve. Slept all night. Quiet. Cooperative. Friendly

and conversational. Appetite good. Do you wish me to omit the time and date?

Q No, I just want the date. I don't care about the time. And the note on the extreme right hand side of that sheet.

. . .

A September Tenth. Early in the morning. Nine A.M. Chart closed as of today. This patient seems to have come along quite well on this ward. He is quiet, cooperative. He is friendly. Will do some ward work if asked. He is oriented in all spheres.

Q What does that mean, that he is oriented in all spheres?

A That would refer to his orientation as far as time, place, and person.

Q Go ahead.

A He eats and sleeps well, offers no complaints, regular diet, no medication. September Seventeenth. Mr. Perroni is oriented in all spheres. His recent and remote memory is good. He is an ambulatory patient who is clean in toilet and personal habits. Eats well and sleeps without complaints. His conversation is rational and coherent. However, he is very suspicious and will tell you that he will talk only to his lawyer as to why he is here. He is quiet and cooperative towards routine. He mingles well with some of the ward cases. Today Mr. Perroni is going to Court at 9:30 A.M. He plays cards, watches TV, and listens to the radio. He does some ward work. He weighs 160 pounds. No medication or treatment.

Q The next day, Doctor? Go ahead.

A September Twenty-first. This patient has adjusted well to ward routine. He is quiet and friendly and sociable. He will assist with ward routine willingly. Neat and clean. Showed no abnormal tendencies so far. Mingles well. Plays cards and watches TV. Eats and sleeps regularly. Receives no medication. September Twenty-sixth. This patient discharged into care of Sheriff of Onondaga County. September Twenty-sixth at 9 P.M. Unimproved.

Q   It is marked "Unimproved," isn't it?

A   Yes.

Q   What kind of improvement could there have been, Doctor, when the day before he mingles well, was adjusted well to ward routine, quiet, friendly, sociable, would assist in ward willingly, neat, and clean, shows no abnormal tendencies so far, plays cards, watches TV, eats and sleeps regularly? What do you mean he is unimproved? Unimproved what for?

A   I don't know. I didn't place that note there.

. . .

Q   How do you account, Doctor, for the continuous notes in your official records to the effect that this man was neat and clean, shaved and showered and so forth? How do you account for that, Doctor?

MR. JORDAN: I object to the question. It is improper in form.

THE COURT: Overruled. If the Doctor knows, he may answer.

A   It was my opinion on the occasions I examined the patient that I would call him untidy in his dress.

Q   Was he shaved at the time you saw him?

A   I can't clearly recall. I recall that on one occasion he had a growth of beard.

. . .

Q   And Doctor, at the time that you examined him were you, yourself, acquainted with the Fifth Amendment to the Constitution?

A   I believe that is the amendment that has to do with a person making statements tending to incriminate himself.

Q   You are aware of that right of a citizen not to talk regarding facts surrounding crimes that he is alleged to have committed?

A   Yes.

Q Did you want him, Doctor, at the times you examined him, to forego that right, Doctor?

A I asked for his cooperation in order that we could better ascertain the facts as he presented them.

Q Doctor, when he refused to answer those questions pertaining to the facts of that particular day that he got into trouble, did you hold that against him in any way?

A I did not.

Q Did you feel he was well within his rights in not answering your questions?

A I did as far as the situation on the date that he was arrested.

. . .

Q You said there was no spontaneity on his part. What do you mean by that?

A At no time did he enter into conversation except in response to a question.

Q Doctor, isn't that normal, rational procedure, when somebody examines somebody else, that he only answers questions and doesn't become enthusiastic in his conversation?

A Many of the patients that I examine spontaneously enter into the conversation.

Q But the fact that this patient, Mr. Perroni—this defendant—merely answered your questions, and did not shoot his mouth off, so to speak—is that any sign of his abnormality?

A Not in and of itself.

Q Did you, Doctor, expect him to pour his heart out to you, is that it, after seven years of confinement?

A I did not.

Q Did you, Doctor, see a note in the clinical records, or read a note—a short time ago that he was spontaneous?

A Yes, I believe there was such a note.

Q Do you know whether or not he is spontaneous with other people on the ward?

A   I do not.

. . .

Q   Now Doctor, none of those things alone that you had mentioned would cause you to arrive at the conclusion that Mr. Perroni cannot stand trial, would they?

A   None of them individually.

Q   And taken together, Doctor, could you tell us what the magic ingredient is that cements these things together and leads you to the conclusion that this man cannot stand trial?

A   Any illness, mental or physical, is marked by a combination of symptoms and signs. The things that I have mentioned are symptoms or, rather, signs of an emotional mental illness that would indicate in my opinion that this man is incapable of—suffering—is in such a state of insanity as to be incapable of understanding the charges, or the procedure, or aiding in his defense.

Q   Doctor, did you at any time note any action or any word on the part of this patient or defendant that you could tag as abnormal?

A   Any action?

Q   Yes, any physical action or word or phrase?

A   On occasion he demonstrated a particular mannerism involving his left palpebral fissure.

Q   His what?

A   His left palpebral fissure.

Q   What is that?

A   The left eye.

Q   What do you mean, he twitched his eye?

A   Twitched or looked upwards in a manneristic way.

Q   What does that indicate, Doctor?

A   In itself possibly nothing, but it is an additional thing that added to the other things is frequently, if not commonly, seen in certain mental illnesses.

Q   How many times did you see him twitch his eye?

A    I could not say.

. . .

Q    Now, the diagnosis that you make that this man Perroni cannot stand trial, is that made purely on a medical basis, Doctor?

A    That is made on a medical basis.

Q    Purely on a medical basis?

A    Yes.

Q    Have you, yourself, ever been a party to a lawsuit?

A    I have not.

    MR. JORDAN: I am going to object to that as being immaterial.

    THE COURT: Overruled.

Q    Have you ever been engaged in litigation, civil or criminal?

A    No.

Q    Do you know, Doctor, what it takes, practically speaking as a layman, to assist an attorney in the defense of a case?

A    I can speak as a psychiatrist.

Q    And speaking as a psychiatrist, where do you get your knowledge from as to what it takes in the courtroom to assist an attorney?

A    It would take judgment, understanding, it would take a memory, it would take a good contact with reality.

Q    All right. What in the clinical notes of your hospital that you read at length into the record—what in those notes do you find contrary to good memory, to orientation—is there anything in those notes that is contrary to this man's ability to understand and help in his defense? I am referring specifically now to the clinical notes of your institution.

    MR. JORDAN: If Your Honor please, I am going to object to it.

    THE COURT: Overruled.

A    These notes were made by people who are not psychiatrists, who are not even college graduates. Their ability to ascertain clearly and completely as to the memory, the orientation of an individual is not entirely clear.

Q  In other words, Doctor, it is your contention—your conviction—that only a man trained in psychiatry, and only a person who has gone through college, can determine whether a person is able to understand a charge against him and to participate in his defense. Is that your conclusion, Doctor?

A  I believe that is it under the law. (To the Court) Is it not, Your Honor?

THE COURT: I don't think you understood counsel's question. (To Reporter) Would you read it?

*Question read by Reporter as follows:*

Q  In other words, Doctor, it is your contention—your conviction—that only a man trained in psychiatry, and only a person who has gone through college, can determine whether a person is able to understand a charge against him and to participate in his defense. Is that your conclusion, Doctor?

A  I don't believe that these people who made these notes had any determination to make as to whether or not the man could stand trial or participate in his defense.

. . .

Q  Let me ask you, Doctor, can Mr. Perroni handle his everyday affairs?

A  I would say no.

Q  All right. Now, as I understand it, you based your answer on the supposition that his judgment is not good?

A  That's correct.

Q  Will you please tell us, Doctor, in what realm his judgment is not good?

A  His judgment in—may I refer to my notes, please?

Q  Yes.

A  I feel that his judgment is affected by his illogical thinking processes.

Q   Doctor, can you give me a single example from the records, from your interview with Mr. Perroni—a single example of any illogical thinking processes?

A   When it was explained to Mr. Perroni the desirability of his cooperating fully for the examinations that we asked him to cooperate in taking, his comment was "What good is that—how is that going to help me?"

Q   Is that the only remark, Doctor, in the entire proceedings?

A   This is one that I clearly recall. There were others.

Q   I see. And can you think of one other, Doctor— just a single one?

A   I cannot recall another one that I am sure of.

Q   Well, Doctor, it is a fact, is it not, that there is such a thing as despair?

A   Yes.

Q   And wouldn't you say, Doctor, that after a man has been incarcerated for seven years, attempting to get out for the purpose of standing trial, that he may feel "What is the use of answering questions"?

A   But it was fully explained to Mr. Perroni that this would add to the objectivity and the completeness of his examination. We very clearly explained to him we had no bias one way or the other. We were trying to determine the state of his mental processes in order to help the Judge in making his decision. We made this very clear to him.

. . .

Q   Doctor, does a person suffering from schizophrenia ever recover?

A   A person suffering from schizophrenia may recover socially.

Q   But not beyond socially?

A   That's correct.

Q   So that once a person suffers from schizophrenia he can never defend a lawsuit, right?

MR. JORDAN: I am going to object unless we know

what kind of lawsuit is concerned. In other words, is it under the Code of Criminal Procedure?

THE COURT: If the Doctor has an opinion on it I will let him express it. Overruled.

A   I don't believe I can answer that question.

Q   You can't answer the question? Is it too broad, Doctor?

A   It seems very broad.

Q   Is there any type of a lawsuit a person suffering from schizophrenia can defend?

A   I don't feel I am competent to get into that area.

Q   You are not competent?

A   I don't feel I can answer that question.

Q   From your examination of Mr. Perroni, will he, in your opinion, ever be able to defend himself against the charges that were placed against him approximately seven years ago?

A   I do not know.

Q   What information must you know, Doctor, in order to form an opinion? What information must Mr. Perroni give you, what questions must he answer for you in order for you to determine whether he will ever be able to defend himself against the charges that were brought against him?

A   It would be necessary for me to find on examination that he had sufficient awareness of reality, ability to reason, and to show absence of the signs that I found on my previous examination of his inability to at the present—

Q   (Interrupting) Doctor, what specific symptoms or signs would he have to rid himself of, or what would he have to acquire or accumulate, in order for you to declare that he was able to stand trial?

A   He would have to demonstrate a more logical process of reasoning than I was able to ascertain previously on my examinations.

Q   What specifically—what would he have to improve in?

A   I tried to, as best I can, indicate some of the specific things that I recall, specific questions. His thought processes when I examined him appeared illogical. Again I go back to the testimony I have given before that he appeared self-absorbed.

. . .

Q   Now, Doctor, is there such a thing as remission in a schizophrenic case?

A   Some individuals suffering from schizophrenia are felt to have remissions.

Q   Do you know whether Mr. Perroni at any time has had any remission, any time in the last seven years?

A   I do not know.

Q   Do you know whether he is in a state of remission at the present time?

A   When I examined him last in March, on March Twenty-fifth, in my opinion he was not.

Q   Now, Doctor, you said the word *insanity* was not a medical term, right?

A   It is not used commonly in medicine. The term that is used is another type.

Q   When you reported to Judge Kirby on March Twenty-seventh, when you signed a written report that Mr. Perroni was in a state of insanity, that is not a medical conclusion, right?

A   It is a translation of a medical conclusion into accepted legal terminology.

Q   And what is the equivalent, Doctor, of insanity in medical terminology?

A   As close as I could come to it would be that of psychosis.

Q   What you are saying to the Court today is that Mr. Perroni is in a state of psychosis, is that right?

A   I am saying today that the last time I examined Mr.

Perroni he was in such a state of imbecility, idiocy, or insanity as to be incapable of understanding the charges, procedures, or making his defense.

Q   Do you mean he was in a state of psychosis?

A   Yes.

Q   Do you have any conception, Dr. Roscoe, of what the defense of Mr. Perroni's case will entail?

A   Not being a lawyer, I am afraid I don't understand the full possibility.

MR. GROSS: That's all.

. . .

DR. MARTIN T. LIPSKY, having been called and duly sworn, testified as follows:

*Direct Examination*

*by* MR. JORDAN

Q   Dr. Lipsky, where do you live, sir?

A   Oakville State Hospital.

Q   And where do you carry on your duties?

A   At Oakville State Hospital.

Q   And in what capacity?

A   As Assistant Director, Administrative.

. . .

Q   Now, Doctor, during the course of your career as a psychiatrist, have you had occasion to have contact with people that are mentally ill?

A   Oh yes, sir.

Q   And have you had occasion to come into contact with people who are mentally ill as far as the criminal law is concerned?

A   Yes, sir.

Q   And will you tell the Court, please, approximately how many people have you come in contact with as far as being criminally insane?

A   On examinations, over three hundred.

Q   And as a result of these examinations you made

various conclusions as to whether a person was criminally insane or not, is that correct?

A    That is correct.

Q    Now, Doctor, did you have an occasion to come in contact with Mr. Perroni?

A    Yes, sir.

Q    Where was that, sir?

A    At Oakville State Hospital.

Q    Do you know when?

A    I was designated by the Director as one of the qualified psychiatrists to make an examination for the Court and to report my results of the examination to the Court. . . . My first examination after the oath was on February the twenty-third.

Q    Where did that take place?

A    That took place in the visitor's room on the sixth floor of the ward where the defendant was presently lodged.

. . .

Q    And can you tell us what the examination consisted of?

A    It was a complete mental examination.

Q    Well, will you please tell me what it consisted of?

A    By observing the defendant, watching his behavior, noting his method of talk, noting his content of thought, noting from the things just related his insight, judgment, and reasoning.

Q    Now, was part of this derived by the interview method, Doctor?

A    Yes.

Q    You asked various questions and he made or did not make various responses, is that correct?

A    That's correct.

Q    Now, what was the length of that examination, if you recall?

A    May I refer to my notes?

Q   If you have no independent recollection you may.

A   The examination on February the twenty-third was fifty minutes.

. . .

Q   What did you observe about him that made you come to a conclusion?

A   Generally, my observations were as follows: His general attitude showed aloofness, an air of superiority, a fixation of posture—he sat erect, arms folded, in most part staring into space. He showed a mannerism—the mannerism being a dilatation in the opening of the left palpebral fissure. He showed personal neglect, suspiciousness, and a psychomotor retardation.

Q   What was that last statement?

A   A psychomotor retardation.

Q   What does that mean?

A   When a question was asked, if an answer was given it was given after a delayed period. It was a definite delayed period before an answer was given to a question. And part of the time there was no answer given.

Q   Was there any time when there was no delay as far as the answers being given?

A   If I recall correctly, only with reference to when he spoke about the judge and the doctors, that the doctors had lied, and "Why doesn't the judge give me a fair trial —a trial by jury?"

. . .

Q   Now, you tell the Court approximately how long in cumulative time your examination took—all the examinations which you had as a result of being a qualified psychiatrist?

A   As a psychiatrist designated by the Director, 135 minutes.

. . .

Q   Now, as a result of your examinations and the other aids that are used, do you have an opinion of reasonable medical certainty as to whether Mr. Perroni is in such a state of idiocy, imbecility, or insanity as to know or understand the charges against him, and to assist counsel in his defense? Do you have an opinion?

A   Yes.

Q   What is that opinion?

A   It is my opinion that Mr. Perroni is in such a state of idiocy, imbecility, and insanity as to be incapable of understanding the charges against him, or the proceedings, or of making his defense.

. . .

MR. JORDAN: You may inquire.

*Cross-examination*

*by* MR. GROSS

Q   Dr. Lipsky, with what is the defendant Perroni charged? With what crime?

A   I was told yesterday it was carrying a gun.

Q   At the time of the examination, what was it?

A   I don't know. All I know is that he was sent in on a Code of Criminal Procedure, under Section 658.

Q   At the time you made your examinations at Oakville, and at the time you signed your opinion on March twenty-seventh of this year, you did not know with what Mr. Perroni was charged?

A   No, I did not.

Q   Did you have any idea at all?

A   No.

Q   Doctor, does it make any difference in your medical opinion with what a man is charged in order to be able to determine whether he can understand such a charge and can help defend such a charge?

A   No. The answer is no.

Q   The answer is no?

A   No. It doesn't matter what he is charged with. My psychiatric examination and opinion would be the same whether he was charged with murder or a misdemeanor.

Q Would it be the same whether the psychiatric examination is for the purpose of defending a case or whether it is for the purpose of drawing a will, or opening a bank account—it would make no difference, would it?

A Your previous question related to charge. Your present question is related to—you are intermingling will with charge. I can't answer the question. Will you break your question up?

Q I want an answer to the question I just asked.

A Would you read it?

*Question read by Reporter as follows:*

Q Would it be the same whether the psychiatric examination is for the purpose of defending a case or whether it is for the purpose of drawing a will, or opening a bank account—it would make no difference, would it?

A It certainly would.

Q It would make a difference?

A It certainly would.

Q All right. Now, is Mr. Perroni—as of March 27, 1962—in a position to draw a will?

A No, sir.

Q Is he in a position to open a bank account?

A I do not know the legal aspects of banking. I cannot answer.

Q Is it necessary to know the legal aspects of banking?

A I don't know. I don't know the legal aspects.

Q I say, is it necessary for you to know, to answer the question?

A Yes.

Q Is it necessary for you to know the process that is gone through in making a will in order to answer the question?

A Yes. I know that.

Q You know that?

A That I know.

Q   Do you know the process that is necessary in defending a criminal case?

A   Yes.

Q   I see. And you say that it makes no difference to you whatever the charge is, just so long as it is a criminal case, is that right?

A   If we keep category within category it makes no difference—the examination would be the same. If you are changing categories there is a difference in our determination.

Q   When you say category, Doctor, what do you mean by category?

A   If a defendant is up on a charge of misdemeanor or felony, the examination in one or the other would be exactly the same, and would give the same weight for both. When it is a determination for a will—for money determination—the question is whether the patient is psychotic. There is a difference between psychosis and mental illness. If the patient is going to open a bank account, I cannot relate. I do not know the laws of banking.

Q   Doctor, would it make any difference whether the crime was a crime that was *mala in se* or a crime which was *mala prohibita*? A crime which is *mala in se* is a crime which is bad in itself. For instance, an act that we don't have to be told by the legislature that the bad act is a crime—for instance, murder, larceny, robbery, arson. On the other hand, we have the type of crime which is *mala prohibita*. In other words, you can't travel more than sixty miles an hour with your automobile just because the lawmakers have said you can't travel any faster, but there is nothing bad in it itself. Now, does it make any difference to you, Doctor, in diagnosing a defendant's ability to defend a case whether it falls into the one category of an act that is bad in itself or an act because it is prohibited?

A   With the illustration as you have cited, thinking of

a vehicle as a dangerous weapon, I would say there would be no difference.

Q Well, Doctor, if Mr. Perroni were charged with speeding, would you say that he isn't able to come into Court, either with or without a lawyer, and say to the Judge—or help his attorney—and say "I was speeding" or "I wasn't speeding"? Would he be able to do that much?

A If he is mentally well or mentally ill?

Q As Mr. Perroni has been during the months of February and March of 1962 under your observation—and if he were charged with speeding—could he come into Court and tell the Judge "I am guilty of speeding" or "I am not guilty of speeding"?

A It depends on his reaction at the time. . . . At times going into Court he may not be able to—at other times, he may be able to.

Q Now, as of March 27, 1962, when you signed the report for Judge Kirby, would you say that at that time and for a few weeks previous that Mr. Perroni would have been able to come into a Traffic Court and tell the Judge "I am guilty of speeding" or "I am not guilty of speeding"?

A I would not, no.

Q You say he was unable to do so?

A That's correct.

Q Now, is it a fact, Dr. Lipsky, that Mr. Perroni regularly during February and March at Oakville State Hospital played cards?

A I don't know.

Q Well, I mean from the clinical notes.

A Of all the notes written that I have inspected, to my best recollection there were several occasions that he had played cards.

Q Would he have been in a position to play cards, Doctor, mentally?

A Yes. Oh, yes.

Q   He can understand that?

A   Oh, yes.

Q   Does that take any intelligence at all, Doctor?

A   A degree of intelligence.

Q   A higher degree than to plead guilty to a traffic charge, Doctor?

A   Well, I don't believe the two are analogous or can be compared. The playing of cards—we find mentally defective children playing cards. It is according to the game they are playing. We find that the two categories cannot be compared. You are trying to compare two categories.

Q   Doctor, you said that one of the reasons that you came to the conclusion that Mr. Perroni could not defend himself was the fact that when a question was put to him he thought out his answer—he delayed his answer and thought about it before he answered, is that so?

A   No, sir.

Q   You didn't say that?

A   I did not say he thought out his answer.

Q   What did you say?

A   I said there was a delayed reaction in answering.

Q   When you say "delayed reaction" what do you mean? A lapse of time?

A   A lapse of time in answering.

Q   Now, you have sat here all day, Dr. Lipsky, until now and you heard Dr. Roscoe testify, did you not?

A   That is correct.

Q   Now, did Dr. Roscoe delay in any of his answers when I put questions to him?

A   At times he did.

Q   At times they were rather lengthy delays, would you not say?

A   Well, you would have to define lengthy.

Q   At times half a minute went by, did it not?

A   No.

Q   Not a half a minute?

A   No.

Q   Thirty seconds did not go by at any time?

A   No, I don't think so.

Q   Doctor, you have delayed answering some of my questions, have you not?

A   That's correct.

Q   Without any personal reflection, does that in any way show a mental aberration on your part?

A   No, sir. The situation is different.

Q   Why is it different, Doctor, between you and me and Judge Kirby and this gentleman here, as to a delay in time in answering a question?

A   When you ask a question some of your questions contain clauses that require figuring out from the past record. When Mr. Perroni was asked a question, he was asked a simple question like "When were you married?"

. . .

Q   You did ask him, Doctor, about the circumstances that transpired on the day that Mr. Perroni was arrested —didn't you ask him that?

A   I asked him what the charges were.

Q   What did he say?

A   "Ask my lawyer" or words to that effect.

Q   Didn't he also tell you the records were downstairs at the office of Oakville State Hospital?

A   That is what he said.

Q   He told you that?

A   Yes.

Q   Isn't that an intelligent answer?

A   Taken out of context it would be considered an intelligent answer, but we are not considering taking a statement out of context.

Q   No, Doctor, we are not talking about taking a statement out of context. You asked the man "What were you charged with?" So the man says to you "The records are downstairs in the office of the Oakville State Hospital." Is that an intelligent answer?

A    As I said, taking a question out of context does not make an answer an intelligent answer. We have got to look at the entire bird's-eye view of the questioning and answers.

Q    I am taking the specific case of your having examined Mr. Perroni on a given date in February or March. I am asking you when you put that specific question to him on that specific date, you asked him what the charges were against him, and Mr. Perroni answered you, "The records downstairs in the office in Oakville will give you what the charges are." Was that an intelligent answer?

A    No, it is an evasive, negativistic answer from a psychiatric point of view.

Q    It is an evasive, negativistic answer from a psychiatric point of view?

A    This is a negativistic evasive answer. . . .

Q    I see. Did you go downstairs to the records room at Oakville State Hospital and try to find out what the charges were against this man?

A    I did not.

Q    You didn't care what the charges were against this man?

A    At the time of my examination I was going to be as objective as possible, and not refer to the previous examinations until my examination was over.

Q    During your examination you did not care what this man was charged with?

A    I did not say that. I said I was going to be as objective as possible and not let the other records influence me in any way.

   . . .

Q    Doctor, did you attempt to find out in any other

way what the charges against this man are other than by looking at old records?

A   I did not.

Q   You didn't think it was important?

A   I knew that the man was charged—he was in the hospital under 658 because that is what the Court order stated, and this is an indictment, and that is all I was concerned about.

. . .

Q   Now, Doctor, you talked about a snicker on this man's face. Can you tell us when and under what circumstances there was a snicker on Mr. Perroni's face?

A   When he was asked the question "Do you think the Judge has been fair with you?" That was when I observed that.

Q   Now, you also asked him "Do you think the Judge is being influenced by someone?" did you not?

A   That's correct.

Q   Did you expect him to answer that question, too?

A   I expected him to answer any question that is put forth in a psychiatric examination if he so desires. That is his privilege.

Q   Did you expect him to answer the questions that involved the circumstances of that particular day on which he was charged with a crime? Did you expect him to answer whether he did carry a gun or didn't carry a gun or what happened?

A   I didn't ask him about the gun because I didn't know if he was carrying it. I asked him what happened. Did I expect an answer? If he wanted to give it. If he didn't want to, he didn't have to.

Q   Doctor, did that in any way affect your psychiatric examination?

A   Oh, no.

Q   But on more than one occasion, Doctor, you repeated that question about what happened that day?

A   That's correct.

Q   And why did you persist in that question when he told you his lawyer advised him not to answer?

A   Because this was an avenue of questioning—a method of questioning—psychiatric questioning. It wasn't a method of acting as an attorney or a legal body. It was purely a method by which I could open up avenues of questioning to determine his mental status.

Q   But once he had refused by telling you his attorney had told him not to answer why did you persist on subsequent occasions to ask him?

A   The reasons I just gave in my previous answer.

Q   Even though the man told you he would not answer?

A   It was purely a point of view of psychiatric examination that these questions were asked.

. . .

Q   Now, Doctor, will you tell us why Mr. Perroni can't stand trial?

A   Would you want me to elaborate?

Q   No, not elaborate. Be specific in telling us why. Give specifics rather than general psychiatric terms.

A   We are psychiatrists. I must use psychiatric terms.

Q   No, I don't want psychiatric terms. I want plain everyday English.

A   If I can without using psychiatric terms. If I do use them you stop me and I will define it. I found the patient to be in general attitude and general behavior aloof, having an air of superiority.

Q   May I stop you there, Doctor, please? When you say a man is aloof, would you try to narrow that down so we can understand in what fashion Mr. Perroni was aloof?

A   I would use a synonym there of a lordly type—a lordly type of behavior reaction.

Q   What did he say or do that gave you that impression?

A   His method of walk, method of talk, his sitting fixed, head high.

Q   He was belligerent?

A   No.

Q   Defiant?

A   No. No, negativistic would be the term.

Q   What does negativistic mean, Doctor?

A   A reaction opposed to a normal reaction expected in a situation.

Q   Expected by whom?

A   By the psychiatrist who is doing the examination.

. . .

Q   It is necessary to have training in psychiatry in order to understand whether a man is able to stand trial or not, is that right?

A   No. If a man knows human behavior. For example, an outright psychotic—one does not have to be a psychiatrist to recognize.

Q   Is Mr. Perroni an outright psychotic?

A   I would say he is psychotic.

Q   But not outright?

A   Not in the gross, overt fashion that could be recognized by all lay people, no.

Q   I see. And you have typed him in what type, did you say?

A   Schizophrenia.

. . .

Q   Doctor, what makes you come to the conclusion that all these separate factors, as you call them—a snicker in one instance, an inappropriate grin—what makes you come to the conclusion that these things added together constitute or add up to an inability to defend himself in a courtroom?

A   When we have a person who shows symptoms of this type, as Mr. Perroni has shown, we can only draw one conclusion, and that is that this man is in such a state of insanity that he cannot defend himself, that he cannot make his own defense or understand the charges against him.

Q    Regardless of the nature of the charges?

A    Would you be specific on the nature of the charges?

Q    Of a criminal charge.

A    You are taking a generalized point of view here. I would like to be more specific.

Q    I say regardless of what the criminal charge is?

A    More or less, yes.

Q    Do you take into consideration at all the clinical notes that were read into evidence this morning?

A    Yes, I do.

Q    Is there a single thing in those clinical notes that indicate any mental illness on the part of Mr. Perroni?

A    There was an observation of seclusiveness in some of the notes.

. . .

MR. GROSS: That's all, Doctor.

THOMAS S. SZASZ, having been called and duly sworn, testified as follows:

*Direct Examination*

*by* MR. GROSS

THE COURT: Gentlemen, at this point, for the record, have The People rested?

MR. JORDAN: Yes, Your Honor.

Q    Dr. Szasz, what is your profession?

A    I am a psychiatrist.

Q    And you reside in the City of Syracuse, do you?

A    That's correct.

. . .

Q    Now, Doctor, at my request and at the request of the brothers of Louis Perroni, the defendant in this case, did you make contact with Louis Perroni sometime in the recent past?

A    I did.

Q   And can you tell us when you first saw Mr. Perroni?

A   I saw Mr. Louis Perroni first on Monday, April third.

Q   And where did you see him, Doctor?

A   At the Cedar Street Jail, in Syracuse.

Q   And could you tell us approximately what time of day it was, morning or afternoon?

A   It was at three-fifteen in the afternoon.

Q   And did you interview or communicate with Mr. Perroni at that time for any length of time?

A   I interviewed him, I talked with him then for one hour and forty-five minutes.

Q   And were you alone with him?

A   I was alone with him, locked in the cell.

Q   And what was the purpose, Doctor, of your interview and communication with him?

A   The purpose of my visit was to ascertain whether or not in my opinion he understood the charges pending against him and could assist counsel. In other words, whether he was fit to stand trial.

Q   And did you arrive at a conclusion after this hour and forty-five minutes, or did you not at that time arrive at any conclusion?

A   I arrived at the conclusion that satisfied me.

Q   I see. Now, did you at any time thereafter, after April the seventh, communicate with Mr. Perroni?

A   I requested that I be given access to the full records in the case, which I wanted to study, and after which I wanted to examine him once more.

. . .

Q   And you told me you wanted to get an order of the Court for the purpose of getting these records?

A   Correct.

Q   That was done, Doctor? Judge Kirby signed an order for that purpose?

A   Correct.

Q   You were given some 120 sheets of records which had been copied with a picture machine at the Oakville State Hospital?

A   Correct.

Q   And did you study those records, Doctor?

A   Yes.

Q   And could you estimate the length of time that you took in studying those records?

A   It was in excess of two hours.

Q   I see. And after you studied those records, Doctor, did you again interview Mr. Perroni?

A   I did.

Q   Where?

A   At the Cedar Street Jail.

Q   And do you remember the date of that visit, Doctor?

A   That was last Saturday, which I believe was the eighth. This past Saturday.

Q   And how long a time did you spend at the Cedar Street Jail with Mr. Perroni at that time approximately?

A   Half an hour.

Q   And when you came away, Doctor, from your second and last visit with Mr. Perroni, did you then have an opinion of Mr. Perroni's ability to understand the charges and to help counsel in his defense?

A   I did.

Q   And then, Doctor, you sat in Court all day yesterday, did you not, at counsel table?

A   I did.

Q   And during the nearly six or seven hours that you sat here did you observe Mr. Perroni who also sat at counsel table?

A   I did.

Q   Now Doctor, do you at this time have an opinion whether or not Louis Perroni, the defendant here, is in such a state of idiocy, imbecility, or insanity as to be incapable of understanding the charge against him, or the proceedings, or of making his defense?

> MR. JORDAN: I am going to object to the question, if Your Honor please. I don't believe a proper foundation has still been laid for the answer to that question.
>
> THE COURT: In what respect?
>
> MR. JORDAN: I don't think we have been told what the examination consisted of. We have heard that he saw him for an hour and forty-five minutes one day, and some other time another day, but we have no testimony in the record as to what the examination consisted of.
>
> THE COURT: Yes, I think I will sustain the objection on that ground.
>
> MR. GROSS: Counselor, do you mean the mechanics of the examination?
>
> MR. JORDAN: Well, just what the examinations consisted of.

Q   Doctor, will you please relate for us and for the record what you did the first time that you visited Mr. Perroni? Did you talk with him?

A   I conversed with him, yes.

Q   And what else—did you ask him questions?

A   I asked him questions.

Q   And what else did you do? You didn't give him a physical examination, did you?

A   I didn't give him a physical examination.

Q   You tell us professionally what you did.

A   I conversed with him.

Q   In other words, did you question Mr. Perroni for the purpose of determining whether or not he was able to stand trial and help in his defense, is that what you did?

A   That is what I did.

Q   Now, when you examined the records that were put

into your possession, what did you do in examining those records, did you read them?

A   I read them.

Q   Did you analyze them?

A   I read them.

. . .

Q   Now, Doctor, may I repeat my original question. In your opinion, Doctor, is or is not Louis Perroni, the defendant here, in such a state of idiocy, imbecility, or insanity as to be incapable of understanding the charge against him, or the proceeding or of making his defense?

MR. JORDAN: I am going to renew my objection, if Your Honor please. As I understand it, the only thing that the reply was as to what his examination consisted of, was that he conversed with the defendant and he also read the record. If that allows the psychiatrist to make an opinion, all right, but just pure conversation—I don't know what the conversation consisted of.

MR. GROSS: I will ask that question.

Q   Doctor, what you did—was that the approved psychiatric method of determining and arriving at a conclusion?

MR. JORDAN: Just a moment. I am going to object to what the approved routine method of examination is.

THE COURT: Overruled.

A   May I answer without saying yes or no?

Q   Any way you want to answer it.

A   In my opinion a correct psychiatric examination is conversation.

Q   And that is exactly the examination that you conducted?

A   Exactly.

Q   Now, Doctor, will you please answer my question then?

A   In my judgment Mr. Louis Perroni is not in such a state of idiocy, imbecility, or insanity as to be unable to understand the charges.

Q   Or the proceedings?

A   Or the proceedings against him.

Q   Or to making his defense?

A   Or to making his defense.

Q   Is there the slightest doubt in your mind, Doctor, about your conclusion?

A   No more doubt than about anything else I have in my mind. I always have doubt.

MR. GROSS: I see. That's all.

*Cross-examination*

*by* MR. JORDAN

Q   Now, Doctor, you are a psychiatrist, sir?

A   Yes.

Q   And will you call yourself—with due respect to modesty, sir—an expert on psychiatry?

A   That is for others to judge.

Q   All right. Are you also a theologian, would you say?

A   No.

Q   Now I am referring, Doctor, to *The Myth of Mental Illness*, written by you, sir. In that book I think you went into the realm of religion—part of that book, would you say?

A   Yes.

Q   And you also made various comments about the historical context of the New Testament and the Old Testament, is that correct?

A   I did.

Q   Did you quote a person by the name of Bridgman in your book, sir?

A   I have.

Q   And if I may read from page 199 in the book *The Myth of Mental Illness*: "More recently Bridgman noted that 'Christian ethics is primarily the ethics of partners in misery. A society like a modern democracy would have been unthinkable to St. Paul.' " Do you agree with that, Sir?

A   I do.

. . .

Q   Would you say that the more democracy we have the less need for the Bible?

A   I don't know about that.

Q   What would you say about that, Doctor? Can you expand on that statement a little bit?

A   Can you be more specific? Explain what?

Q   That statement you made in your book.

A   Can you read it again, perhaps two or three sentences before it, because I am not certain of the context.

Q   The sentence before it is "Lincoln said, 'As I would not be a slave, so I would not be a master. This expresses my idea of democracy. Whatever differs from this, to the extent of the difference, is not democracy.' "

A   I like that.

Q   You like that statement?

A   I like that statement.

Q   Who said that?

A   Lincoln.

Q   Lincoln said that?

A   Yes.

Q   And then you differ from Abraham Lincoln's definition of democracy in your book, is that correct?

A   That is not correct.

. . .

Q   Now, Doctor, you call it *The Myth of Mental Illness*. In my layman's terms would that mean that mental illness doesn't exist?

A   You could put it that way.

Q   So you are of the belief, Doctor, that there is no such thing as mental illness, is that correct?

A   That is fairly correct. Only fairly.

Q Only fairly? Well, Doctor, I want to be fair. You tell me what it is.

A I will be glad to. It means that the phenomena—the human behaviors which some people call mental illnesses—do indeed exist. But I think that calling them mental illnesses is about as accurate as to call them witchcraft, which they used to be called. Many people behave badly, annoy society—as the defendant has done socially—but to call him mentally ill is to do him a grave harm.

Q Could anybody be mentally ill, Doctor?

A I have just explained my objection to the term. If you define mental illness as social misbehavior, then certainly people can be mentally ill.

. . .

Q Doctor, are you a qualified psychiatrist?

A Qualified by whom?

Q Isn't there a term in the State of New York "a qualified psychiatrist"?

A You mean qualified by the State Department of Mental Hygiene?

Q Yes.

A No.

Q You are not?

A No, I am not.

Q Now, if you would say that there is a myth of mental illness, if you examined Mr. Perroni and, say, one hundred other people, would you ever come to the conclusion that any one of those people are mentally ill?

A I was not hired to examine Mr. Perroni to determine whether he was mentally ill.

Q Will you please answer my question, sir?

A You have asked a hypothetical question. In my professional life I have gone out of my way to be sure I would not be put in the position of having to do what you are asking me to do, namely of having to pronounce somebody mentally ill—because this is like branding him a criminal without a trial in this day and age. I would not do this. I would not accept the position.

Q   Doctor, isn't it true that in the development of the law, that one of the great beauties of the law is that a mentally ill person is not responsible for his acts?

A   I consider this is one of the most catastrophic things in American law.

Q   Would you rather have it this way, that a person who would be called mentally ill at the time he killed somebody should be hung or sent to the electric chair?

A   I am also opposed to the death penalty.

Q   Given life sentence, Doctor?

A   I think that every person accused of crime should stand trial. This is my bias.

. . .

Q   Doctor, did you make any notes on your examination of Mr. Perroni?

A   No.

Q   You made no notes at all?

A   No notes at all.

Q   And how long were you with Mr. Perroni?

A   Approximately one hour and forty-five minutes the first time, one half-hour the second time.

Q   What did your examination consist of, Doctor?

A   Conversation.

Q   Conversation? Would that take the form of a narrative or questions and answers?

A   A friendly conversation, questions and answers, but not a stoical "Did you do this?" or "Did you do that?"

Q   What questions did you ask him, Doctor?

A   I asked him about what happened when he was first apprehended. I told him to tell me only what he wanted to tell me because I may have to reveal in Court whatever he tells me.

THE COURT: Did he respond to that question?

A   He responded just as humanly as we are responding

to each other, I would say. I also asked him about his marriage. I asked him about many of the things that were covered in the previous testimony.

Q You have come to the conclusion that this man is not in such a state of idiocy, imbecility, and insanity as to be incapable of understanding the charges against him?

A Yes.

Q How many people have you examined, Doctor, as a psychiatrist?

A Total people?

Q Say, in the last two or three years. Say, in the last two years?

A In the last two years—very few.

Q Fifty?

A Less than that, I am sure.

. . .

Q Can you diagnose schizophrenia as a result of a conversation with an individual?

A This is a loaded question because I don't believe in the diagnosis—

Q (Interrupting) You don't believe in diagnosis, Doctor?

A No, I don't believe in diagnosis. I know how to make one. But I disbelieve in it.

Q You don't believe such a thing as schizophrenia exists?

A Not otherwise than as ink marks on a piece of paper. It is a name. But that the disease exists, no, I don't believe it.

Q You don't believe the disease exists?

A No.

Q What about pneumonia—do you think that disease exists?

A Yes, I think that disease exists.

Q How do you distinguish—how do you know it exists and schizophrenia does not exist?

A   I know that by virtue of the fact that pneumonia refers to a physical-chemical alteration in the human body. That exists in the same sense as a table exists. It is an object. But schizophrenia is supposed to be, even according to those who use it—it is like patriotism or democracy. It is a theoretical term. An abstraction. It can exist only as an abstract idea exists.

Q   It helps us from one person communicating to another to use a word?

A   It helps us. And it does something else even more —it hurts and confuses us.

Q   Would you say that for all psychiatry, Doctor?

A   I would say that for all psychiatric diagnostic terms. I think psychiatry is a fine enterprise if practiced properly.

Q   Would you be of the mind to redefine all psychiatric terms?

A   Why should I do that?

Q   In other words, if you say all psychiatric terms confuse us?

A   I didn't say that. I said diagnostic terms.

Q   Diagnostic terms? Would you substitute other terms?

A   No.

Q   Less confusing?

A   No. I would retain them. I would retain the terms we have. I don't believe in adding more words.

Q   So even though the terms we now have are confusing you would still retain them?

A   Yes. I would do something else, too.

Q   What would you do?

A   I would make clear the social context—the social situation—in which they originate historically and in which they are used. May I illustrate?

Q   Sure, go ahead.

A   If you came to me as a private patient—nobody knows about this—and if I say "You have schizophrenia.

You should come and see me for interviews and maybe I can help you," this will not affect you directly, socially. If you want to come, you come. If you don't, you don't. You will not lose your job, nothing dire will happen. But if I use the word *schizophrenia* outside of my office or in a courtroom it is a terrible thing. It is not the word—it is the context in which you say it that matters. . . . So these diagnostic terms have a tremendous social impact. To be called mentally ill is like being called a Negro in Alabama or a Jew in Nazi Germany—or to be called a schizophrenic in a courtroom. You are finished, unless somebody defends you. You can't stand trial, you have no rights, you can't get out of the hospital. Everybody is protecting you. Even the District Attorney is protecting you. Once this word gets out, particularly in the courtroom, you are finished. You have no more rights. Everybody all of a sudden wants to help, and you have no more enemies. Someone said "Protect me from my friends, and I will take care of my enemies." The so-called patient has no enemies; everybody wants to help. Has it occurred to his friends that letting him stand trial would be good for him?

Q  Doctor, someday when I may have a little more time I would like to answer some of your questions, but right now I want you to do the answering.

A  Well, I have answered, I think, your question.

Q  Do you think everybody is against Mr. Perroni in this case?

A  On the contrary. I have just tried to explain that everybody is for him. You should be against him and then he could stand trial. This is my point. You shouldn't be for him; be against him. Let Mr. Gross be for him and me. Don't let Dr. Lipsky be for him, but let him be his adversary. I believe in the American adversary system of justice. It may be old-fashioned but I believe in it. But I don't believe that people opposed to the defendant should be allowed to retain a psychiatrist. I think this is gross mis-representation.

Q   Didn't you hear the psychiatrists say who examined him as a result of the Court order that they had no disposition whatever, didn't you hear that?

A   No disposition? I am sorry.

Q   They didn't care one way or the other which way it went.

A   I heard it and I do not believe it for a moment. As a human being I believe, I know as surely as I am sitting here, that it is impossible to be impartial in a case like this. How can you be impartial? This case has been in the papers for seven years.

. . .

Q   Well, Doctor, you don't like a man being examined by a psychiatrist who you think is against him because they come out prejudiced, is that correct?

A   Correct.

Q   What about psychiatrists retained by the patient or his agents to examine him—do they come out prejudiced?

A   I have been trying to tell you about my prejudice for the last hour. I don't claim to be impartial. But I would say more. Not only do I not claim to be impartial, but it is my opinion that no psychiatrist is impartial in a case like this. I may be wrong. This is my opinion.

Q   You are of the opinion that this man was not insane before you even saw him, right?

A   No, that is not my opinion. In fact, I would like to tell you how I was retained in this case, if I may, because I think it is relevant at this point.

Q   Go ahead, Doctor.

A   I told Mr. Perroni's brother when he asked me to see Mr. Louis Perroni that I would not accept the case until I have had a chance to talk at sufficient length with Mr. Louis Perroni to see whether or not he is really out in left field—whether or not he thinks he is Jesus Christ, or that right is left, or day is night—or if he is completely disoriented. . . . So I said to Mr. Perroni's brother that I would like to talk to Mr. Louis Perroni, and if he seems to know what is going on then I would be glad to take his case. Otherwise, I would not—would have nothing to do with it. But you are quite right in one respect. In no circumstances would I be willing to examine him, take his money, then testify that he is mentally ill.

. . .

Q   Did you tell the brothers of Mr. Perroni that you will continue to treat him?

A   The subject never came up.

Q   So you aren't there to treat Mr. Perroni, are you, sir?

A   Certainly not.

Q   Just to examine him?

A   No, not to examine him. To give this testimony. The examination is just a preliminary. This was the point of my intervention, as I understood it. This was what I was hired for.

Q   To give testimony?

A   To give testimony.

Q   Not·to examine him?

A   The examination was a preliminary, a necessity, in order for me to give rational, relevant, meaningful testimony.

. . .

Q   Now, Doctor, I believe you testified before the United States Senate—a Committee of the United States Senate, is that correct?

A   I had that privilege.

Q   Now, did they ask you to define mental health or mental illness?

. . .

A  Yes.

Q  Now, do I assume that you do not subscribe to the general definition of mental illness as used today?

A  No, you cannot assume that. My objection is not so much to the definition as to the social consequences of using the term.

Q  Your objection is to the social consequences?

A  Of using the term.

Q  All right, Doctor. What definition would you give to get away from the social consequences of using the term?

A  I would not look for a remedy in definition. I would look for a remedy in expressing as emphatically as possible the terrible social consequences which happen to a person when he is called mentally ill in a courtroom.

Q  Do you feel that it is detrimental to a person to be called mentally ill in a courtroom?

A  I do not believe it is a question of what I think. It is a question of fact, Mr. Jordan.

Q  Who is it detrimental to, sir?

A  It is detrimental to the so-called patient. May I elaborate? You asked how is it different to be called mentally ill than from having pneumonia. A person who has pneumonia loses none of his civil rights. But a person who is said to be mentally ill to the extent of being hospitalized loses his civil rights—he can't walk around as a free man.

Q  You feel that the sections of the law dealing with insanity pertaining to a man accused of a crime is a detriment to that person?

A  No, sir, not to a man accused of a crime. Of any man on whom the label "mental illness" is pinned against his own will in a public proceeding by a superior person. If an inferior person pins this label on him it doesn't make much difference. But if a socially superior, that is to

say, more powerful, person pins it on him it is detrimental.

. . .

Q  Would you assume then, Doctor, that two psychiatrists designated to aid the Court, would be against the
interest of the person they are examining?

A  They might be against his interests as the defendant
himself defines his interests. They need not be against his
interests as the Court defines his interests.

. . .

Q  Now, did you discuss the charge with Mr. Perroni?

A  I discussed the charge insofar as I knew what the
charge was.

. . .

Q  Did he discuss it with you?

A  Yes. Very freely.

. . .

Q  What do you look for, Doctor, in determining
whether a man is able to stand trial, or assist his counsel
in defending the charges against him on a criminal
charge?

A  Maybe to me psychiatry is simpler than to some
people, but I just like to ascertain whether he can talk
to me reasonably, like anybody else, whether he is mentally clear and rational.

Q  You came to the conclusion that Mr. Perroni did
not have any mental illness, is that correct—that Mr.
Perroni does not have any mental illness?

A  Oh, no. I didn't try to examine him for mental illness. I have already told you my reservations about mental
illness.

Q  You came to the conclusion Mr. Perroni is not in
such a state of insanity he couldn't prepare for his defense?

A  As I understand it.

Q  Did you ever examine anybody else pertaining to
a criminal charge?

A   Very few people.

Q   Very few?

A   Very few.

Q   The people that you did examine, did you ever come to the conclusion that they were in such a state of insanity they couldn't stand trial?

A   No.

Q   So that nobody you have ever examined pertaining to a criminal charge has ever been in such a state of insanity that he didn't know what the charges against him were or couldn't help his counsel in preparing for his defense?

A   This is correct. The total number I examined may be less than four, I would say.

Q   In your, say, fifteen years of experience?

A   I tried to explain that I have avoided these cases.

Q   Oh. That you don't take in your practice, either?

A   That's right. I have avoided being a qualified psychiatrist because I don't want to do—what I call prosecute people for mental illness. If I find somebody mentally ill who doesn't want to be mentally ill I become the prosecutor. This would be my definition of it. I don't want to prosecute anybody for mental illness.

Q   Are you a medical doctor?

A   Why, certainly.

Q   If I come to you and I say "I need an examination. Please don't find cancer." And then you do find cancer. Would you say I had cancer?

A   As a practical question?

Q   Yes.

A   As a practical matter, I would ask you to go to another doctor who does this examination. I am not that kind of doctor.

Q   You don't cover that, either?

A   This is an age of specialization.

Q   What about hypothetically, Doctor?

A Hypothetically, I would proceed as follows. I would ask you: If you don't want me to find cancer, why do you ask me to examine you?

Q That would be the question you ask me?

A Well, you are the patient. This is what I would tell you.

. . .

> MR. JORDAN: Thank you very much, Doctor.
>
> MR. GROSS: No questions.
>
> (Witness excused)
>
> THE COURT: All right. The evidence is closed. The Court will reserve decision.

\* \* \*

Approximately six weeks after the hearing, Judge Kirby handed down his decision: he found Mr. Louis Perroni incompetent to stand trial. Mr. Perroni was thereupon transferred from the Cedar Street Jail in Syracuse to the Matteawan State Hospital in Beacon, N.Y. Appeals from the Court's ruling have failed. At the time of this writing (February 1965), Mr. Perroni remains confined at Matteawan. He has now been incarcerated for nearly ten years.

## III

It would be superfluous to comment on this tragic story. What could one say?

I should, however, like to call attention to two issues which we encounter in this case and in many others in which the accused is forced to submit to pretrial psychiatric examination. One is the pressure on the defendant to incriminate himself to the psychiatrist, and the dire consequences of his refusal; the other is the prosecution's prerogative to request and obtain not just one pretrial psychiatric examination but several.

The defendant forced to submit to court-ordered psychiatric examination before trial is under strong pressure to "cooperate" with the examining psychiatrists. However, it is a euphemism to speak of "cooperation" here. For the accused is in a bind: he is damned if he cooperates and damned if he does not.

When Mr. Perroni was arrested in 1955 and ordered to undergo pretrial psychiatric examination, he cooperated with the psychiatrists. (He had, incidentally, no counsel until after he was declared unfit to stand trial and committed to Matteawan.) Mr. Perroni trusted the psychiatrists who came to see him. He talked to them. He explained his reasons for acting as he did. The psychiatrists regarded his reasons evidence of mental illness and declared him unfit to stand trial. Thus, by "cooperating" with the court-appointed psychiatrists, Mr. Perroni incriminated himself as "mentally ill."

Seven years later, assisted by defense counsel, Mr. Perroni was less cooperative: he declined to discuss the circumstances of his alleged offense. Yet, despite his assertion that he was doing so in an effort to protect himself, the court-appointed psychiatrists persisted in quizzing him about the details of his crime. It is important to note that information elicited in this type of examination is not protected under the principle of medical confidentiality, and is admissible in court as evidence against the defendant. Nevertheless, the examining psychiatrists maintained that their questions served a purely psychiatric purpose and interpreted Mr. Perroni's refusal to answer, not as an exercise of good judgment, but as "lack of cooperativeness" and "negativism" which added up to "mental illness."

This invitation to self-incrimination, as guilty, mentally sick, or both, is present in all such examinations. The habeas corpus hearing of Mr. Abraham Hoffer (Chapter 5) provides another illustration of this.

Of equal or perhaps greater significance is the issue of the prosecution's privilege to request, and obtain, not just one but several pretrial psychiatric examinations of the defendant.

This must be contrasted with the single chance of the district attorney to prosecute. At the conclusion of a criminal trial, if the defendant is acquitted, the prosecutor cannot appeal and request a retrial; however, if convicted, the defendant can appeal. This asymmetrical arrangement serves to protect the weak citizen from the strong state.

No such rule constrains the prosecution in its efforts to obtain a psychiatric "conviction." Since a psychiatric finding of unfitness to stand trial (with subsequent incarceration in a hospital for the criminally insane) is not considered a "verdict" like one reached at the conclusion of a criminal trial, the district attorney may request repeated examinations of the defendant. Once the "logic" of the medical view of this situation is accepted, it is reasonable that he should do so; after all, it is always possible that the defendant might have become "sick" again since his most recent examination.

In practice, this means that even if a defendant declared mentally unfit to stand trial manages to reverse this finding in a habeas corpus hearing and succeeds in being returned to court for trial, instead of being tried he may be ordered to submit to a fresh psychiatric examination. This is precisely what happened to Mr. Perroni. In June 1961, after spending approximately six years at the Matteawan State Hospital, Mr. Perroni and his attorney obtained a favorable ruling in one of their numerous habeas corpus hearings. Mr. Perroni was returned to court in Onondaga County (where the alleged crime had been committed). But again, despite the decision of a State Supreme Court Judge in Dutchess County that Perroni was fit to stand trial, the district attorney moved that he was not fit and should be examined by psychiatrists. Again the court concurred, ordered the examination, declared

Perroni unfit to stand trial, and recommitted him to Matteawan.

In brief, it is possible—and legally proper—to force a defendant to submit to any number of pretrial psychiatric examinations, thus increasing the likelihood, which is high in any case, that he will be found mentally incompetent to stand trial. This practice was adopted or attempted in three of the four cases here reported. (It was not applicable in the Lynch case, where psychiatric incarceration was secured through a forced plea of "not guilty by reason of insanity" rather than through a forced pretrial psychiatric examination.)

# 5 THE CASE OF MR. ABRAHAM HOFFER

¶ If freedom is humiliated or in chains today, it is not because her enemies had recourse to treachery. It is simply because she has lost her natural protector. Yes, freedom is widowed, but it must be added because it is true: she is widowed of all of us.*

## I

On July 3, 1960, I received a letter from an inmate of the Matteawan State Hospital, an institution for the so-called criminally insane in New York State. It read, in part, as follows:

Box 307
Beacon, New York

DEAR DR. SZASZ:

I am about to tell you my true tale of woe, and I do hope you can help me out. . . .

I was arrested on or about October 20, 1958, later indicted for a crime, and after six months detained in county jail, the prosecution directed the County Judge to send me to a "legal no man's land," a mental hospital. . . . My case happens to be a "mistaken identity," and I claim to be innocent. I protested my innocence since my arrest. My co-defendant received a verdict dismissal on or about January 29, 1959, but I was unfortunate. I was sent to a mental hospital where I am writing you at the present time.

I am getting no treatment, and I do not claim, in my honest

* Albert Camus, "Bread and Freedom" (1953), in *Resistance, Rebellion, Death*, p. 89.

144

opinion, to be mentally ill or insane, but rather "sane." I understand the quality and nature of the alleged act I am charged with. I have witnesses in my behalf, and I certainly can put up a strong defense. All I ask for is justice, and I am refused a chance to go back to the original court and put in a plea of "not guilty."

I have been to court at Poughkeepsie on a Writ of Habeas Corpus but I was turned down, due to the doctor's report claiming me "sick," of unsound mind, who cannot make out right from wrong; and which isn't true, in my honest opinion. . . .

I am a veteran of World War II. I participated and saw several battles in North Africa and Italy. I was wounded in Italy. I was sent back to the States and treated, and finally received my honorable discharge from an Army mental hospital. . . .

Doctor, all I ask for, but I am refused, is to stand trial on my alleged indictment. I am charged with kidnapping. . . .

> Respectfully,
> ABRAHAM HOFFER*

I answered Mr. Hoffer's letter and we proceeded to correspond. It developed that Mr. Hoffer was a well-educated person—he had been to college; also, that he had considerable funds—but no access to them, having been adjudged legally incompetent to manage his affairs.

The first thing Mr. Hoffer needed was an attorney to represent him. He had none, and knew of none he could approach. I recommended Mr. William F. Mann, of New York City. Mr. Hoffer contacted Mr. Mann, who, after visiting Mr. Hoffer at Matteawan, accepted him as his client. We agreed that I would act as Mr. Hoffer's psychiatrist if, after examining him, I considered him mentally fit to stand trial; if I did not consider him fit, I would withdraw from the case.

* The dates and the names of persons, places, and institutions (except mine, the Dutchess County Court's, and the Matteawan State Hospital's) are fictitious; otherwise the account is factual.

Since Mr. Hoffer had been adjudged legally incompetent to manage his affairs, he had no authority to retain either counsel or psychiatrist. Thus, first, Mr. Mann had to be retained by Mr. Hoffer's "committee" (legal guardian) as his counsel; then, I as his psychiatrist. It was a long and tedious procedure, the details of which I will omit.

After Mr. Mann was appointed Mr. Hoffer's attorney by his committee, he filed a petition for a writ of habeas corpus on behalf of his client. At long last I received court authorization to examine Mr. Hoffer and his hospital record. I visited him at the Matteawan State Hospital on January 27, 1961, and found him fit to stand trial. I informed Mr. Hoffer of my opinion and subsequently, in writing, his committee and Mr. Mann.

What else did I learn about Mr. Hoffer, from talking to him and from studying his records? The most important facts for our understanding of what had happened to Mr. Hoffer so far, and what was to happen to him later, are that his current confinement at Matteawan stemmed from his being indicted, on November 29, 1958, by the Bronx County Grand Jury and charged with the following offenses: kidnapping; rape in the first degree; sodomy in the first degree; assault in the second degree; attempted rape in the first degree; and impairing the morals of minors. The charge of rape in the first degree had been dismissed prior to his commitment to the Matteawan State Hospital, but the other charges were still standing. (Specifically, he was alleged to have engaged in sexual activities with two girls, aged eleven and thirteen. He denied having done so.)

Furthermore, Mr. Hoffer had received a neuropsychiatric discharge from the Army and was receiving compensation, having been diagnosed as suffering from schizophrenia. He had also had several previous arrests and a few convictions for minor offenses.

After several postponements, the habeas corpus hearing was set for May 17, 1961.

# II

The hearing was held at the Dutchess County Court House in Poughkeepsie, New York, on May 17, 1961. The following persons participated:

ABRAHAM HOFFER, Relator.

DR. BRIAN HIGGINS, Superintendent, Matteawan State Hospital, Respondent.

HON. JAMES B. CAMPBELL, Justice of the Supreme Court.

EDWARD M. KANTOR, ESQ., Assistant Attorney General, New York State, attorney for the respondent.

WILLIAM F. MANN, ESQ., attorney for the relator.

PHILIP I. ROSENBERG, M.D., psychiatrist for the respondent.

THOMAS S. SZASZ, M.D., psychiatrist for the relator.

MR. KANTOR: May it please the Court, this is a habeas corpus proceeding commenced by the relator, Abraham Hoffer, with his petition verified the fourteenth day of August 1960 and the writ of habeas corpus issued thereon by the Honorable John F. Daly, Deputy Clerk, Appellate Division, the Honorable Frank Murdock presiding. The return to the writ is verified the sixth day of September 1960. The matter having been adjourned from September 19, 1960—that is, having been adjourned on several occasions up to today.

THE COURT: All right.

MR. KANTOR: I will also produce the original commitment of this relator to Matteawan. The relator is here.

ABRAHAM HOFFER, being first duly sworn, testified as follows:

*Direct Examination*
*by* MR. MANN

Q   Mr. Hoffer, you are the relator in this proceeding?

A   That's right.

Q   And you are now in Matteawan State Hospital?

A   That's right.

. . .

Q   Now, prior to your commitment from Bronx County, had you been indicted for any criminal acts in Bronx County?

A   I was indicted for the crimes of rape in the first degree, two counts of kidnaping in the first degree, sodomy in the first degree, attempted rape in the first degree, two assault counts, and the Penal Code Law 483, Subdivision 2, impairing the morals of a minor.

Q   In other words, there were how many counts of the indictment?

A   There were nine counts. . . .

Q   At the time of your arrest were you arrested with another man?

A   A co-defendant by the name of James Doolan.

. . .

Q   Did you understand later that James Doolan had made a statement to the police of New York that you were his accomplice or partner?

A   That's right. I was told that at the Police Precinct, the Bathgate Avenue Police Precinct, in the Bronx.

. . .

Q   And you claim to be innocent of these charges that were made against you?

A   I claim to be innocent of the charges against me in this particular case. And I have never seen the co-defendant. I was working at the Hotel Willoughby.

. . .

Q   Did you commit the crimes mentioned in the indictment?

A   I never committed the crimes mentioned in the indictment.

Q   Now, were you ever tried on this charge, on the indictment?

A   I was never tried on this indictment.

Q   Did you ever have a preliminary hearing in the City Magistrate's Court of the City of New York, after your arrest?

A   I never had any hearing at all on this particular indictment.

Q   Were you ever confronted by the person or persons mentioned in the indictment?

A   I never was confronted with the two children mentioned in the indictment.

. . .

Q   And do you remember the names of the doctors who examined you at Bellevue Hospital?

A   Dr. Demuth and Dr. Ross.

. . .

Q   Did they examine you jointly or separately?

A   Separately.

. . .

Q   Now, can you say how long Dr. Demuth examined you?

A   I would say that Dr. Demuth examined me for about fifteen minutes.

Q   How long did Dr. Ross examine you?

A   For about five or ten minutes. . . .

Q   Now, do you know what they said about you?

A   Dr. Ross made a statement that "We are going to send you to Matteawan State Hospital where you belong. You were there before, you are going back." That's all. And he said, "Good-bye."

. . .

Q   Mr. Hoffer, then you understand what this proceeding is about today?

A   The proceeding today is that I would like to go

back to the Bronx County to be adjudicated in the right manner.

Q You mean to be tried?

A To be tried on my indictment.

. . .

Q Do you understand the nature of the charges against you?

A I do.

Q Have you conferred with counsel in defense of these charges?

A I have.

. . .

Q How many times have you conferred with me?

A Oh, I would say on several occasions, about five or six times.

Q During those occasions did you give me all of the details and the facts constituting your defense to the indictments?

A I did.

Q Did you give me the names and addresses of witnesses?

A The names of witnesses, right.

. . .

Q Did you discuss thoroughly and in detail all of the counts in the pending indictment against you?

A I did.

Q Did you also, besides telling your attorney personally about your defense to these charges, did you also write him a number of letters?

A I did.

. . .

Q Did you also inform your own doctor of the facts constituting your defense to these charges?

A I told Dr. Szasz all about my pending indictment and my medical background, my service record, whatever was asked. I did confer with Dr. Szasz, in a right and orderly manner, and whatever question was put to me I did answer to my best knowledge.

Q   Now, Dr. Szasz, you say, is here in Court today?

A   That's right. . . .

Q   Did he visit you at Matteawan State Hospital?

A   He did, on approximately January 27, 1961.

Q   Did he talk to you about your case?

A   He did.

Q   Well, now what has been your record while you have been at Matteawan for the last approximately two years?

A   I would say I have conducted myself in an orderly manner, polite to everyone, obeyed orders, and I worked on a job.

Q   What job?

A   I worked in the dining room. The second month I was here I got a job from a doctor, Dr. Hotchkiss, and I worked for Mr. Stanton at the reception. I worked for Mr. Richard Norton at the Old Building.

Q   What is your occupation or livelihood in civilian life?

A   Hotel clerk.

. . .

Q   Now, tell me, during your confinement at Matteawan State Hospital, how do you while away your time?

A   Well, I would try to locate magazines, books from the library, and I would while away my time by reading books, watching the television, watching discussion programs, "Meet the Press," whatever can be had at that particular time in Matteawan. Also I would read the newspapers. I would buy *The New York Times,* I would buy the New York *Journal-American.*

. . .

Q   Have you been keeping abreast of current events?

A   That's right.

Q Will you tell us how you were able to contact Dr. Szasz as the psychiatrist in this matter?

A I first read about Dr. Szasz at Syracuse in *The New York Times* in an article on the Senate hearings, where Dr. Szasz was fighting for civil rights. And I got the name and address, and I did write to him, from that article.

Q What did the article say?

A Well, it said that Dr. Szasz is fighting for patients' civil rights, and for having patients go to trial on criminal proceedings, if they have a charge lodged against them, back to the original court, and have a trial by jury.

. . .

Q While at Matteawan, besides watching the television programs and reading books and *The New York Times,* what else did you do for recreation?

A Nothing.

Q Did you gamble?

A I did gamble, yes.

Q What kind of gambling?

A I gambled on the different sports like football, baseball, hockey. And I would pick many winners.

Q Now, in talking about gambling on football, do you mean on the results of football games?

A Yes.

Q What did you bet with?

A I bet with cigarettes.

MR. KANTOR: Your Honor, this is all immaterial, I think. Why he gambled and what he gambled for.

THE COURT: No, I assume that he wants to show that he had the mental capacity. I don't know whether that's a test of sanity or not, to be honest with you.

MR. MANN: To show judgment.

THE COURT: Well, I don't know about that. I will let you ask the question.

. . .

MR. MANN: All right, your witness.

*Cross-examination*

*by* MR. KANTOR

Q   Mr. Hoffer, what are you doing in Matteawan? Why are you in Matteawan?

A   I was sent here by two psychiatrists at Bellevue, Dr. Demuth and Dr. Ross. . . .

Q   Now do you feel that you belong in Matteawan?

A   I do not feel that I belong in Matteawan.

Q   Then why do you think you wound up in Matteawan? Why did they place you in Matteawan?

A   Dr. Ross said that I have a mental background and that I was in Matteawan before, so the best place for me is back at Matteawan.

Q   Have you a mental background?

A   I have.

Q   Could you give us a brief review of it?

A   In 1944, in Italy, I was hospitalized. I was sent back on a hospital ship to the Stark General Hospital at Charleston, South Carolina—that's a stopping-off point. I stayed there a few weeks, about three or four weeks, and then I was sent to Mason General Hospital, Brentwood, Long Island.

Q   What were you hospitalized for?

A   I was hospitalized—they had a diagnosis of dementia praecox, hebephrenic.

Q   This is while you were in the service?

A   That's right.

. . .

Q   All right. Now, in what other mental institution have you been?

A   I was at Kings Park State Hospital, Kings Park, Long Island, New York.

Q   What date?

MR. MANN: Now, if Your Honor please, I will object to the question unless it related to some period of time not more than two years ago, because we are not interested in this patient's mentality or competency more than two years ago. We are interested at the present time.

MR. KANTOR: I wish to show—and I will tie it in, Your Honor—that all these commitments relate to the same particular type of charge, the same type of mental illness that has been consistent throughout this man's life. . . .

. . .

MR. MANN: The Matteawan records show that he recovered, that he was discharged on any prior commitment. The report of any prior commitment ends with the words that this patient has recovered and is therefore discharged. So therefore, going back into that ancient history of what happened several years ago I don't think is material. We are interested in this man's mental capacity today, to understand the nature of the charges pending against him.

THE COURT: Yes, I think you are correct in that.

MR. KANTOR: Your Honor, I rest my entire case on the question of this person's mental condition today.

THE COURT: Yes.

MR. KANTOR: But I wish to show that the very crime for which he is presently charged is similar to several other commitments and other arrests in the past, to show that this man's mental capacity with respect to these particular offenses is still the same as it has always been.

MR. MANN: Well, the Attorney General overlooks the fact that on a prior offense he was discharged and acquitted by a jury. And if we are going to go into this history of what happened before—

THE COURT: Well, I will sustain the objection.

. . . .

Q  Do you feel you are mentally sick now, Mr. Hoffer?

A  I do not feel that I am mentally sick right now.

Q  Do you feel you have ever been mentally sick?

A  I figure that I probably was mentally sick—well——

Q  Be careful what you say now.

A  I am going to be careful. I was never mentally sick.

Q  Never mentally sick?

A  That's right.

Q  Now, you have been in conflict with the law before, haven't you?

A  I was.

Q  And always with crimes or charges involving young girls. Is that correct?

MR. MANN: Just a minute, I object to that.

MR. KANTOR: That's a matter of record.

MR. MANN: It may be a matter of record, but we are not going back into ancient history.

THE COURT: Well, I don't know what you are trying to prove. Are you trying to prove a continuing criminal tendency?

MR. KANTOR: Yes, that this man is mentally sick with respect to this thing. And I submit again, Your Honor, that this is a matter which the doctors have examined and which they find this man is still mentally sick with respect to.

THE COURT: I will take it subject to the doctor's connection.

MR. KANTOR: Thank you.

MR. MANN: I object to the statement made by counsel because the issue here is not whether this man is mentally sick. Because he can still be mentally sick and in this proceeding there are only two issues—whether he understands the nature of the charges; whether he can confer with counsel. If he is sick otherwise, it is not material.

THE COURT: That's right.

MR. KANTOR: I will not oppose that statement of counsel.

THE COURT: All right.

. . .

Q   Now, what are you charged with at the present time?

A   I am charged on a nine-count indictment—at the present time it is eight counts. One count, the third count—

Q   You mentioned that there are eight counts against you now.

A   There are eight counts against me.

Q   And not just one?

A   There are eight counts against me right now.

THE COURT: Do you know what disposition was made against your so-called co-defendant?

MR. HOFFER: As far as I know, the disposition was made, that he got time served for Section 483 of the Penal Code Law, Subdivision 2, he got time served. He was sent from County Court by the Honorable Judge Timothy L. Mentiss to Kings County and later on transferred to Bellevue Hospital for psychiatric—declared to be a schizophrenic, et cetera. And then sent back to Court, and the attorney took back the original plea of not guilty to the indictment and he pleaded guilty to Section 483 of the Penal Code Law, Subdivision 2, impairing the morals of a minor, and he got time served for it.

Q   You say he was diagnosed as a schizophrenic?

A   From the records that I did see from my attorney, Mr. Mann.

Q   Isn't that the same diagnosis that you have?

A    From the records, yes.

. . .

Q    Mr. Hoffer, have you been in Kings Park Hospital on two previous occasions?

A    I was.

Q    And have you been in Bellevue Hospital on several occasions?

A    I was.

Q    And have you been in—

MR. MANN: Now, just a minute. I object. Counsel is going back earlier than two years ago.

THE COURT: Yes, I think we are just encumbering the record. I think the doctor is going to testify as to his previous incarceration. He probably has to have that to form a medical opinion. The mere fact that he was previously incarcerated in and of itself does not mean anything, if he was discharged.

. . .

MR. KANTOR: All right, no further question.

MR. MANN: That's all, Mr. Hoffer.

THE COURT: All right, you may step down, Mr. Hoffer.

. . .

THOMAS S. SZASZ, M.D., being first duly sworn, testified as follows:

*Direct Examination*

*by* MR. MANN

Q    Doctor, are you a duly licensed physician of the State of New York?

A    I am.

MR. KANTOR: We will concede the doctor's qualifications, if Your Honor please.

MR. MANN: All right.

Q    Now, Doctor, did you have the occasion to examine Abraham Hoffer, the relator in this proceeding?

A   Yes.

Q   When and where did you examine him?

A   At Matteawan State Hospital.

Q   When?

A   Towards the end of January—on January 27 or 28.

Q   1961, this year?

A   This year, yes.

Q   Prior to the time that you examined him, did you have the opportunity to examine the Matteawan State Hospital records concerning Mr. Abraham Hoffer's confinement therein?

A   I did.

Q   After studying that record, and after interviewing Mr. Hoffer at the hospital in January of this year, were you able to form any conclusions based upon your own knowledge and training in the field of psychiatry, based upon the study of his hospital records? Now, have you formed any opinion as to his mental condition?

A   I formed an opinion as to his mental condition to stand trial, to understand the charges and to stand trial, yes.

Q   Have you formed any opinion as to his capability of understanding the indictment against him?

A   I have. . . .

Q   And as to his capability of conferring with his counsel in defense of those counts?

A   I have.

Q   And what is the opinion that you have formed?

A   My opinion is that he is capable of understanding the indictment and he is capable of conferring with counsel.

. . .

Q   Now, generally speaking, the doctors who are on the staff of Matteawan State Hospital, are they able to gain the confidence of the patient when they interview the patient at the hospital and make their notes or comments on his condition?

MR. KANTOR: I object to that again, Your Honor.

THE COURT: Sustained.

Q Are they in a similar position to a doctor who is retained by the patient privately, or through the patient's attorney—are they in the same position, medically speaking and psychiatrically speaking, as the doctors who are on the staff of the state institution like Matteawan State Hospital?

THE COURT: Can you answer that, Doctor?

DR. SZASZ: Yes, sir. It is my personal opinion that doctors not retained by a patient, and especially doctors representing opposing interests, are in no position to render any psychiatric service, in the correct sense of the term, to that patient. The analogy would be that if you, Your Honor, apply for life insurance and are referred to a physician who examines you, he is not your doctor, he is the life insurance company's doctor; if you are sick, you call your own doctor. By the same token, the doctors at the state hospital may be good doctors, but they are not Mr. Hoffer's doctors, they are his adversary's doctors.

MR. KANTOR: I am going to object to the witness' statement, and I will move to strike it from the record because from the witness' statement he infers that because these doctors are retained by Matteawan State Hospital that their interests are adverse to those of the inmates of the institution, and that does not necessarily follow.

THE COURT: I will let it stand and take it for what it is worth. . . .

Q Well, now these doctors whose comments are contained in the hospital record, they are doctors employed by the State of New York, is that right?

A    That is correct.

Q    Are they on the staff of a hospital which is under the jurisdiction of the Department of Correction of the State of New York? Is that right?

A    That is my understanding.

Q    And Matteawan State Hospital is not under the jurisdiction of the Department of Mental Hygiene?

A    That is correct.

Q    So that Mr. Hoffer is now in a correctional institution?

A    That would be my definition of the institution.

. . .

Q    Now, have you seen notes in the hospital record, Relator's Exhibit Number 4, where there are comments made by the doctors in Matteawan, in which they say that this patient still denies or keeps on repeating his denial of having committed the crime and he still insists upon his innocence?

A    I have.

Q    How do you interpret those opinions?

A    I should like to read this entry and make one comment on it: "December 29, 1959: He continues to deny the crime he had been indicted for."

I interpret this in two possible ways: One, he is innocent and is asserting the facts. Two, he is guilty and knows that if he admits the crime, this will be held against him because the doctors will immediately report it. This will essentially be self-incrimination and therefore he is exercising his good mental judgment in protecting his rights, even if he is guilty.

Q    So, in either event he is exercising good judgment?

A    This would be my interpretation.

. . .

Q    Now, from your examination of the record and of the patient, privately at the hospital, and from your observation of the relator in Court here today, did your observation of the relator here in Court today confirm your opinion as to his ability to stand trial, his competency to stand trial?

A    In my judgment, the patient's behavior here today speaks for itself. Moreover, the manner in which the patient went about securing my services, corresponding with me, conferring with Mr. Mann, arranging for this hearing, and so forth—all these things are, to my mind, prima facie evidence not of mental health or illness, but of his capacity to understand the predicament he is in and of trying to get out of it.

. . .

Q    Now, Doctor, psychiatric opinions which are formulated by a psychiatrist, do they in some degree depend upon the personal background of the doctor giving that opinion?

A    I believe they do.

Q    To what extent?

A    I believe they depend upon the doctor's own cultural and moral standards.

Q    So that, for example, if one of the doctors who made a comment or an opinion in the hospital records, Relator's Exhibit 4, if he made a comment adverse to Mr. Hoffer, you would say that to some extent that psychiatric opinion given by that doctor on the staff was influenced by his own private background, his own moral upbringing, and so on?

A    I would, yes. And so is mine.

Q    And so is your opinion?

A    Yes.

Q    And so are the opinions of all these psychiatrists. Is that right?

A    That is correct, that is my judgment.

. . .

Q    All right. Now, do you think, Dr. Szasz, that you could correctly diagnose a patient who considered himself to be jailed by the one who is interviewing him, or kept in jail by the one who is interviewing him?

A   I would consider that this is impossible.

Q   And if, because of the opinions given by the doctors at the Matteawan State Hospital staff, an inmate of said hospital is kept continually confined therein, would that particular patient consider that doctor to be his jailer?

A   I think he would.

Q   And under those circumstances, could that jailer who is called a doctor, could he correctly diagnose the patient psychiatrically?

A   I think he could not.

Q   And is friendship and cooperation and confidence, are they elements which must exist in order to have a true diagnosis of one's mental condition or in order to make a true diagnosis?

A   I think this is so.

. . .

*Cross-examination*
*by* MR. KANTOR

Q   Dr. Szasz, if you carry out your last statement to its logical conclusion, then in your opinion, no doctor in an institution like Matteawan can adequately treat a patient. Is that correct?

A   That is correct.

MR. MANN: Can adequately treat?

MR. KANTOR: Yes. He has already answered the question.

MR. MANN: I mean, my question was, could correctly diagnose, not treat.

Q   Or diagnose?

A   No, not mental illness. Organic illness, like syphilis or pneumonia, yes; but not so-called mental illness.

Q   Would you say the same thing is true with respect to other mental institutions in which these patients are confined and are run by the State of New York?

A    I would not.

Q    You would not?

A    No.

Q    Where does the distinction take place, Doctor? How would you distinguish them?

A    The first distinction is whether the patient is voluntary or involuntary; the second distinction is whether the patient is hospitalized while he is under criminal charges or without criminal charges.

Q    You know there are patients in other mental institutions, that they are in there involuntarily?

A    Certainly.

Q    Now, with respect to those, could the doctors do a fair job?

A    I do not think so.

Q    So, wherever the patient feels that the doctor who is treating or examining him is the one who may keep him confined in the institution, then there cannot be any rapport between the doctor and the patient?

A    That is correct.

. . .

Q    Now, is it possible, Doctor, for a patient such as Mr. Hoffer here, to give the wrong answers to any questions that you may ask him—and I am referring to you specifically, you, Dr. Szasz—would it be possible, in your opinion, that he might give you answers which he feels will make a better impression upon you, is that possible?

A    It is not only possible, it is highly probable.

Q    And it may be also possible, Doctor—is it possible for a patient like this to so delude himself and to be in such a mental condition that he himself does not realize he is doing this?

A    May I answer this without a yes or no?

THE COURT: Yes, you may, Doctor.

A    Mr. Kantor has built into his question the proposition that this hypothetical patient is mentally sick already; this is built into the question.

Q   It is possible, isn't it—I mean, that such a condition could exist?

A   Well, this is built into the question. You are forcing me to say that he is mentally ill.

Q   All right, not referring to this patient—

A   The hypothetical patient is mentally ill. You are forcing me to say that he would be mentally ill.

Q   I am not referring to Mr. Hoffer now. Let's take a general question: Is it possible for a patient—

A   To do what?

Q   Who is mentally ill, of course I am saying this, who is mentally ill, who will give you certain answers to questions that you may propound to him, where he would not realize that he is giving you these answers, and which would certainly indicate that he is ill. Now, for example, what I am leading to is this, Doctor: This patient has said that he was not in this particular place where he was found. Let's assume that he was in another place where he was picked up . . . that he was actually picked up in his place of business where he was working, would that make a difference?

A   It would make a difference in what?

Q   With respect to your analysis as to his mental condition, as to whether or not he could stand trial and confer with counsel. Let's assume he actually believes this to be the truth, that he was picked up in Weber's Cafeteria where he was eating, says he; if on the other hand the records show that he was picked up in his place of business, would that make any difference with respect to your analysis?

A   Yes, I would conclude that he lied about it.

. . .

Q   All right, if the facts disclose that the two girls

actually identified Hoffer as being in the place when this occurred—

A   If I may answer other than yes or no.

Q   Yes, you may.

A   What you are getting at, as I understand it, is that supposing that you could demonstrate that Mr. Hoffer is an inveterate, no-good liar—

Q   Either a liar or he doesn't actually remember the facts.

A   No, wait a minute, that's just your interpretation. I think mine is the simpler one. In science, one always takes the simplest explanation—

Q   Which is?

A   That he might be lying.

. . .

Q   How can he stand trial when he deliberately lies to all the occurrences and to all the facts that occurred?

A   That's a problem for the jury and the Judge.

Q   That is your analysis?

A   The world is full of liars. Yes.

. . .

Q   This patient was in Matteawan before.

A   I know that.

Q   And he did tell the doctors the truth.

A   How do you know that?

Q   Because they let him go back.

A   Well, that may mean that he fooled them. And he may be fooling me. But that's not the issue as far as I can see.

Q   Well, then, how can you honestly say that he can confer with counsel? He may be fooling counsel and you and everybody.

A   To me, that's not the problem. That's for the Judge to determine. Here I have the evidence; he corresponded with me; he wrote to me; he used the mails. He talks and writes to me like a human being. That's enough for me.

Q Now listen, Doctor. You know, I hate to tell you this, you are the expert, but you know that people that are ninety-nine per cent well oriented, who are able to do everyday work—in fact, we may have a lot of them in the streets today, but you wouldn't say they were completely sane, would you?

A I don't use these words *sane* and *insane*.

Q Well, I got to use these terms, otherwise I can't express myself.

A Well, how can you tell what's sane and insane?

Q Depending on what this particular man is being charged with. This man is an intelligent man. You heard him testify here. He can recall dates and events, he is a very bright man. There is no question about that. But he can still be mentally ill.

A Can you give me a definition of mental illness, Mr. Kantor?

Q I am not a doctor.

A Well, you are using the term mental illness. I submit it is a dirty word that is pinned on people, in order to incriminate them, to get them.

. . .

Q Well, is this patient schizophrenic or not?

A You give me a definition and I will answer you.

Q What is your diagnosis of this patient?

A I was not hired to diagnose him.

Q You were not hired to diagnose him?

A I was not hired to diagnose him.

Q Have you seen the diagnosis in the record?

A I have.

Q And you disagree with it?

A To me it is a meaningless term. Or rather, it has only one meaning to me.

Q What is that?

A It is like saying "Let's not treat Mr. Hoffer as an

American citizen any more. He has no more rights. He is a mental patient, with capital *M* and capital *P*."

Q You feel because he is a mental patient and because he is confined to Matteawan, all his rights are being denied him?

A Not all of them, only a great many.

MR. KANTOR: That's all.

THE COURT: Doctor, may I ask you a question: Can you tell me whether or not Abraham Hoffer is in such a state of insanity, idiocy, or imbecility, as to be unable to understand the nature of the charge pending against him and to make his defense?

DR. SZASZ: Your Honor, in my judgment, he is not in such a state.

THE COURT: And he is able to prepare his defense. Is that your testimony?

DR. SZASZ: That is my testimony.

THE COURT: And what do you base that on, Doctor?

DR. SZASZ: I base that on the manner in which he secured my services, his correspondence with me, my examination of him at Matteawan in January, and my observation of him here this afternoon.

. . .

THE COURT: And you have examined all the records, Doctor?

DR. SZASZ: Yes, I have examined the records carefully, Your Honor.

THE COURT: Of the hospital?

DR. SZASZ: Yes, sir.

THE COURT: And your statement is based on your examination of the patient, as well as the examination of the hospital records, the correspondence he has had with you, and the type and nature of the correspondence he has had with you, and the manner in which he retained your services. Is that right?

DR. SZASZ: Yes, sir, that is absolutely correct.

THE COURT: All right.

. . .

PHILIP I. ROSENBERG, M.D., being first duly sworn, testified as follows:

*Direct Examination*

*by* MR. KANTOR

Q Dr. Rosenberg, you have already testified before His Honor on previous occasions, have you not?

A Yes, I have.

MR. MANN: I concede Dr. Rosenberg's qualifications.

THE COURT: All right.

DR. ROSENBERG: Thank you.

Q Dr. Rosenberg, do you know this patient, Abraham Hoffer?

A Yes.

Q Have you had occasion to observe this patient and to speak with him while he has been confined in Matteawan State Hospital?

A Yes, on several occasions.

. . .

Q Doctor, are you familiar with the case history of Abraham Hoffer that has been introduced in evidence?

A Yes, I am.

Q Now, Doctor, from your familiarity with the case history of this patient, from your own observations of the patient, and from your medical background and experience and education, are you able at this time to form an opinion regarding the mental condition of Abraham Hoffer?

A Yes, I am.

Q What is the diagnosis, Doctor?

A The diagnosis is schizophrenia, pseudo-psychopathic type.

Q On what do you base that opinion, Doctor?

A The opinion is based on a longitudinal section of

the patient's previous behavior. He has been arrested many times and behaved like a psychopath; that means as a person who does not learn from his experience, who is sick primarily in terms of society. And his adjustment or culture is—we call them pseudo-psychopaths, because he is not a simple psychopath. The term has been changed ten or fifteen years ago to differentiate from a real psychopath.

Now, in contrast to my learned colleague, I would like to emphasize that I am in good company with Kraepelin, the first scientific psychiatrist, who made the first classification. He said mental disorder is a disturbance of thinking and of feeling and of acting.

Now, this patient has not only shown behavior disorder in the way of a psychopath, he has shown other disorders which have been diagnosed, since 1944, in eight different hospitals about fourteen times, and by different doctors, some of them outstanding in the field, as schizophrenia, but with another type. He was diagnosed as schizophrenia, catatonic type; he was diagnosed as schizophrenia, paranoid type; and finally in our hospital as schizophrenia, pseudo-psychopathic type.

. . .

Q  Now, Doctor, in your opinion, from your examinations of the patient and from your examination of this record, is this patient able, at this time, to understand the nature of the charges now pending against him in the Bronx County?

A  Not at the present time.

Q  Can he confer with counsel?

A  Not at the present time.

Q  Can he prepare his defense of the said charges?

A  Not at the present time.

Q  And why do you say that this is so, Doctor?

A  That I will try to prove, now. This patient, up to today, this is the first time he changed one point. He always told me all the charges have been dropped. I read it to you: "A lawyer told me that the indictment for kidnaping"—this is also in the record—"is a technical charge to hold me and to recommit me to Matteawan State Hospital."

He claimed several times that all the other charges have been dropped. So that I felt that in order to have an idea if the patient is lying or if he is self-deluded, I asked our Director to write to the District Attorney. And the District Attorney confirmed that all the charges are standing. I don't know if I might read it: "Hoffer will have to stand trial on all the"—

Q    Well, he has admitted that there are nine counts.

A    Okay.

Q    No, eight counts.

MR. MANN: Yes, eight counts presently standing.

Q    All right.

A    The patient also told me that the girls never identified him, they have never seen him. So I called the District Attorney personally and asked him to give me in writing what happened—to give me the information in order to find out if the patient is lying or is self-deluded, as my learned colleague said these two possibilities are given.

. . .

THE COURT: Well, Doctor, can I ask you a question: Have you had an opportunity to observe the demeanor of the witness on the witness stand today?

DR. ROSENBERG: Yes, I have.

THE COURT: Would you say that has any effect on your testimony?

DR. ROSENBERG: No. It only confirms my conviction that this is a bright, intelligent young man who has distorted thinking, who unfortunately never in his life could make a go of his life because of his— that's my opinion—of his perverted sexual develop-

ment, for which I don't reproach him. But unfortunately, because of it, he always came in conflict
with the law.

Now, this is my opinion. And I feel very sorry
for him. Because I had to decide if this patient is
lying or is self-deluded. I wrote this letter to the
District Attorney and made two examinations with
other psychiatrists. . . .

MR. KANTOR: I have no further questions.

THE COURT: All right, Doctor, your opinion, as I get
it from your testimony, is that the defendant is in
such a state of insanity, idiocy or imbecility, as to
be unable to understand the nature of the charge
pending against him, and to make his defense
thereto; is that correct?

DR. ROSENBERG: At the present time, yes.

THE COURT: At the present time?

DR. ROSENBERG: Yes, at the present time.

. . .

*Cross-examination*
*by* MR. MANN

Q   Doctor, you have heard Mr. Hoffer testify in Court?
A   Yes.
Q   You heard his testimony that he consulted with me
as his attorney in defense of the pending charges against
him?
A   Yes.
Q   And despite that testimony, you still say that he is
unable to confer with counsel, even though he has already
conferred with counsel. Is that correct?
A   Yes. . . .
Q   Yes?
A   Yes. In your opinion, he has conferred.
Q   Well, does that make sense, Doctor?
A   It makes sense because it is your feeling that he has

given you the right answers, but it is our feeling that he is deluded.

Q  Now, Doctor, how do you know what is in the back of his mind, that he is deluded? How do you know that? Are you able to peer into the innermost recesses of his mind?

A  I have had several interviews with him. And as I told you, at a certain time I believed the things he said, but I found out later. So there can be two possibilities. He is lying or he is deluded. And from the whole picture, from his letters I have read, he is very circumstantial—

. . .

Q  But, Doctor, seriously talking, what more do you expect Mr. Hoffer to do than what he did do in conferring with his attorney on at least four or five occasions, discussing all the details and circumstances of the charges against him, giving his attorney the names and addresses of witnesses, detailing the places where he was and what he was doing at the time involved in the indictment? What more must Mr. Hoffer do to satisfy you that he is capable of conferring with counsel?

A  He has made many contradictory statements. He has, as I said, continuously told me until today—that he has changed today—that all charges have been dropped, so that I was forced to find out what is really going on. And that the kidnaping charge was only kept up by the District Attorney in order to have a hook to recommit him to Matteawan.

Q  Now, let me ask you this question, Doctor: If, for example, a prior attorney representing Mr. Hoffer two years or so ago, who subsequently was discharged as his attorney—if his prior attorney at that time told Mr. Hoffer that his charges were dismissed, and Mr. Hoffer had no official communication from the Court to show him what the facts actually were, and suppose Mr. Hoffer repeated to you what he was told by a previous attorney, which was apparently mistaken, would you hold that against him?

A  Absolutely not. I told him I could not only not convince him—he told me that his attorney—and I think this is paranoid thinking—the attorney Mr. Essig—he told me twice that Mr. Essig shanghaied him into Matteawan in order to get rid of his money. Now, if this is not a paranoid—

Q  Well now, Doctor, did you read the voluminous records in the County Clerk's office of Bronx County, and have you read what the charges were against Mr. Essig by the Veterans Administration? Have you examined all those papers?*

A  No.

. . .

Q  Dr. Rosenberg, are you serious in maintaining, after hearing Mr. Hoffer today, that he is unable to talk intelligently and rationally to his counsel?

MR. KANTOR: The witness has already answered that question, if Your Honor please.

THE COURT: I will let him answer that again.

A  I cannot form an opinion on the basis of one appearance in Court. I have seen this patient very often, not just one time.

. . .

Q  Aren't you really laboring under the belief that Mr. Hoffer has some sort of mental illness which you don't like, from your own moral background, and isn't that the real reason why you are keeping him in?

MR. KANTOR: I object to the question.

A  No, I must really protest against this kind of insinuation. For me it is absolutely unimportant what crime the patient has committed. In this case it has something to

---

* Mr. Mann was referring here to the fact that Mr. Hoffer's "committee" (i.e., his legal guardian) did indeed find Mr. Essig to be derelict in his duties and removed him as Mr. Hoffer's attorney.

do with the diagnosis. The other hospital doctors made the diagnosis of pseudo-psychopathic, and I continued it because I agree with them.

Q When you heard Mr. Hoffer say from the witness stand, when I asked him "What are you charged with?" and you heard him answer that question, you still say he does not know what he is charged with? Do you still say that?

A Yes.

Q Didn't you hear him testify in detail, the sections of the Penal Code, the subdivisions of the Penal Code, the nature of the crime, and you still say that he does not know what he is charged with?

A Mr. Kantor, could I get this—there is an opinion of the Attorney General, where he writes—

MR. KANTOR: That's not necessary.

A It is the opinion of the Attorney General in a similar case, where he wrote us that it is not important that the patient just knows, he has to understand. He doesn't understand. He claims that he was never mentally sick before, so all the doctors were wrong . . . knowing what the patient is charged with doesn't mean understanding.

Q Now, Doctor, in your opinion as a psychiatrist, wouldn't further confinement in Matteawan State Hospital—indefinitely in the future—cause Mr. Hoffer to become mentally ill?

A Not mentally ill, to become more paranoid, that's possible.

. . .

MR. MANN: All right, Doctor, that's all.

. . .

THE COURT: Do you gentlemen want an opportunity to submit anything or not?

MR. MANN: No, that's all, Judge.

MR. KANTOR: That's all.

MR. MANN: We rest.

MR. KANTOR: The State rests, too.

THE COURT: All right, the relator will be remanded pending my decision.

\*     \*     \*

On August 21, 1961—three months and four days after Mr. Hoffer's petition for a writ of habeas corpus was heard in court—Justice James B. Campbell issued an order dismissing the petition. "In the opinion of the Court," wrote Justice Campbell, "the relator has failed to establish his capacity to meet the statutory test expressed. Accordingly, the writ is dismissed and the relator remanded to the custody of the respondent."

## III

Mr. Hoffer did finally gain his freedom. On December 14, 1962, he was declared competent to stand trial by the psychiatrists at the Matteawan State Hospital and was remanded to the Criminal Division of the Bronx Supreme Court for disposition of the indictment there pending against him.

The District Attorney thereupon requested that Mr. Hoffer be committed to Bellevue Hospital to determine, once more, if he was competent to stand trial; Judge Milliken of the Bronx Supreme Court authorized his commitment.

Mr. Hoffer remained at Bellevue Hospital for twenty-seven days and was returned to the court as competent to stand trial. He finally appeared in court on March 5, 1963, and was "induced" to plead guilty to one of the charges—impairing the morals of a minor. (He was represented by counsel, but not by Mr. Mann, in this proceeding.) His guilty plea was accepted by the court, the other charges against him were dismissed, and he was sentenced to time served at the Matteawan State Hospital —that is, to three years and nine months. Inasmuch as the time served at Matteawan was credited against his sentence, he gained his freedom immediately upon sentencing.

It is evident that Mr. Hoffer had little to gain from insisting on his innocence. At best, he could have pleaded "not guilty" and thus have forced the court to try him and acquit him as innocent. At worst, he would have courted the risk of again being pronounced mentally unfit to stand trial and recommitted to the Matteawan State Hospital or of being found guilty and sentenced to an additional term in prison.

One thing was certain: the time served at Matteawan could not be erased by an acquittal. Thus, Mr. Hoffer had really no choice but to accept the offer to "cop a plea"— that is, to plead guilty to a lesser charge in order to avoid standing trial for a more serious one.

The fact remains that Abraham Hoffer—however suspicious a "character" he may seem—was charged with a crime and confined in an institution operated by the New York State Department of Correction without first having been tried, found guilty, and sentenced. Instead he was imprisoned first, then allowed to plead guilty to a crime for which the "just" sentence turned out to be exactly the number of years and months he had already served.

## IV

In conclusion, I should like to comment briefly on Abraham Hoffer's habeas corpus hearing.

1. It was conceded by everyone present—explicitly by Mr. Kantor, Mr. Mann, Dr. Rosenberg, and me, and implicitly by Judge Campbell—that Mr. Hoffer was an intelligent young man, in good contact with his environment.

2. It was clear that Mr. Kantor, who was ostensibly representing the Superintendent of the Matteawan State Hospital, was actually prosecuting Mr. Hoffer—not for crime, to be sure, but for mental illness. He made no

attempt to show that Mr. Hoffer was mentally unfit to stand trial; instead, he tried to incriminate Mr. Hoffer as mentally sick.

3. Mr. Kantor and Dr. Rosenberg placed repeated emphasis on Mr. Hoffer's having a "history" of mental illness. It was thus implied that he was still mentally ill and incompetent to stand trial. This is like trying to incriminate someone as guilty of a recent crime by citing his past misdeeds—a tactic barred in the courtroom of every civilized country.

4. It is significant that in this case—as in so many others—a person defined as a mental patient cannot adequately protect himself from actual occurrences being viewed as fantasies by his adversaries. Mr. Essig, an attorney who had represented Mr. Hoffer in the past, was found to have acted improperly in handling Mr. Hoffer's affairs and was removed by his committee. When Mr. Hoffer related this to Dr. Rosenberg, the latter regarded it as a symptom of his "paranoia."

5. Despite the evidence of Mr. Hoffer's behavior on the witness stand, including his responses to aggressive cross-examination by the Attorney General—which furnished prima facie evidence of his competence in the courtroom situation—the court found Mr. Hoffer mentally unfit to stand trial.

# 6 THE CASE OF
## MR. EDWIN A. WALKER

¶ [T]he executioners of today, as everyone knows, are humanists.*

## I

In the midst of the integration crisis at the University of Mississippi precipitated by the enrollment of James Meredith, former Major General Edwin A. Walker was arrested, charged with crimes, and then committed against his will for pretrial psychiatric examination. Without doubt, this is the most widely publicized case ever reported in the American press of an attempt to deny an accused person the right to trial by branding him insane and hence incompetent to stand trial.

General Walker, it should be recalled, commanded the federal troops in the desegregation crisis at Little Rock, Arkansas, in 1957. In 1961, Walker resigned from the U.S. Army. When, in late September 1962, federal troops were sent to the University of Mississippi to enforce James Meredith's enrollment, Mr. Walker went to Oxford, allegedly to aid Mississippi segregationists. After two stormy days of disturbances in Oxford which made the headlines throughout the world, on Monday, October 1, General Walker was arrested. He was charged with: "1. Assaulting, resisting, or impeding U.S. marshals. 2. Conspiring to prevent discharge of duties. 3. Inciting, assisting, and engaging in insurrection against the authority of the United

* Albert Camus, "Reflections on the Guillotine" (1957), in *Resistance, Rebellion, Death*, p. 230.

States. 4. Conspiring to oppose by force the execution of any law of the United States."

"Taken before U.S. Commissioner Omar Craig, Walker waived his hearing after conferring by telephone with an unidentified attorney. 'Is it proper to ask that if I waive this hearing, I will be assured that it [the trial] comes back to Mississippi?' General Walker asked."*

Craig assured Walker the trial would be held in a U.S. District Court in Mississippi. Thereupon Walker waived his hearing. He was held, pending his posting one hundred thousand dollars bond. Shortly afterward, on Monday night—while Walker was making arrangements to post bail—he was placed in a border patrol plane, flown to Springfield, Missouri, and confined at the U.S. Medical Center for Federal Prisoners.

How could this happen? And was it legal? It was "legal," and this is how it happened.

On the afternoon of October 1, 1962, Dr. Charles E. Smith, Medical Director and Chief Psychiatrist of the Federal Bureau of Prisons was called by telephone by Mr. Carl Belcher, an attorney in the U.S. Department of Justice. "Mr. Belcher asked Dr. Smith if, on the basis of what he knew of the Walker case, he thought it would be reasonable to make a statement concerning General Walker's condition. Dr. Smith replied in the affirmative. At 7:30 P.M. that day, Dr. Smith was asked by Mr. Belcher to examine the following material:

"1. A report by Mr. Van A. Savell of the Associated Press to a Department of Justice official which stated that General Walker led toward the Lyceum at the University of Mississippi a group of students armed with rocks and sticks.

"2. A transcript of General Walker's testimony at hear-

* Syracuse *Herald-Journal*, October 2, 1962. See also William F. Walsh, "A Postscript to the Meredith Case," *Western Reserve Law Review*, *15*: 461–478, (June) 1964.

ings before the Special Preparedness Subcommittee of the Committee on Armed Services, United States Senate, 87th Congress, second session beginning on April 4, 1962, reported in the United States Government Printing Office document entitled 'Military Cold War Education and Speech Review Policies, Part IV';

"3. Certain news reports relating to General Walker's activities shortly before Oct. 1, 1962; and

"4. Certain of General Walker's army medical records. The earliest report was dated 1927 and the most recent 1958."*

Dr. Smith studied these documents for approximately six hours. On October 2, he prepared a brief memorandum summarizing his impressions of these documents. He submitted this memorandum to James V. Bennett, Director of the U.S. Bureau of Prisons. Subsequently, Dr. Smith put his summary in the form of an Affidavit, reproduced here.

## AFFIDAVIT†

I, Charles E. Smith, Medical Director and Chief Psychiatrist of the Federal Bureau of Prisons, Department of Justice, having been duly sworn, do hereby certify that I have examined carefully various news reports concerning the actions and behavior of former Major General Edwin Walker, including his appearance before the Committee of the United States Senate on Armed Forces in April of this year and news reports of his appearance on the Campus of the University of Mississippi during the past several days. Some of his reported behavior reflects sensitivity and essentially unpredictable and seemingly bizarre outbursts of the type often observed in individuals suffering with paranoid mental disorder. There are also indications in his medical history of functional and

---

* "General Walker and Dr. Smith. Opinion of the Judicial Council Concerning Complaints Received Against Charles E. Smith, M.D." *Journal of the American Medical Association, 185:* 36–37, (July) 1963.
† *Ibid.,* p. 36.

psychosomatic disorders which could be precursors of the more serious disorder which his present behavior suggests. From this and other information available to me I believe his recent behavior has been out of keeping with that of a person of his station, background, and training, and that as such it may be indicative of an underlying mental disturbance.

This affidavit was immediately transmitted to Mr. H. M. Ray, U.S. Attorney in Oxford, Mississippi, who was handling the government's case against General Walker.

"On October 2, Mr. Ray filed a motion in the United States District Court for the Northern District of Mississippi to have General Walker given a psychiatric examination. In addition, Mr. Ray asked the Court to designate a suitable hospital or other facility to which General Walker might be committed for this examination. This motion was filed pursuant to the authority of Section 4244, Title 18, United States Code."[*]

On the basis of Mr. Ray's motion, of which Dr. Smith's affidavit formed a part, Judge Claude F. Clayton, the District Judge in the U.S. District Court for the Northern District of Mississippi, Western Division, ordered a psychiatric examination of Mr. Walker.

Actually, Mr. Walker had already been arrested and transferred to the Medical Center for Federal Prisoners in Springfield, Missouri. "This had been done because only county jails of minimal standards were available for the incarceration of federal prisoners in Mississippi. The court determined that a competent psychiatric staff was available at the Springfield Medical Center and directed that the psychiatric examination be made at that institution."[†] (A neat coincidence indeed.)

On October 3, the New York *Herald Tribune* reported these events in a front-page story. The large headline read:

---

[*] *Loc cit.* For the statute authorizing this procedure, see pp. 46–47.
[†] *Ibid.*, p. 37.

A U.S. COURT'S FORMAL PSYCHIATRIC ORDER. WALKER MENTAL TESTS. "SEDITION" BAIL IS DENIED HIM.

According to the *Tribune,* the order committing General Walker for psychiatric study was issued by Judge Clayton "on the basis of a statement by Dr. Charles E. Smith, staff psychiatrist for the U.S. Bureau of Prisons. The attorney [Clyde J. Watts] said he had asked Dr. Smith if he had seen Mr. Walker, and the psychiatrist said he had not."

Although the day after he was committed Walker had the $100,000 bail ready, he could no longer obtain his release in this way. U.S. District Attorney F. Russell Millin of Kansas City said "the psychiatric examination order prevents Walker from obtaining his release under a $100,000 bond set Monday at his arraignment . . . he understood the psychiatric examination would take 60 to 90 days and that during that period Walker could not be freed on bail."*

Immediately there were many protests against Walker's psychiatric incarceration. Clyde J. Watts, himself a former Army general and one of Mr. Walker's attorneys, announced his intention to file a petition for a writ of habeas corpus. In the meantime, he had advised his client to give the psychiatrists at the federal Medical Center "only his name, rank, and serial number—the same as an American soldier who has been captured."† Mr. Watts characterized the commitment order as "simply fantastic," adding that he had talked at length with General Walker during the preceding two days and found him "in complete possession of all mental faculties."‡

Other attorneys for General Walker, headed by Mr. Robert Morris of Dallas, Texas, sent a telegram to the

---

* Syracuse *Post-Standard,* October 3, 1962.
† *Ibid.*
‡ New York *Herald-Tribune,* October 4, 1962.

Senate Judiciary Committee, asking it to investigate the former general's "political" confinement.*

The American Civil Liberties Union also filed a protest. In a letter to Attorney General Robert F. Kennedy, the Union "told the Justice Department . . . that it might have violated due process of law in holding former Maj. Gen. Edwin A. Walker for psychiatric examination." Mr. Edward Angell, chairman of the American Civil Liberties Union, complained that "The psychiatric examination of Mr. Walker was ordered in a court hearing at which neither Mr. Walker nor his lawyer were present and at which a psychiatrist who had not examined Mr. Walker testified."†

On Thursday, October 4, Walker's attorneys filed a petition for a writ of habeas corpus. Thereupon U.S. District Judge John W. Oliver issued a show cause order requiring that the government demonstrate by Tuesday, October 9, that it has "proper reason to keep Walker . . . in custody without releasing him on bond."‡

The government did not even attempt to prove that it had "proper reason" for confining Walker at the U.S. Medical Center for Federal Prisoners. On Saturday, October 6, Walker was released on $50,000 bond, "on an order signed at Oxford, Miss., by United States Judge Claude Clayton. It was specified that within five days after his release, Mr. Walker must undergo a psychiatric examination in Dallas."§

Judge Clayton's order directed General Walker to report to Dr. Robert Stubblefield, chief psychiatrist at the Southwest Medical Center in Dallas. It further specified that he was "to be examined by Dr. Stubblefield and

* *The New York Times,* October 3, 1962.
† *Ibid.,* October 5, 1962.
‡ Syracuse *Herald-Journal,* October 5, 1962.
§ *The New York Times,* October 8, 1962.

another psychiatrist to be selected by the Government to determine if he is mentally competent to stand trial."

Reported *The New York Times:* "Clyde Watts of Oklahoma City, one of Mr. Walker's attorneys, said today he welcomed the examination. 'All we want is a fair and impartial examination,' he said. 'The question was raised whether Walker was capable of understanding the charges against him,' he declared. 'Certainly he understands. It was also questioned whether he is capable of assisting in his own defense. He has been and is. This is so obvious that it's futile to raise such questions.' "*

To others, as we shall see, the answers to these questions were not so obvious. On the contrary. While preparations were made to examine General Walker, the news media— or at least many important newspapers and magazines— had begun to speak of Walker as if it had already been established that he was mentally ill. On October 4, *The New York Times* ran a story captioned MILITARY MEN SAY WALKER CHANGED AFTER HE BECAME A GENERAL. It began:

The case of former Maj. Gen. Edwin A. Walker has focused attention once again on career military officers, and many persons are asking the question: How does a man like Walker rise to two-star rank in the Army?

At the Pentagon, where the former general has been disowned emphatically, they say that men like him do not rise to high command. The man has changed, they say. As one officer put it:

"He's gone through a metamorphosis. He is not at all the man he was when he was a combat officer" [p. 30].

On October 12, in a long article on the riots at Ole Miss, the readers of *Time* were given this picture of Walker as a crazy man:

* *Ibid.*

The only prisoner with a claim to fame was Edwin A. Walker. He had arrived in Mississippi the day before the battle, proclaiming that the court orders on Meredith were part of "the conspiracy of the crucifixion by anti-Christ conspirators of the Supreme Court." On the night of the battle, he was observed by newsmen and a campus minister to be holding forth at a sort of informal command post. Every now and then somebody would run up to him and ask for military counsel. One man who got close to him reported that *there was a wild, dazed look in his eyes.* Late that morning, soldiers at a roadblock arrested Walker *as he was attempting to leave town* in a car. He was arraigned on charges of insurrection and seditious conspiracy and sent to the U.S. prison and medical center in Springfield, Mo., for observation [p. 21; emphasis supplied].

An article in *Life,* too, referred to General Walker's behavior in Oxford, Mississippi, as "bizarre."\* It did not refer to Governor Barnett's behavior as bizarre.

Finally, as is invariably the case, the public was told that those wishing to declare Mr. Walker insane and unfit to stand trial were really trying to help him. Wrote Walter Winchell in his syndicated column: "Former General Walker's friends don't know how really lucky he is. Sedition calls for death by the firing squad or hanging. Gov't is really giving him a break trying to have him declared Gluggy."†

On Thursday, October 11, General Walker kept his court-ordered appointment with Dr. Robert L. Stubblefield at the University of Texas Southwest Medical School. After twenty minutes Walker left, "put on 24-hour notice for the decision on when he should report for psychiatric tests."

After Walker left, Dr. Stubblefield appeared for a press conference and said: "When I am notified officially by the

\* *Life,* October 12, 1962, p. 42.
† Syracuse *Herald-Journal,* October 8, 1962.

court of the second psychiatrist, we will decide what is a reasonable psychiatric examination." At the same time, it was reported that the government named Dr. Winfred Overholser, former superintendent of St. Elizabeths Hospital in Washington, D.C., "as its psychiatrist in the case."*

By a curious coincidence, a special report to *The New York Times* from Oxford, Mississippi, dated the same day —October 12—disclosed that Governor Barnett was planning to bar James Meredith from the University of Mississippi as "mentally incompetent." "Mr. Barnett was said to have told Mr. Tubb [Mr. Thomas Jefferson Tubb, Chairman of the Board of Trustees of State Institutions of Higher Learning] that he knew of at least one psychiatrist in Jackson, the state capital, who was prepared to testify that Mr. Meredith was insane." (Nothing came of this.)

Before the day was over, however, Walker had won what was probably the most important round in his fight to be allowed to stand trial: a federal judge upheld the protest of his attorneys against the government-appointed psychiatrist in the case:

U.S. District Judge Claude Clayton dismissed Dr. Winfred Overholser from the case after a Walker attorney complained that the psychiatrist was a "man who presses for commitment to mental institutions." . . . Originally, two psychiatrists were to examine Walker . . . [but] Judge Clayton Friday dismissed Dr. Overholser after Walker's attorneys complained that the psychiatrist, who formerly headed St. Elizabeths Hospital—a government mental institution in Washington—had spent most of his life as a Government psychiatrist and had pressed for commitment in many cases. The question of Walker's sanity now rests entirely with Dr. R. L. Stubblefield, appointed by Walker's own attorneys.†

* Dallas *Morning News,* October 12, 1962.
† Detroit *Free Press,* October 14, 1962.

The psychiatrist appointed to examine Mr. Walker now moved cautiously. First he consulted with Charles Weber, a professor of law at Southwestern Methodist University. Then it was announced that Dr. Stubblefield "will confer with Dr. Titus Harris and Dr. Andrew Watson . . . to discuss what is a reasonable psychiatric examination."*

Finally, on November 9, Mr. Walker entered Parkland Hospital in Dallas to submit to the court-ordered psychiatric examination. He was released two days later. On the eve of the examination, Mr. Robert Morris, one of Walker's attorneys, was quoted as having stated that: " 'The tests will show General Walker is fully capable of standing trial.' Morris said that Dr. Stubblefield knows what is necessary to conduct the tests and that the Walker attorneys are satisfied with all that Dr. Stubblefield has done to date."†

On November 20 and 21, 1962, a hearing was held before U.S. Judge Claude F. Clayton in the Northern District Court of Mississippi at Oxford. Its purpose was to receive Dr. Stubblefield's report and determine if Mr. Walker was mentally competent to stand trial. In addition, Judge Clayton heard a motion from Walker's attorneys "to strike from the record a memorandum by a Government psychiatrist, Dr. Charles Smith, who said there was cause to believe Mr. Walker was suffering from a mental disturbance." The Government presented a countermotion which, "in effect, urges the court to deny the defense motion."‡ The following excerpts are from the stenographic record of that hearing. As will be seen, the government was not content to abide by the favorable report rendered by Dr. Stubblefield, but instead moved to obtain an order for another pretrial psychiatric examination of Walker.

* Syracuse *Herald-Journal,* October 17, 1962.
† Fort Worth *Star-Telegram,* November 9, 1962.
‡ *The New York Times,* November 21, 1962.

## II

### CHARLES E. SMITH

called as a witness by the United States of America, having been first duly sworn, was examined and testified as follows:

*Direct Examination*
*by* MR. RAY:*

Q   Please state your name.
A   Charles E. Smith.
Q   What is your profession, sir?
A   I am a physician.
. . .
Q   Dr. Smith, what is your connection with this case?
A   If I may, I would like to relate to you just how I did enter into this case.
Q   Please do so.
A   On the afternoon of October 1—I was called to take a phone call from Mr. Carl Belcher in the Department of Justice. Mr. Belcher put to me a query of something in the order of a curbstone query. . . . The query was much as follows: "Doctor, given what you know about the Walker situation, or the Walker case, do you think that it would be reasonable to consider his mental condition?" I would say this was the gist or the import of his question; and I indicated to him on the basis of what I had heard and seen that I thought that it would be reasonable to consider it. Subsequently, I was advised that he had, that Mr. Belcher had, certain material which he wished me to examine. This was stated to be medical records in addition to some other material which was not at the moment defined, and I examined this material with the—how shall I put this? —with the approval of Mr. James Bennett, the Director of

* Mr. H. M. Ray, U.S. Attorney, representing the government.

the Bureau of Prisons, to whom I am immediately responsible. The examination of this material took place Monday night in the office of the Attorney General at the Department of Justice. I spent several hours there examining this material, and then continued to review some of it at home later in the evening, and the following morning I spent another several hours on it. I would estimate that I spent approximately six hours of this time in reviewing the material which had been provided. Subsequently, around midmorning of the second, Tuesday, I prepared a brief memorandum to the Director reporting the substance of my impressions of this material. This in turn, as you know, was referred to this Court, and to the United States Attorney here, and at Mr. Bennett's direction I had it put in affidavit form, and this was my understanding that this was subsequently provided to this office. I think that is essentially the way in which I entered into this case. I might say in this connection, if I may, that this inquiry which I got is similar to inquiries which I received from time to time from attorneys in the Department, and which make up a part of my ordinary duties.

Q    Now, what did you examine, sir?

A    If I may, I would like to make a summary statement of this material. I ask this privilege since there have been so many questions raised as to just what I did see or did not see. The sources of my information in this case included news reports; they included the hearing before the Special Preparedness Subcommittee of the Committee on Armed Services, United States Senate, Eighty-seventh Congress, Second Session, identified as Part 4, of a document entitled "Military Cold War Education and Speech Review Policies"; a report of a statement which was made by a newsman to a Department of Justice official. This, I believe, is in the hands of counsel; and Army medical reports, which I have brought here with me. These are copies of the reports which I examined.

Q  May I interrupt, Doctor. Is this the memorandum?

A  This is a copy of the document which was provided to me.

Q  How would you identify that?

A  The document is identified as dictated by Harold Reis by telephone, October 1, 1962, from Oxford, Mississippi; further identified as by Van H. Savell, correspondent with the Jackson office of the Associated Press, 1910 Whitman Terrace, Jackson, Mississippi.

Q  Would you read that, please.

A  This document reads as follows: "He went out on the campus at about 5:00 P.M. and he wandered about. After the first tear gas bomb was shot, which was estimated to be about 7:30 P.M., he got in a group of about five hundred students which had separated themselves from the other students and started what they said would be a charge to the steps of the Lyceum. They stopped at the flagpole and returned roughly to where they started, about where the Confederate Soldier statue is, and at that point someone hollered, 'Where is General Walker?' Walker appeared at the front of the group and did not make a speech. Some student asked Walker the following: 'Will you lead us to the steps?' At the time they were asking Walker that question, they had bricks and sticks in their hands. Walker nodded his head in an affirmative manner, then huddled with about sixteen students. The witness was about six feet from them at the time they huddled. They talked low, and he could not hear what was said. The group then turned about and headed toward the Lyceum. Walker said, 'Well, we are ready.' They and the larger group moved toward the Lyceum. The students had rocks and sticks. Walker carried nothing. The whole group turned and fled when they were flooded with tear gas. They ran back to where they had started. About ten minutes later, Walker got up as high as he could on the Confederate statue and told the students in essence: 'Barnett has not lost the fight. You can still fight and we are ready to fight *possibly to the death.*' He is positive about this last phrase. Then he said they should return to their homes. After making this speech, Walker got down from the statue and was still in the area about 12:30. This man has met Walker and knows him well. . . ."

. . .

Q   What else did you examine, Doctor?

A   As I indicated, I examined this document which I have already identified, the report of the Subcommittee, Special Preparedness Subcommittee of the Committee on Armed Services, United States Senate; and Army medical records, of which there are copies with one exception . . .

. . .

Now, considering briefly the news reports, in substance these news reports preceding the Oxford incident reported that Mr. Walker exhorted the public to come to Oxford in large numbers and to join in a coordinated movement, and later it was reported that he led persons against the United States marshals. These reports contributed to my memorandum opinion to the extent that they showed to me evidence of behavior out of keeping with that of a person of his station, background, and training.

In the medical history which was available to me, there were recurrent complaints of gastrointestinal trouble, headaches, backache, and chronic fatigue and insomnia, which in several instances were found to be without apparent organic basis. In addition, I had a report which indicated that Mr. Walker was hospitalized in 1960 because of complaints leading to the suspicion of brain tumor and possible personality changes. This record was requested, and I have examined it since my original affidavit was submitted.

All of these reports were considered in reaching the conclusions in the memorandum report, which I have referred to and which subsequently was put in affidavit form.

Q   May I interrupt a minute—

A   Yes.

Q   —Dr. Smith, and ask if— You mentioned an affidavit form. Do you recognize this paper?

A   Yes. This appears to be a copy of my affidavit, the affidavit to which I referred.

Q   Would you read that affidavit?

A   I, Charles E. Smith, etc. . . .*

This was signed and sworn to before Donna A. Cowden, a notary public in the District of Columbia.

Q   What day did you do that?

A   The date is the second day of October of this year.
. . .

MR. RAY: If it please the Court, we have no further questions.

THE COURT: You may cross-examine.

MR. WATTS: Thank you, sir.

*Cross-examination*
*by* MR. WATTS†

Q   You have been a psychiatrist since when, Dr. Smith?

A   I entered the field of psychiatry in December of 1945.

Q   And for whom have you worked since then?

A   Counselor, I complete twenty-one years of Government service in June of this year.

Q   And you have worked constantly for the Government during all your period of time that you have been a psychiatrist?

A   Yes.
. . .

Q   Did you understand, Doctor, that you were, by this examination or alleged examination of news reports, the pamphlets you have there, and Walker's medical reports,

* The full text of this affidavit, which Dr. Smith read into the record, is reproduced on pp. 180–181.

† Mr. Clyde J. Watts, attorney representing General Walker.

that you were furnishing evidence to commit a man to imprisonment in a federal prison to from sixty to ninety days?

 A Quite the contrary—

  MR. BARKIN: I object, Your Honor.

  THE COURT: What is your objection?

  MR. BARKIN: I believe this is a legal conclusion.

  THE COURT: The witness is on cross-examination. It is proper to inquire into what his understanding was as to the effects of what he was doing. The objection is overruled.

*by* MR. WATTS

 Q Do you understand the question?

 A Yes, I do; and my response is quite the contrary.

 Q What is the response?

 A I made no recommendations whatsoever for any type of commitment.

 Q I believe you misunderstood my question. My question was: Did you understand that your affidavit was being used by the Government to commit this defendant for the type of psychiatric examination as you have outlined? Yes or no.

 A I am not certain that I was fully informed of what use the Government might make of this affidavit.

 Q What use did you understand they were about to make of it?

 A The use which, as I indicated to you at the outset, the question was put to me, whether there may be some reason to consider this defendant's mental condition.

 Q Consider in what manner and where?

 A Well, I would say to you that this is a very broad sort of a, a very broad kind of a concept as to just how you might consider it, and—

  . . .

 Q What did Mr. Belcher say to you and what did you say to him?

A   As I have already stated, I have tried to state the import of the call as nearly as I can recall it. I can not remember verbatim what the exact words were.

Q   I understand.

A   There was no transcript made, to my knowledge.

Q   As nearly as you can repeat it.

A   At least there was no transcript made on my end.

Q   As nearly as you can repeat verbatim. I'd appreciate what you can recollect of what he said.

A   The question which he put to me was something in the nature of a curbstone query, something as follows: "Given what you know about Mr. Walker, do you think it reasonable to consider his mental condition?"

Q   And what did you know about him at that time?

A   What I knew about him at that time I think was a combination of things which I had read and heard over the radio, the usual sorts of things that one might read about a public figure.

. . .

Q   And then did you talk to Mr. Belcher again, please, sir?

A   I did.

Q   When and where?

A   I had another telephone call from him, which as I recall, at about 7:30—excuse me—6:30 that evening, at which time he advised me that he had some material which he wished me to examine.

Q   Where were you then? Home, or still at the committee meeting?

A   I was just sitting down to dinner.

Q   When and where?

A   In the office which I will identify as the office of the Attorney General at the Department of Justice, and I arrived there about 8:30 P.M., I have here on my note.

. . .

Q   Dr. Smith, were you at any time given access to a

United Press news report which said: "During a lull in the rioting, General Walker mounted a Confederate statue on the campus and begged the students to cease their violence. He said, 'This is not the proper route to Cuba.' His plea was greeted with one massive jeer. Walker, who commanded Federal troops which were sent to Little Rock five years ago, was seen striding toward the demonstration wearing a big Texas hat." Did you ever see a newspaper report of that kind?

A    I haven't any definite recollection of it.

. . .

Q    Directing your attention here to the Defendant's Exhibit 2, I'll ask you if, had you received this medical report, it would have changed your opinion. This is a letter dated 11 September 1961, from Joseph H. McNinch, Major General, Medical Corps, Surgeon:

"This is to certify that I, Major General Joseph H. McNinch, have been on continuous active duty as a medical officer in the U.S. Army for over thirty years, and since August, 1960 have been assigned as the Surgeon, U.S. Army, Europe. As the senior Army medical officer in Europe, I have complete access to any information from U.S. Army hospitals in Europe, more specifically Army hospitals in Augsburg, Munich, and Landstuhl in Germany, relative to the mental and physical health of Major General Edwin A. Walker, U.S.A. On the basis of first-hand knowledge, I categorically affirm that medical records of Major General Edwin A. Walker indicate no evidence of brain tumor, central nervous system disease, or any findings of mental disease or mental incompetency. From my experience as a medical officer in the U.S. Army, I can also categorically state that career Army officers, such as General Walker, receive superior medical attention and observation from qualified physicians of the U.S. Army, wherever they may be assigned. For many years, all officers of the Regular Army have been required to undergo an annual, complete physical examination (except during World War II). Findings of physical or mental unfitness are causes for mandatory retirement from the services. To my knowledge, General Walker has never been found other than fit for full duty and free from serious physical or mental disease."

Q Had you been shown that by the Department of Justice, would that have changed your opinion?

A I don't think that I could definitely state that it would.

. . .

Q Do you feel that everyone who is apprehensive that there may be some Communist infiltration in our government is a lunatic?

A I certainly do not.

Q Do you recognize that the Communist enemy is the most effective infiltrating enemy in the history of the world?

A I am not an authority on that.

Q Do you feel that we are immune as their number-one target from such infiltration?

A I can't answer that.

Q Do you think, Doctor, that any commander or major general in the Army who is apprehensive of this infiltration is a lunatic?

A If I may say so, I would rather confine myself to the statements I made here rather than to discuss—

Q Well, Doctor, I understood you to say—

A —communism.

Q —that there were three things upon which you based the conclusion you came to that he was mentally defective, or the apprehension that he was mentally defective; one was that he felt unidentified forces were running the Army and caused his dismissal; second, that his dismissal was caused by a secret apparatus who resented his efforts at indoctrinating his troops, if I am accurate; and third, that he was a scapegoat of a policy of collaboration with the enemy. Now, was that—is that a fair statement of the conclusions you draw from his over-all appearance before the Senate Subcommittee?

A   If it were true that these things were true, then they would have one significance; if they are not true, then they may have another.

Q   In other words, if he imagined all this, he's a fugitive from the psychiatrists; in simple language, that's what it is?

A   I wouldn't use such terminology.

Q   Well, I'm just a lawyer. Excuse me for my inaccurate terminology.

A   Well, I don't like to think of anyone as fleeing from us. However, I must say that there is a large body of persons who do fear the ministrations of the practitioners of mental health. This has been a traditional sort of thing that's gone on for a long time.

Q   If there may have been in General Walker's mind reasonable cause to believe that there was some influence there that he couldn't identify that caused his dismissal from the Army and established a no-win policy, and he was sincere in that, that would not necessarily indicate either paranoia or psychosomatic disorder . . . If he had reasonable grounds to believe that, and he sincerely felt that way, that would not indicate either paranoia or psychosomatic disorder, would it?

A   I would say this, Counselor; that until these theories or ideas are affirmed, there may be reason to suspect—

Q   Suspect what?

A   Some abnormal suspicions.

Q   But, Doctor, without your knowing what he knew, and what went on in his mind to motivate that conclusion, it would be honestly, fairly, scientifically impossible for any honest psychiatrist to say that his apprehensions in those directions indicated paranoia or psychosomatic disorders?

A    I think that's a matter of opinion.

Q    I'm asking you: What is your opinion?

A    I stated my opinion.

Q    Well, you mean to say without knowing what was in his mind, he could—you could still state that this was indicative of paranoia and psychosomatic disorder?

A    I stated that what he stated insofar as it reflects what is in his mind is suggestive of a paranoid trend.

. . .

MR. WATTS: That's all.

THE COURT: Any redirect examination?

MR. RAY: We have no further questions of this witness.

. . .

MANFRED GUTTMACHER, called as a witness by the Government, having been first duly sworn, was examined and testified as follows:

*Direct Examination*
*by* MR. RAY

Q    Would you state your name, please.

A    I am Dr. Manfred Guttmacher.

Q    What is your profession?

A    I am a psychiatrist.

. . .

Q    Doctor, what is your connection with this case?

A    I was called by Mr. Bennett, I think somewhere around the third or fifth of October, and asked whether I would be willing to be one of a member of a board to examine Mr. Walker. He named as the other probable members Dr. William Menninger of the Menninger Foundation, and Dr. Winfred Overholser, who was then retired from St. Elizabeths Hospital, and the idea was that we were to go to Springfield, Missouri. I told Mr. Bennett that I was tied up in many things and I couldn't go immediately, and I couldn't spend a great deal of time there, and he said that the case would be worked up thoroughly by the staff there, that we would have all of the material available to us, and then, of course, I learned that Mr. Walker was no longer there, and I heard nothing further about the matter. Again I'm not certain of dates, but Dr. Felix, Dr. Robert Felix, who is head of the Mental Health Division of the U.S. Public Health Service, and is director of the National Institute of Mental Health in Washington—we are old friends—asked me whether I would be willing to review a series of documents which would be furnished me and give my opinion as to whether I thought on the basis of this material, which he said contained medical reports and various other things, as to whether I thought there was enough suspicion of General Walker's or Mr. Walker's mental condition to warrant a full psychiatric study, and I said that I would be willing to do that. Then a couple of days later, I think it was, Mr. Belcher called me—I had never been in contact with him previously—and said that he had had word that I would serve in this capacity and that he would be sending me very soon a batch of material. Then I got a letter from, I believe, Mr. Miller, it is—I don't know him either; he is, I believe, an assistant to the Attorney General—verifying the fact that I would be asked to do this, and a large cardboard carton was delivered to my office with a good deal of material in it.

Q    What material was in this carton?

A    Well, there were the movie reels of the press conference that was held in Dallas, I believe, on October the twenty-seventh. There was the investigation, the general report of the investigation of General Brown; there was, I was told, a full copy of all of the medical records that General Walker had had while he was in the service; and there was the printed document of his testimony before the Senate Committee; and then there were a great series of newspaper clippings, many of which I just glanced through and paid very little attention to, dealing with Mr. Walker, particularly the recent situation, some that had to do with the situation that developed here in Oxford, and I remember particularly I paid attention to one that was done by Mr. Savell, I think it was, and one by, I think a man named Rogers from Denver, which seemed to give some on-the-spot material as to behavior at the time. I believe that these are the sources of my information, sir.

. . .

Q    Did you review this material and study it?

A    Yes. I kept count of it. I devoted some eighteen to twenty hours going over the material.

Q    Would you summarize what you did and what your findings, if any, were?

A    Well, I have some notes here. I don't know what order is best to give them, but in the Army medical records there are a number of things that I think are of importance. It was recorded that General Walker was in the hospital with encephalitis in 1950 from which he made a full recovery. At that time it was diagnosed as viral encephalitis. He had a very high white-cell count in the spinal fluid and all of the symptoms of a rather severe infection of the central nervous system. What effect that can have later I think is hazardous to say. I certainly am in no position to maintain that he is now suffering from any residuants from this. On the other hand, it certainly is not conducive to strengthening the nervous system.

There are a series of examinations—two examinations in 1953—where he complained of insomnia on several occasions, and then he has been plagued with gastrointestinal symptoms for at least a decade, and when he was cleared for release from the Army, the thirty-first of October, 1961, they found the residual of an old duodenal ulcer which apparently he's had for a number of years. There had been a great deal of complaint of backache, which in most instances has not been identified by X ray or other means as definitely organic, and a number of consultants in the Army records have suggested that this is of a psychosomatic nature. In an examination made on December 11, 1959, there were signs of sclerotic changes in the vessels of the retina . . . it was noted at that time that there was prominent nicking of the veins at the arterial-venous junctions. This, I think, can be of significance.

Then—the patient was admitted on the third of November 1960 to a hospital in Munich where he was suspected of having a brain tumor. The history that was given at that time was that he had minor headaches—this is for six months—and had felt as if his lips were thick recently, and the day before he had a backache with severe generalized headache which lasted until four in the afternoon, at which time he vomited. . . . It was thought there was some minor paralysis of the lower facial nerve, a weakness of the nerve. Otherwise, nothing consequential was noted. . . . It was recommended by one of the medical officers that he be transferred to a general hospital, but then after the matter was further considered he was returned to duty.

Now, none of these things are diagnostic of definite neurological or organic brain disease; on the other hand, I think that they point to what I consider desirable, and that is a full study and exploration. The denting of the veins noted by the ophthalmologist can be consequential. The symptoms that were present in November, 1960, and which disappeared, I think now that there's a period of two years elapsed, it seems to me they should certainly be further explored, because it is very likely, or at least possible, that there might be findings of a definite nature now which would not have been present at that time.

. . .

Q  Dr. Guttmacher, I believe you were testifying concerning some indications of mental disorder when Court recessed yesterday afternoon. Would you take up where you were and continue your testimony?

A   Yes, sir. I think that there were three categories of material that I thought suggestive, thought significant from the Senate hearing, and the first one dealt with what I thought was evidence of mental confusion, and the second one dealt with what I felt were feelings of suspicion, and with that some feelings of grandeur.

. . .

On page 1523 Mr. Walker was testifying, and he said: "I suggest that the whole area should be reappraised by the Congress. I want it perfectly clear that my complete testimony should conclude for all, as it certainly does for me, that I was framed in a den of iniquity represented by co-existence, no-win, collaborating, soft on communism, national policy. This is the hidden State Department policy being implemented now by Mr. Rusk and being withheld from public view. It was the policy that I ran into head-on. The commissariat system is set up to insure conformance by our military to the soft, no-win policy."

. . .

I have seen newspaper articles, articles on the testimony in which it was said that after the hearing a reporter asked Mr. Walker whether he would disavow the support of Mr. Rockwell, and this led to an altercation. Mr. Walker is alleged to have struck the reporter. This seems to me also not good judgment certainly.

I would then like to consider very briefly the motion picture which was sent me by the Government which was alleged to have been, and I am quite sure that it was, a press conference held in Dallas on October the twenty-seventh—

Q   Doctor, was that October or September?

A   I'm sorry, sir. September the twenty-seventh.

. . .

I felt that Mr. Walker's replies were unusually slow,

and there seemed to be some confusion as to the meaning
of the questions. The chief points that I made from this
film were two. First of all there was the element of what
I have called grandiosity here. I recall that he said, and
I think this is a correct quote, although it may not be word
for word: "There are thousands going to Mississippi, not
only because of my interest." I think that this has significance in suggesting the very important role that he was
playing in this situation. He said he was being flooded
with thousands of cables and telegrams and telephone
messages.

. . .

In addition to that, I have paid particular attention to
the newspaper accounts that were written by Mr. Van
Savell and dated October the third, published in the
*Evening Star* in Washington, and then the one that was
published in the Washington *Post* on October sixth, it
was from Oxford, Mississippi, by John Rogers of the
Denver *Post*, and the material in this, I think, has already
been brought to the attention of the Court, but it seemed
to me here again that General Walker was playing a role
that didn't seem to me to show good judgment, and was
using tactics and carrying out this mission without the
judgment and the control that one would feel appropriate
to a man of his type and of his long and very honorable
Army record.

I believe, sir, that's the extent of my observations.

Q   Did you form any conclusions from those observations, Doctor?

A   Well, I think the only conclusion that I could
draw is that there is a real possibility that there has been
a deterioration in the mental processes of General Walker
in the past year or two. I certainly would not want to be
understood to say that I would hazard a diagnosis or that
I would hazard an opinion as to competency. I think that
this is impossible without a very detailed and very com-

plete examination, but I do think there is sufficient smoke here to feel that one ought to look to see whether there's any fire.

MR. RAY: If it please the Court, we have no further questions of this witness.

THE COURT: Before tendering the witness for cross-examination, I have a question. I get, of course, the implication of your last answer, Doctor, but I want to be a little more specific about it. From your study of the materials which you have identified, what is your opinion with respect to whether or not a complete psychiatric examination is indicated to determine the competency of this man under the provisions of the statute with which we are concerned, and with which you are familiar, that is Section 4244 of Title 18 of the United States Code?

THE WITNESS: I have no doubt, sir, in stating an opinion that I think to meet the requirements of this statute that a full psychiatric study would be highly advisable. I might further add that I think for Mr. Walker's own good from a medical point of view I feel that such a study is advisable.

THE COURT: Thank you, sir. You may cross-examine.

*Cross-examination*

*by* MR. MATTHEWS*

Q   Sir, I can't help but think of you in looking at you and listening to you as a professor. Do you have any objection to me calling you Professor?

A   It's very unusual, but I think I can get used to it.

Q   All right, sir. It's your image and your background. I mean that very respectfully.

A   Thank you, sir.

Q   Do you understand the nature of this hearing and the purpose of this hearing and the purpose of your testimony?

* Mr. Joe W. Matthews, attorney representing General Walker.

A Well, I hope I do. I have never previously been involved in a hearing involving this statute, but my understanding is that the statute provides that if a man is charged with a Federal offense, the Government has the right and duty to be sure that he is fully competent mentally to protect his own best interests by being able to confer with his counsel and present his defense in a logical and clear way. That's my understanding. Now, I may be wrong about it, but that's my understanding of it, sir.

Q And do you understand the purpose of your testimony in this hearing, sir?

A I understand that the purpose of my testimony is to see whether I as a psychiatrist would feel in the light of the material which has been given me that there is some reason to question the patient's mental health and his competence.

Q Would you think it a fair statement of your understanding that the purpose of your testimony is to show reasonable cause for having Edwin A. Walker committed to a Government prison hospital for examination for sixty to ninety days?

A No, I am very clear that that's not my understanding. My understanding as given me by Mr. Belcher . . . when he phoned me was that I was to very narrowly face the issue as to whether I thought there was enough to indicate the need of a psychiatric examination presently, and not to concern myself, and consequently I have not concerned myself, with whether had I been there or done this or done that I would have recommended admission to a hospital. That has not been my consideration.

Q Well, sir, now let's look carefully at what we have here. Do you understand that the hearing we are having today and that we had yesterday is based upon the Government's motion to have Edwin A. Walker committed to Springfield at the Federal Medical Prison Center there for psychiatric examination for sixty to ninety days?

A  I am not a lawyer, sir, even though I do lecture in a law school, and I am not too clear about this. I thought my mission was quite clearly as to whether psychiatric examination was indicated now, and I haven't tried to familiarize myself with the statutes. I think when doctors play lawyers they make pretty much of a mess of things, so I haven't read the statutes, and I just tried to stick to my own particular mission.

Q  I take it then, it's a fair statement that you did not realize that the motion before the Court today and yesterday in this case is to have Edwin A. Walker committed to Springfield for sixty to ninety days, a sixty-to-ninety day observation?

A  Well, of course, I was here during the opening statements, and I was able to get that much, that this was an issue, but I didn't think I was involved in that issue.

Q  Well, sir, now let's go one step further. You understand, of course, that the testimony elicited from you by Government counsel, and the very question asked you by the honorable Court, went directly to the question of the interpretation of Section 4244 and your opinion as to whether or not reasonable cause existed for such an examination under 4244, is that not a fair statement?

A  I think whether it exists—I didn't understand the existence—

MR. RAY: If it please the Court, may I make this observation?

THE COURT: All right, sir.

MR. RAY: The statute nor the motion of the United States, and neither does— May I refer to the motion?

THE COURT: Yes.

MR. RAY: The last phrase of it [is]: "and for the purpose of this examination the defendant be committed to a suitable hospital or other facility to be designated by the Court." That's the language of the statute. It was His Honor that committed this defendant to Springfield.

THE COURT: I recall what you said in your opening presentation on the defendant's motion that you gathered the implication when you were there in Springfield from him that it was normal to keep some of the people there from sixty to ninety days.

MR. WATTS: Stronger than that, sir. He specifically told me that they intended to keep Walker in the institution for a period of sixty to ninety days to complete the examination of Walker.

THE COURT: Well, he wasn't kept there—

MR. WATTS: No, sir, he got out on bond.

THE COURT: Got out on an order of this Court resulting from a stipulation of the parties and had an examination which you say took only about two days.

Let's get back on the track. I'm not trying to confine you, but we went all over the football field and the stadium as well yesterday. Let's get back into the playing part of it.

. . .

*by* MR. MATTHEWS

Q Well, the only point I am making, Professor, is, whatever the Government's thinking, you recognize the purpose of your testimony is to get an order requiring Edwin A. Walker to be examined to determine his sanity and mental competency?

A To be examined, yes, that's right, but not to be committed. I didn't realize that that was involved.

Q Well, you have read Section 4244, have you not?

A No, sir, I have not.

Q You have never read it?

A Never read it, as far as I know.

Q You understood, I am quite sure, from prior publicity and prior conference that Edwin A. Walker had already been committed under 4244 once, did you not?

A   I heard this, and I think I knew—I didn't know under what section he had been committed, because as I told you, I am not familiar with this code at all, but I knew that he had been committed to Springfield with the idea of having an examination made.

Q   You knew that this was a hearing under Section 4244, did you not?

A   No, sir.

Q   You did not?

A   No, sir.

Q   You did not inquire?

A   No, sir.

Q   All right, sir. Now, you recognize that this is a case where the raising of a question of a man's sanity influences public opinion in just about every community in our country concerning this particular man, do you not?

A   Not in every community, no, sir, but I think it's of broad general interest, yes, sir.

Q   Well, I am quite sure that you recognize that representatives of the press and wire services, AP, UP, et cetera, are here. Have any of them talked to you or asked you any questions?

A   No. I have handed out prescription blanks so they would get my name accurately; that's all.

. . .

Q   Well, sir, in all fairness and honesty, you recognize that the testimony you give here today and the opinion you render here today goes out across our country on the news media, as to this man's sanity and the inferences concerning this man's sanity, don't you, sir?

A   Yes. I think it's a serious responsibility, and I have tried to carry it out in that way.

Q   And, Professor, I think it's reasonable to assume from your demeanor and the way you have answered questions on direct examination that you recognize that a professional man should be very cautious in expressing opinion as to a man's sanity? In public or in court or at any place.

A   I recognize that.

. . .

Q   Now, how many times have you testified over the years, Professor, in criminal cases concerning psychiatry, just roughly?

A   Well, I have been doing this now for thirty years, over thirty. Yes, thirty years, because I was in the Army for four years. I would say that I do it probably thirty times a year. I would think that's a fair estimate, so if you multiply that, why it's a good many times.

Q   Yes, sir. Now, how many times during that period have you testified for the authority seeking to have a person committed? What percentage of the time, I think would be more pertinent, sir.

A   Well, specifically, I don't recall being involved in that particular type of proceeding. Our law is quite different, and we are always dealing with the question of whether an individual is committable or not, and we make out certificates when we feel that a man is committable, and we, of course, testify in the trials as to whether a man is not responsible on the basis of mental disease, but the vast majority of patients in our mental hospitals in Maryland are there on two doctors' certificates or on voluntary commitment. A large majority are there as voluntary patients. I don't recall actually—my memory doesn't serve me correctly—it may have been once or twice that I was actually involved in a court proceeding as to whether a man should be committed or not.

Q   Let me ask you this question, sir: Have you ever in your thirty years gotten on the stand and testified giving your opinion where the purpose of the litigation is to determine whether or not a man should be committed or not committed and you were called by the man in order to prevent commitment?

A    As I said, I don't think I have done it either way. I don't recall doing it.

. . .

Q    All right, sir. Now, you are paid by the Government for doing this?

A    I hope I am. I mean, I certainly— They said they would pay me.

Q    What is the basis for this payment? Is it an hourly thing, or is it a flat fee, or what?

A    Well, they said whatever my usual charges were for being employed in work out of Baltimore, and they would also pay me the usual fee charged for time spent in going over records. They didn't name any specific fee.

Q    Yes, sir. Now, at that time was it discussed as to whether you would later be called on to testify, or was it mentioned?

A    I don't think it was mentioned. I think I made that assumption.

Q    All right. Now, where did you examine these records? In your office in Baltimore?

A    No, in my home in the evenings and on Sunday.

Q    Now, did you discuss these records as you went over them with anyone?

A    I showed my staff at the clinic the movie. I have two other psychiatrists who work as my associates and two psychologists and a social worker, and I was interested in getting their views as well as having them have the opportunity of seeing this material, and that's the only thing that I ever discussed with anybody.

Q    After you finished on October eighteenth, did you discuss with anyone the records and your opinion?

A    I did with Mr. Ray when I came here.

Q    And up until that time no one?

A    No, I am sure I haven't. I may have mentioned it

to my wife, who is a psychiatrist, but I don't think I discussed it with her.

Q  Do I understand, Professor, that the Government sent you all these records and you spent all this time, and when you got through and had your opinion that nobody in the Government phoned—

A  Well, now, wait a minute. That's not true. Mr. Belcher, I had another conversation with Mr. Belcher. I called him particularly because I knew about the electroencephalogram and the head X ray taken at Munich on the third of November 1960, and I called him about that. I didn't have the record, and there was some conversation that I felt that there were abnormalities present. I also want to correct another thing. I am not an electroencephalographer myself. I am very unskilled in interpreting these, so I took them over to Professor Curtis Marshall who is head of this at Hopkins, and I ran through the record with him. I know I spoke to Mr. Belcher about that, and he said he would look and find the material and so forth.

. . .

Q  Turning, sir, to your instances of grandiosity—

A  Yes.

Q  —and confusion, et cetera. You mentioned page 1394, I believe, yesterday.

A  Yes, sir.

Q  And you read a sentence from that page. Would you read that sentence again, please.

A  "It seems from this that my case is not merely unusual, but unique."

Q  Now, your statement was that this indicated grandiosity.

A  "The forces back of it must be extraordinary. These forces cannot be fully identified, but, in general, the Walker case can be recognized as basically a fight between the internationalist left and the nationalist right with control of part of the U.S. Military Establishment at stake." I think the whole thing to me suggests grandiosity, yes.

Q   Now, when you say grandiosity, what do you mean?

A   An exaggerated opinion of one's importance in the world in which one lives and works.

Q   I take it, then, that you feel that at that time General Edwin A. Walker did not occupy as important a position in the world as indicated by that statement?

A   That's my opinion, sir, yes, sir.

Q   Without going to the various pages throughout this report, do you recall seeing his various assignments from, say, 1951 to 1959?

A   I don't know whether I know of all of his assignments.

Q   Well, as reflected by this record, do you recall whether or not it shows in there that from '51 to '53 he was Deputy to the Commanding General for Prisoner-of-War Affairs over in Korea?

A   Yes, that's right.

Q   And also the senior advisor to the Commanding Officer of the Republic of Korea, there being only two corps? Do you recall that?

A   Yes.

Q   Do you recall that from '53 to '55 he was Assistant Division Commander of the 82nd Airborne Division? Do you recall that in there?

A   I don't recall it, but I'm sure that it's true.

Q   Do you recall that in 1955 he was advisor, the United States advisor and the Chief of Staff to the Chinese Nationalist Army on Formosa? Would you answer out loud, please, sir?

A   Yes.

Q   Do you recall that from '56 to '57 he was the Artillery Commanding Officer for the 25th Infantry Division in Hawaii?

A   Yes.

Q    Do you recall that in '57 and '58 he was in Little Rock?

A    Yes, sir.

Q    Would you say that a person like that would be of extreme interest to Communists?

A    One of a great number of many people that have similar assignments in the Army of one kind or another.

Q    Wouldn't you say that these are assignments primarily devoted to combating our common enemy, the Communists?

A    Yes, I think that most of them are.

Q    Would it not be proper to assume that our own government should have a complete file and a complete dossier and be extremely interested in the background and activities of a Communist general occupying relatively the same position on the other side?

A    I imagine that there is.

Q    Well, using your own—I don't know whether a psychiatrist recognizes common sense—

A    Yes.

Q    All right, sir. Now, going to that statement, the paragraph before where you started quoting, please, sir—

A    Was that page 1394?

Q    Yes, sir.

A    "Last September, in reply to a question by Senator Saltonstall, Secretary McNamara said: 'The only case that I can recall involving discipline of any kind relating to a public statement by an officer or civilian employee of the Department of any kind, including statements relating to communism, is the discipline applied to General Walker' (hearings, page 11)."

Q    Now, start with your quote again, that first sentence.

A    "It seems from this that my case is not merely unusual, but unique."

Q   Now, wouldn't you say, sir, that that is a pretty accurate statement?

A   Yes, I think more. The grandiosity part is "The forces back of it must be extraordinary. These forces cannot be fully identified, but, in general, the Walker case can be recognized," et cetera. I don't think the unique part is so important as the rest.

. . .

Q   All right, sir. I'll try to shorten this as much as I can. The point I am trying to make with you, sir, in all fairness I think you will recognize that the various words that you have picked out here indicate, sir, that when you put them back into context it does not have the connotation that you would have had us believe yesterday, is that not true?

A   Well, I think there are two ways of looking at most things, and my own clinical judgment indicates the way I look at it, and your judgment indicates otherwise. Now, I think that this is where the real difficulty lies.

Q   Are you still of the same opinion as to the use of the phrase "the whole world"?

A   Well, I'm willing to amend this if it's just a figure of speech, but I'm not sure that it was, knowing other things here and knowing General Walker's behavior at the time this conference in Dallas in front of the movies, and knowing news reports of his behavior here, and I believe he, if I had to say what my opinion is, I think he literally meant the whole world just the way I would mean the whole world if I spoke of it.

Q   Professor, let me submit to you, sir, that it might be, in fairness to everybody concerned, proper for you to analyze your feelings, your unconscious feelings concerning the way you went into the investigation of these records. Do you think it would be possible that unconsciously because you were given the job of going through the records and picking out things to indicate mental disturbance, et cetera, that it might have unconsciously caused you to start picking things out that you might not otherwise do?

A    I tried to be fair.

Q    Now, that's not an answer to my question.

A    I tried to be fair. Certainly it's very difficult to rule out entirely an unconscious bias when one is employed by one group or another. This is our method of trial procedure in America, and I think that it does throw a certain onus on the part of the witness, which I tried to guard against, but I admit that it's quite impossible to be certain that one is guarding against it completely.

Q    Thank you kindly for recognizing this fact.

A    Yes, sir.

Q    Now, you mentioned news reports of Mr. Savell; is that correct, sir?

A    And Rogers of the Denver *Post*.

Q    I will hand you what has been marked Defendant's Exhibit 1, and direct your attention to the second paragraph, and ask if you were also furnished with this news report.

A    I would gather that it probably was in all the material. I didn't go through all the material, as I say; it would have taken me—I didn't think it was worth the Government to pay me the extra money that it would require to go through these hundreds of news reports which they sent me; so it may be there, and I may have missed it.

Q    Did you go through these news reports to see if they were inconsistent; you did do that, didn't you, sir, in all fairness to Edwin A. Walker?

A    I know there were some reports which said that he had tried to use a quieting influence at times, that's right.

Q    Would you read that statement out loud, please, sir; this paragraph?

A "During a lull in the rioting, General Edwin Walker mounted a Confederate statue on the campus and begged the students to cease their violence. He said, 'This is not the proper route to Cuba.' His plea was greeted with one massive jeer."

Q All right, sir. Now, that is just inconsistent, isn't it, sir, with the attitude of a man that—

A I think it would show, if both are true, a good deal of confusion as to just what his role was in the situation.

Q Are you not willing to assume, sir, that there might be an inaccuracy in one of the statements, since they are diametrically opposed, in all fairness?

A I haven't read this whole statement. This is just one statement of what he did at the Confederate monument. It doesn't cover the whole situation as far as I know, and it's possible that he was confused as to what his role was. This is the only statement made about him —the rest were just—

Q Just taking that statement that you read out loud, sir.

A If that is correct, and the other is incorrect, then of course that changes the picture. Naturally, I think it would.

Q Would it not change your whole concept of everything that you have said?

A Well, it would certainly make me doubt the strength of my views. Certainly I would say that. It would certainly considerably throw more doubt into my mind as to whether there is enough here to merit exploration, but I think I would still feel that it would be desirable to have a psychiatric examination, psychiatric evaluation, but I think that I certainly would not feel as strongly about it.

. . .

Q All right, sir. Now, we are taking up a lot of the

Court's time going over your testimony, sir. I would like to ask you one other basic series of questions. You stated that you have taught in law school, is that not correct, sir?

A   I have given lectures in law school.

Q   You are familiar with forensic medicine, and you are familiar with courtroom procedures; I think you testified, you stated that you testified in an average of thirty cases a year over a period of thirty years. I would say, based on that, that you have a fair working knowledge of what hearsay is, do you not, sir?

A   Yes, I think so.

Q   Now, in all fairness, Professor, in all fairness to Edwin A. Walker, would you do this for us, please, sir, and in all fairness to the Court, would you please in your mind eliminate from what you have seen all hearsay statements, other than government medical records and this Senate hearing—

A   Now, wait a minute. I can take this into consideration?

Q   You can take other than the hearsay statements in there. You can take his own statements. Would you be kind enough to do that, sir? Eliminate other people's suspicions, other people's opinions, and confine yourself to recalling specifically his own statements. Now, doing that, after you have done that, eliminate all this hearsay, all this unverified information that you have considered—

A   General Brown's material, too?

Q   Yes, sir. Everything that you have considered, washing that from your mind, if that is possible, can you say under oath to God and to this Court that there is reasonable cause to believe that a fine American like Edwin A. Walker is probably insane, or probably mentally incompetent, and I use the word "probably" in contrast to "possibly," if you please.

A   No, I certainly couldn't.

MR. RAY: I object.

MR. MATTHEWS: Thank you, sir.

THE COURT: Does this conclude your cross-examination?

MR. MATTHEWS: Yes, sir.

THE COURT: Is there any redirect?

MR. RAY: No further questions of this witness, Your Honor.

THE COURT: You may stand down, Doctor.

## III

On November 22, 1962, the court declared Mr. Walker fit to stand trial. In an order and an accompanying memorandum, dated December 6, 1962, Judge Clayton summarized his opinion in the case and the reasons for his decision. I shall quote excerpts from these documents to round out the factual presentation of this case.

The order asserts:

The alternative motion of the United States for a psychiatric examination of Edwin A. Walker, the defendant, shall be and is hereby sustained. . . . [T]he report of Dr. Robert A. Stubblefield of the psychiatric examination heretofore conducted by him of the said Edwin Walker, as stipulated by counsel for both parties, shall be and is taken and considered as the report of the psychiatric examination which has this day been ordered. Said report of psychiatric examination having been read and considered by the court in accordance with the foregoing stipulations, the court finds it essentially negative; that is to say, no opinion is expressed therein that Edwin A. Walker is presently insane or presently incompetent within the meaning of Section 4244, Title 18, United States Code.*

A memorandum of some 2800 words, attached to the order, consists largely of a recapitulation of the various

* "Editors' Addenda," in Walsh, *op. cit.*, p. 471.

judicial steps taken following Walker's arrest. Of special interest are the following points made by Judge Clayton:

The basic, underlying question . . . which I have characterized as narrow is: Does the United States Attorney have reasonable cause to believe that a person so arrested, that is to say, arrested on a Federal charge, does the United States Attorney have reasonable cause to believe that such a person is presently insane or otherwise so presently incompetent as to be unable to understand the proceedings against him, and is the motion frivolous, or is it filed in bad faith?

. . . In the context of the situation then existing here in Oxford, it appeared that the United States Attorney had such reasonable cause, and I had no reason or basis then to say that his filing of this motion was in any way frivolous or motivated in the slightest by bad faith. It is my view that those proceedings were valid.*

This is a statement by the court, made in the proper spirit of judicial detachment, concerning the legitimacy of a petition for the psychiatric examination of the defendant, filed by the United States Attorney. It shows that Judge Clayton felt constrained to order a psychiatric examination of Mr. Walker, even though, on the basis of his own information and observation, he considered Walker fit to stand trial.

In his memorandum, Judge Clayton spoke of Mr. Walker as follows:

. . . for the protection of this man, about whom it would be improper for me to express my personal views—I do think, however, it would be proper for me to say that I know his career as a soldier and as an officer personally to a much greater extent than has been developed in the record here. I have long admired the character of his service in that capacity. I had, and still have, the greatest respect for him for that out-

* *Ibid.,* p. 475.

standing service in which he followed the flag wherever duty called.*

Somewhat earlier, in the course of the hearings, Judge Clayton is quoted as having remarked:

[F]rom the appearance of Edwin A. Walker on the witness stand, his response to the questions put by counsel, *from a layman's standpoint* as distinguished from the psychiatric standpoint, if I had limited my consideration to that and that alone, on a hearing where I had to make a judicial determination thereof, I would necessarily have found, *as I am sure most of you would have,* that this man is competent within the meaning of the statute, capable of advising and assisting his counsel in the preparation of his defense in such criminal charges as may be presented against him by the Grand Jury of this Court [emphasis supplied].†

Mr. Walker, it must be recalled now, had not yet been indicted. He had only been charged with certain offenses. The final act in this drama occurred on Monday, January 21, 1963.

Headlined the Syracuse *Post-Standard* the next morning: U.S. DISMISSES CASE AGAINST GEN. WALKER. JURORS FAIL TO INDICT ON RIOT CHARGES. After what had happened to Walker, it was hardly surprising that the Mississippi jury that heard the evidence refused to indict him.

There is an interesting postscript to this story. During 1963, Mr. Walker filed several suits for damages, charging that he had been libeled and slandered. The largest was a $2-million libel suit against the Associated Press for a story, carried in the fall of 1962, alleging that Walker had led a student charge against U.S. marshals during the rioting at the University of Mississippi.

* *Ibid.,* p. 476.
† *Ibid.,* pp. 466–67.

At the time I write this (January, 1965), only one of Walker's suits has reached court. On June 20, 1964, *The New York Times* reported that Mr. Walker had won an $800,000 libel judgment against the Associated Press. "A state district court jury found the A.P. guilty of falsely describing Mr. Walker as the leader of student rioters who charged United States marshals on the Mississippi campus September 30, 1962." The Associated Press said it will appeal.

Again, it is a curious coincidence (if such it is) that this Associated Press report, declared libelous and "actuated by malice" by a Fort Worth, Texas, jury, was listed in first place as the document submitted to Dr. Charles E. Smith for examination and from which he concluded that Walker's "recent behavior . . . may be indicative of an underlying mental disturbance."

## IV

The attempt by the prosecution to incriminate a defendant as a mental patient and thus deprive him of the right to trial is clearly displayed in the Walker case. It is evident that a person so attacked cannot effectively defend himself if he does not have the funds to procure the legal talent necessary for the task. In effect, anyone but a Very Important Person is defenseless against the prosecution's ostensibly benevolent "suspicion" that he is "too sick" to stand trial.

The case of Mr. Edwin Walker supports this conclusion. Certain aspects of this affair now deserve to be re-emphasized.

1. Although committed to the U.S. Medical Center for Federal Prisoners at Springfield, Missouri, Walker was released on bail. This is exceedingly unusual (I have never heard of a similar instance), because defendants ordered to undergo pretrial psychiatric examinations are

considered involuntary mental patients. Hence they are no longer regarded as suspected criminals and are therefore ineligible for bail.

2. Having been ordered by the court to submit to pretrial psychiatric examination, Walker was allowed to exercise two important prerogatives. He could select one of the psychiatrists; and he could object to the psychiatrist chosen by the government and thus disqualify him from being an examiner. As a result, Mr. Walker was examined by only one psychiatrist, the one he had selected. Significantly, this man was a professor of psychiatry in a medical school in Dallas, where Mr. Walker resided. Ordinary, noncelebrity defendants can never choose their psychiatric examiners.

3. Before examining Mr. Walker, the psychiatrist who was to examine him announced that he was consulting with two other experts "to determine what might be a reasonable psychiatric examination" of the defendant. Psychiatrists called upon to examine men like Hoffer, Lynch, or Perroni never have any problems about what constitutes a reasonable examination for *them*.

4. In the hearing held to determine Mr. Walker's competence to stand trial the adversary nature of the proceeding was clearly demonstrated. In other, similar hearings, the impression is allowed to linger—clearly encouraged by the presiding judge—that the prosecuting attorney and his psychiatric agents are somehow trying to "protect" the accused.

This was not allowed to happen in the Walker case. Thus, it was clearly established that Dr. Smith was an employee of the U.S. government and had acted as its agent.

Dr. Guttmacher's testimony resembled more closely the opinion usually given in this type of case. Although it was clear that he was testifying for the prosecution, Dr. Guttmacher was not a full-time employee of the government. Moreover, he emphasized his medical concern for the defendant by consistently referring to Mr. Walker as "the patient," and by asserting that a "full psychiatric study" of Walker was necessary not only to "meet the requirements of this statute" (Section 4244, Title 18, U.S. Code), but also "for Mr. Walker's own good from a medical point of view."

However, the effort by Dr. Guttmacher to deny that he was here acting as Mr. Walker's antagonist—and not as his friend or physician—was swiftly and effectively blocked by Mr. Matthews: first, by the device of addressing Dr. Guttmacher as "Professor," which, I think, hammered home to everyone present the significance of name-calling in the whole proceeding. Second, by eliciting several important contradictions in Dr. Guttmacher's testimony; for example, in reply to Judge Clayton's question, Dr. Guttmacher acknowledged being familiar with Section 4244, Title 18, of the U.S. Code; yet, when questioned by Mr. Matthews, Dr. Guttmacher admitted that he was "not familiar with this code."

Indeed, so evident was it in the Walker case that physicians had acted as the antagonists of a "patient" (who, of course, was not a patient, but a defendant), that the American Medical Association, having been deluged with complaints against Dr. Smith, issued, through its Judicial Council, a statement concerning it. After a summary of the salient facts, the statement concluded:

After considering all this information the Judicial Council concludes as follows:

It is the judgement of the Judicial Council of the American Medical Association that Doctor Smith did not violate the Principles of Medical Ethics, did not violate professional confidence and did not make a diagnosis in regard to the mental condition of General Walker.

The Judicial Council expresses concern about possible

future situations wherein a physician might be subject to political control in order to pervert his medical opinion or be used as a tool for political purposes. The Council urges physicians to be alert to such possibilities and to refuse to give such opinions which might be used for political purposes.

The Council points out that a physician employed by government or others may never distort or color his opinion to satisfy either the political purposes or business interests of his superiors.*

The American Medical Association thus justified Dr. Smith's actions largely by claiming that he did not make a "diagnosis." This, however, was not the government's understanding of what Dr. Smith had done. When Walker's lawyers appealed to Judge Clayton to strike the government's petition seeking a psychiatric examination of Walker, the United States Attorney filed a brief which included the following: "In the instant case the Government and the Court relied on the psychiatric diagnosis of an expert psychiatrist who based his conclusions on extensive medical histories of Walker ..."†

What constitutes a "diagnosis" of a mental condition? The American Medical Association did not long hold to the view it expressed in the Walker affair. When, in the fall of 1964, 1189 psychiatrists declared that Senator Goldwater was "psychologically unfit to be President of the United States"—many offering a diagnosis of paranoid schizophrenia as the basis for their judgment‡—the American Medical Association denounced the poll and the physicians' willingness to lend their opinions to such an enterprise.§ But what is the difference between Dr. Smith's "diagnosis" of General Walker and the nearly

* "General Walker and Dr. Smith," p. 37.

† Walsh, *op. cit.*, p. 465.

‡ "The Unconscious of a Conservative: A Special Issue on the Mind of Barry Goldwater." *Fact* (September–October) 1964.

§ *A.M.A. News,* October 12, 1964.

1200 psychiatrists' "diagnosis" of Senator Goldwater? If one is ethical, why not the other? In each case, psychiatric intervention serves the same strategic purpose: to prevent the subject from playing a particular role. In the case of General Walker, the aim was to prevent his assuming the role of accused; in that of Senator Goldwater, the role of President. Never has the art of slander been developed to greater perfection.

# 7 THE CASE OF MR. FREDERICK LYNCH

¶ [T]he characteristic of the world we live in is just that cynical dialectic which sets up injustice against enslavement while strengthening one by the other.*

## I

The cases presented thus far illustrate how a person may be denied his right to trial by being ordered by the court to submit to pretrial psychiatric examination. If the accused is declared unfit to stand trial, he is incarcerated for months, years, or sometimes for life in an institution which, though ostensibly psychiatric, is actually penal in character.

In our day of psychiatric enlightenment, there has evolved still another method for depriving a person accused of an offense of his right to trial. Although considered fit to stand trial, the accused is not permitted to plead as he and his counsel wish; instead, he is coerced by the court to plead "not guilty by reason of insanity." Since this is done in cooperation with, indeed on the instigation of, the prosecution, it follows as day after night that the defendant will be acquitted. This does not mean, however, that he goes free. On the contrary. Although declared "innocent" by the court, the accused is, without further examination of his sanity, also declared insane and in need of immediate and indefinite mental hospitalization.

This travesty, not only on justice but on everyday com-

* Albert Camus, "Bread and Freedom" (1953), in *Resistance, Rebellion, Death*, p. 92.

mon sense, logic, and psychiatry, has been made possible by the Durham decision and by the subsequent work of its defenders. The coerced plea of "not guilty by reason of insanity" thus stands as probably the single most terrible manifestation of evangelistic psychiatry riding roughshod over civil liberties and human dignity. Despite its absurdities and the violence it inflicts on our sense of justice, many jurists and psychiatrists earnestly defend this method of handling accused persons as both legally sound and psychiatrically therapeutic.

I shall first present a summary of the Lynch case. I shall then cite the opinions of authoritative spokesmen for and against the coerced plea of "not guilty by reason of insanity."

## II

On November 6, 1959, Frederick Lynch, a realtor and former lieutenant colonel in the Air Force, was arrested in Washington and charged in the Municipal Court for the District of Columbia with a violation of the "Bad Check" Law of the District of Columbia.* This was Lynch's first encounter with criminal justice—and, as it turned out, his last.

Frederick Lynch's offense was that he overdrew his checking account by $100 and failed to make restitution within a period of five days after notice to do so. Lynch appeared in Municipal Court on November 6, 1959, without counsel and a plea of not guilty was recorded. He was

* I wish to thank Mr. Richard Arens and the Editors of the *Catholic University Law Review* for kindly granting me permission to quote from the article cited, and Mr. Arens for providing me with a copy of his brief. The account of this case which follows is based on: (1) Richard Arens, "Due Process and the Rights of the Mentally Ill: The Strange Case of Frederick Lynch," *Catholic University Law Review, 13*: 3–38 (Jan.) 1964. (2) *Lynch* v. *Overholser,* 369 U.S. 705, 1962 (the decision rendered by U.S. Supreme Court in the Lynch case), in 30 *Law Week,* 4369, May 22, 1962. (3) *Lynch* v. *Overholser,* Brief for the Petitioner, Filed in the Supreme Court of the United States, October Term, 1961, No. 159, Richard Arens, Esq., Counsel for Petitioner.

thereupon committed under D.C. Code Section 24-301 (a) to the District of Columbia General Hospital for a mental examination to determine his competence to stand trial. The record of the hearing in Municipal Court does not reveal the basis for the trial court's action. It should be noted, however, that Lynch did not plead not guilty by reason of insanity.

On December 4, James A. Ryan, M.D., the Assistant Chief Psychiatrist at the District of Columbia General Hospital, reported that Lynch was "of unsound mind, unable to adequately understand the charges and incapable of assisting counsel in his own defense."* Lynch remained under "treatment" at the General Hospital.

On December 28, 1959, Dr. Ryan sent a letter to the court, advising that Lynch was now mentally fit to stand trial. However, Dr. Ryan did not limit himself to reporting this opinion, but added that at the time of the offense Lynch "was suffering from a mental disease, i.e. manic-depressive psychosis . . . so that the crime charged would be a product of his mental disease. At the present time, Mr. Lynch appears to be in an early stage of recovery from manic depressive psychosis. It is thus possible that he may have further lapses of judgment in the near future. It would be advisable for him to have a period of further treatment in a psychiatric hospital."†

The following day, December 29, 1959, Lynch was brought to trial in the Municipal Court before a judge without a jury. Represented by counsel, Lynch now sought to withdraw the early plea of not guilty (entered when he had been declared incompetent to stand trial), and instead sought to enter a guilty plea. The trial judge refused to allow the guilty plea, presumably on the basis of Dr. Ryan's letter, which had alleged that Lynch's offense was "the product of mental illness." (According to

* Arens, op. cit., p. 5.
† Loc. cit.

the Durham formula, this entitled the accused to acquittal as not guilty by reason of insanity.)

In the trial which followed, the conventional positions of the participants were reversed. The defense sought Lynch's conviction, the prosecution his acquittal—to be sure, by reason of insanity, so that he would be automatically committed to St. Elizabeths Hospital. Over Lynch's objection, a government psychiatrist testified that the accused had been a victim of mental illness as of the time of the overdrawn checking account and that the crime was the product of his illness. Despite the defendant's persistent objections, the judge acquitted him by reason of insanity. Then, without holding a hearing or making a determination of his state of mind or need for hospitalization at that time, the judge ordered him committed to St. Elizabeths Hospital pursuant to D.C. Code Section 24-301(d). Lynch was thereupon confined in St. Elizabeths Hospital and housed in a department which contained 1000 patients and provided two psychiatrists for their care and treatment.

On June 13, 1960, after having been incarcerated for approximately six months, Lynch petitioned for a writ of habeas corpus in the District Court. The petition asserted "That commitment of Frederick Lynch, pursuant to an involuntary insanity defense, violated due process of law, . . . and circumvented the safeguards of the Civil Commitment Law."*

After a hearing, held on June 16, 1960, the District Court held that the Civil Commitment Law had indeed been improperly circumvented. In an order dated June 27, 1960, the District Court sustained the writ and declared that "the Municipal Court lacked jurisdiction to effect such a commitment and thereby permit the government to obtain commitment of the petitioner [Lynch] as of unsound mind by use of criminal proceeding in substi-

* *Ibid.*, p. 9.

tution for civil commitment procedures established by law . . . [and] . . . that petitioner, therefore, was illegally detained at St. Elizabeths Hospital."*

Despite this judicial finding Lynch was not released. The officials of St. Elizabeths Hospital and the prosecution were offered a choice: accept the District Court's ruling or appeal it? They appealed. Lynch was therefore held in confinement at the hospital pending the outcome of the appeal.

The appeal was based on the claim that the Municipal Court exercised proper discretion in rejecting the guilty plea. The prosecution argued that it was the court's duty to reject this plea because of the information it had about Lynch's mental illness. (The prosecution also maintained that the possibility that Lynch might be incarcerated at St. Elizabeths Hospital for a period longer "than the maximum imprisonment possible under the offenses to which he desired to plead guilty" was not relevant to a determination of the legality of his detention.) Once again, the hospital superintendent and the prosecutor, acting as his legal representative, claimed to be representing the best interests of the petitioner (Lynch), not those of his adversary (the government). They sought to support this Orwellian strategy by arguing that the "acceptance of his [Lynch's] guilty plea would have created a double stigma —conviction of crime and insanity."†

Thus, although Lynch was now declared competent to stand trial and was advised by counsel, the prosecution and its psychiatric agents arrogated to themselves the privilege of deciding how best to protect Lynch from social stigmata.

On January 6, 1961, the United States Court of Appeals reversed the order of the District Court and sustained the commitment of Frederick Lynch by the Municipal Court

* Loc. cit.
† Ibid., p. 10.

as a proper exercise of judicial discretion. The Court of Appeals held:

"1. That a defendant could be validly denied the right of entering a guilty plea to a misdemeanor even though it was conceded that he was mentally competent [to stand trial]. . . .

"2. that an insanity defense could be thrust upon a defendant by either court or prosecution upon the basis of a history of some mental illness; and

"3. that upon acquittal by reason of insanity . . . the defendant was properly subject to indefinite commitment in a lunatic asylum without any hearing as to his then existing mental state."*

Strangely, in rendering their judgment, the majority of the Court of Appeals reiterated that confinement such as Lynch's is not punitive, but "remedial," and added that "now . . . [that Lynch] has received treatment he is well on the way to unconditional release without the probability of repeat offenses."†

Perhaps this smug prediction was based partly on the fact that even before the court's decision was handed down, Lynch had been given a "conditional release" from St. Elizabeths Hospital. He was incapable, however, "of persuading any prospective employer that he was worthy of any but the most menial and routine of jobs."‡ Soon Lynch passed several more worthless checks and, on April 7, 1961, his conditional release was revoked and he was returned to the hospital.

A petition for certiorari (review) was filed with the Supreme Court and was granted on June 19, 1961. Peti-

* *Ibid.*, p. 12.
† *Ibid.*, pp. 12–13.
‡ Lawrence Speiser, "Statement," in *Constitutional Rights of the Mentally Ill.* Hearings before the Subcommittee on Constitutional Rights of the Committee of the Judiciary. Eighty-seventh Congress, First Session; Part 2—Criminal Aspects; (Washington, D.C.: U.S. Government Printing Office, 1961), p. 561.

tioner's brief, filed by Mr. Arens, contended that Lynch's confinement was in violation of due process of law and in circumvention of the Civil Commitment Law. The American Civil Liberties Union filed an independent brief as *amicus curiae*, urging the reversal of the judgment of the Court of Appeals.

Eleven months later, the Supreme Court reversed the judgment of the Court of Appeals and held Lynch's commitment by the Municipal Court null and void.

Speaking for the majority, Justice Harlan declared that it was unnecessary to consider the constitutional claims of the petitioner and stated that the Supreme Court "read Section 24-301(d) as applicable only to a defendant acquitted on the ground of insanity and not to one, like petitioner, who has maintained that he was mentally responsible when the alleged offense was committed."*

He further explained that "it was not Congress' purpose to make a commitment compulsory, when, as here, an accused disclaims reliance on a defense of mental irresponsibility."†

Justices Frankfurter and White took no part in the decision of this case. Justice Clark dissented.

In his dissent, Justice Clark made several significant points. He asserted that the "Court did not reach the constitutional issue. Its failure to do so is, I believe, a 'disingenuous evasion.' "‡ He went on to say that:

I would uphold the statute. . . . [P]etitioner has no constitutional right to choose jail confinement instead of hospitalization. . . . There is no reason to believe that the doctors, or for that matter, the judge would be improperly motivated. . . . It must be remembered that here the constitutionality of Section 24-301(d) is at issue, not the wisdom of its enactment. That is

* Arens, *op. cit.*, p. 14.
† *Loc. cit.*
‡ *Lynch* v. *Overholser*, p. 4377.

for Congress. So long as its choice meets due process standards it cannot be overturned.*

Additionally, Justice Clark stressed the "medical" aspects of the problem. Noting that Lynch has not claimed "that he is now sane," nor has he made effort "to secure his release on the ground of being cured," Justice Clark suggested that Lynch ought to be "required to make such an effort before asking the Court to strike the statute. . . ."† In other words, he felt that the petition lacked merit because Lynch was still mentally ill.

In a sense, Lynch was vindicated. He had carried his case to the highest court in the land, obtained a hearing there, and won. Had he been a criminal, he would have been set free. He might even have been a hero. But Lynch was a mental patient, confined in a hospital, not a prison. Instead of setting him free, the hospital authorities initiated proceedings for his civil commitment.

On January 22, 1962, four months before the Supreme Court handed down its decision on his appeal, Lynch wrote to Arens that "the conditions here are almost more than anyone can bear—the monotony—78 cents per day per patient food budget, no laundry, and above all no treatment. This hospital . . . is a human warehouse." Prophetically, he added that "Even if the Court does rule in my favor, it is the kind of a case where the operation was a success but the patient died."‡

Perhaps Lynch felt that he had become some sort of "test case" and that the authorities in charge of him would go to any length to prevent his discharge. His retention in the hospital after winning his case may have confirmed this impression. On August 23, 1962, three months after

* *Ibid.*, p. 4378.
† *Loc. cit.*
‡ Arens, *op. cit.*, p. 38.

the Supreme Court's decision and while still confined at St. Elizabeths Hospital, Frederick Lynch threw himself under the wheels of a slow-moving truck on the grounds of the hospital. "The apparent suicide of the 45-year-old Air Force Lieutenant Colonel came on the eve of a new court hearing today in which the Government, which lost the case before the Supreme Court, sought a civil hospital commitment. The Government had its fingers crossed in the Lynch case, because for a while it appeared that he might not be sick enough to qualify for civil commitment."*

The government could now uncross its fingers. Frederick Lynch, the bad-check-passer, was no longer stalking the streets of Washington.

## III

Is it possible to justify what was done to Mr. Lynch? To my mind it is not. It is widely believed, however, that there are two sides to every question. Barrows Dunham called this idea a myth, and I agree with him. Like all myths, however, this one too serves a useful function: it justifies inaction. For this reason it appeals "chiefly to people of not very acute moral perceptions, people whose satisfaction with their own lot leaves them merely puzzled by others' misery."† In addition, people are persuaded by other reasons, peculiar to the Lynch case, that the treatment afforded to this man was fair, just, and reasonable.

We may begin with Justice Clark, who dissented from the majority decision of the Supreme Court. He objected to reversing the decision of the Court of Appeals because he felt that the Supreme Court would create "a loophole for those who seek to plead guilty."‡ But, according to

* Washington *Evening Star*, August 24, 1962.
† Barrows Dunham, *Man against Myth* (1947) (New York: Hill & Wang [American Century Series], 1962), p. 119.
‡ *Lynch* v. *Overholser*, p. 4378.

Anglo-American legal tradition, except in a capital case a defendant has the right to plead guilty.

Basically, Justice Clark approved Lynch's coerced psychiatric confinement because he considered Lynch a "sick" man, and because he accepted the whole semantic deception inherent in the notions of "mental illness" and "mental hospitalization." Thus he spoke of persons such as Lynch as "unfortunates among us that know not what they do. . . ."* But Lynch was declared competent to stand trial by the government's very own psychiatric experts. On what ground, then, does Justice Clark hold that Lynch did not know what he was doing when he elected to plead guilty? The answer can only be because Lynch had a history of mental illness.

The principles behind the Lynch case, and the practices to which they gave rise, were examined in some detail at hearings before the Senate Subcommittee on Constitutional Rights in Washington on May 2, 4 and 5, 1961. Several of the witnesses who testified before the Committee expressed approval of the automatic commitment statute in force in the District of Columbia and also of the propriety of the prosecution's raising the question of the defendant's insanity.

Commenting on the Lynch case, Mr. Oliver Gasch, a Washington attorney, said: "He is in a mental hospital right now receiving care and treatment. Of course, he will probably in due course be rehabilitated and released."† The naïve complacency with which Mr. Gasch equates confinement in St. Elizabeths Hospital with "receiving care and treatment" is shocking to those who know what that institution is like.

Mr. Gasch also expressed opposition to Lynch's right to plead guilty: "We are not trying to keep these people there [at St. Elizabeths Hospital]. But we do feel that when

* *Loc. cit.*
† *Constitutional Rights of the Mentally Ill*, p. 572.

they have violated the law, and when there is reason to believe that they are not guilty because of a disease or defect from which they suffer at the time the act was committed, that in conscience the court should not accept a plea of guilty."*

Dr. Winfred Overholser, the Superintendent of St. Elizabeths Hospital, also spoke in support of the psychiatric incarceration of alleged offenders. In particular, he defended as morally proper the government's privilege of foisting a psychiatric defense on an unwilling defendant: "It seems to me, as an interested layman, only proper that the prosecution should be allowed to bring in all of the evidence, whether favorable or unfavorable, to the defendant. Certainly it should hardly be compulsory upon the state to prosecute a defendant whom it knew to be mentally ill and in need of treatment."†

As to the right of the defendant, competent to stand trial, to have his guilty plea accepted by the courts, this, Dr. Overholser stated, was a matter of "law and ethics [rather] than of psychiatry. I certainly do not speak as an expert in either of these fields, but it is my impression that it is of doubtful propriety ethically to permit a person to stultify himself by allowing him to plead guilty to an offense which was the outgrowth of mental illness. I agree, in other words, with the conclusions of the majority of the court of appeals as expressed in *Overholser* v. *Lynch*."‡

Since Dr. Overholser disclaimed expertness in the field of ethics (as if this were a domain reserved to qualified ethicists), and since he gave his conclusions not as his own but as those of a court of law with whose judgment he was in agreement, one must wonder how he reconciled his views with the Supreme Court's judgment in the Lynch case.

* *Loc. cit.*
† *Ibid.*, p. 589.
‡ *Ibid.*, p. 590.

Still another witness who testified in favor of coercive psychiatric confinement was Samuel Polsky, Professor of Law and Legal Medicine, Temple University School of Medicine. The following exchange illustrates Professor Polsky's views:

Q. (Mr. William Creech, Chief Counsel of the Subcommittee). I gather you believe that at present society is justified in indefinitely hospitalizing these people [i.e., alleged "sociopaths" accused of crime], even though it has not been ascertained that treatment or cure will be available, rather than giving them short-term prison sentences, which many of them would receive because not all of their anti-social activities would subject them to imprisonment for a long period.

A. (Mr. Polsky.) Yes. (There followed an explanation of this answer.)"*

Several witnesses assailed the Durham decision and its consequences, and criticized specifically the treatment accorded Mr. Lynch.

Mr. Lawrence Speiser, Director of the Washington office of the American Civil Liberties Union, recommended that "as long as the present automatic commitment law stands, legislation . . . be adopted forbidding the use of an insanity defense by the Government or the court against the wishes of a competent defendant aided by counsel."†

Similarly but somewhat more narrowly, Mr. Abe Krash, a Washington attorney, stated that he did not believe "that either the judge or the prosecution should be entitled to force a defendant to stand trial on the insanity issue in misdemeanor cases over his objection."‡

Dr. Leon Salzman, Professor of Clinical Psychiatry at Georgetown Medical School in Washington, called atten-

* Ibid., p. 680.
† Ibid., p. 561.
‡ Ibid., p. 616

tion to the antitherapeutic aspects of involuntary mental hospitalization. He noted that "The prisoner can only view the decision to send him to the mental hospital as a sentence in a hospital in lieu of a prison. He sees the action as a means of substitute punishment and not the benevolent action of a concerned community. Psychiatric therapy cannot even start, let alone develop, under such circumstances. . . . This must be borne in mind particularly if the hospital to which the prisoner is sent is insufficiently staffed or has inadequately trained personnel to deal with the problem. Here the automatic commitment may be even more severe than a jail sentence where the prisoner may have a better chance of receiving adequate therapy."*

According to Dr. Salzman, the automatic commitment procedure "is a fence-straddling device, because we are afraid or unwilling to discharge the accused when he is found to be of unsound mind at the time of the crime. Instead, we distort the role of the mental hospital and the psychiatrist in order to appease what we think will be community censure, and thereby discredit the psychiatrist and psychiatry."†

Though I agree with the objectives of Dr. Salzman's argument, I think it is misleading to say that "we distort the role of the mental hospital." As a group, mental hospitals and psychiatrists have two antithetical roles: to help patients with their problems in living, and to protect communities from the annoyance and harm of so-called mental patients.‡ One of the important traditional functions of the mental hospital is to serve as a kind of jail. This role is not a new role, foisted on the mental hospital

---

* Ibid., pp. 625–26.
† Loc. cit.
‡ Thomas S. Szasz, Law, Liberty, and Psychiatry: An Inquiry into the Social Uses of Mental Health Practices (New York: Macmillan, 1963), pp. 79–88.

by recent legislation in the District of Columbia, but on the contrary is an old role, merely given greater scope and significance than it has had before.

Dr. Salzman further observed that "we find [that] those individuals who are enthusiastically supporting the Lynch decision, are also primarily detractors and derogators of psychiatry and its possibilities. They are delighted to use psychiatry as an agent of punishment, while they have disrespect for its therapeutic potentialities."*

This is a cogent observation. It should remind us that when basic human rights are trampled upon, those who are crushed are not the only ones harmed; they are merely injured first. Next come those who do the trampling, even though their actions may be sanctioned by the government. They too become debased, and are soon injured as well. Finally everyone suffers—the whole society that has stood by idly and permitted a majority to injure a minority.

The following exchange between Mr. Creech and Dr. Salzman is pertinent here:

*Mr. Creech.* Doctor, you have mentioned the Lynch case, and cases such as the Lynch case, where the plea of insanity is interposed by the prosecution. Is it your feeling that interposition of insanity at this point may be such a traumatic experience as to have, not a disastrous effect, but perhaps a worsening effect upon the mentally ill defendant's condition?

*Dr. Salzman.* That is certainly a real possibility that would have to be considered. The prosecution presenting a plea, a statement of the unstable nature of the accused person, can hardly be viewed as a compassionate act. I do not see how it is anticipated that in a contentious situation, which a trial very clearly is, that the man who is designed to be your grave digger, so to speak, makes a tender suggestion about your need for hospitalization and treatment. Now, it may be perfectly true, but in that setting it cannot serve to do anything but

* *Constitutional Rights of The Mentally Ill,* p. 628.

encourage whatever distorted attitudes and feelings the prisoner may have. He cannot view this act as an act of benevolence.*

Perhaps the strongest criticism of psychiatry as a weapon of law enforcement was voiced by Hugh J. McGee, an attorney and Chairman of the Committee on Mental Health of District of Columbia Bar Association. To begin with, he noted that "To suggest that psychiatry has accepted the challenge hurled at it by Durham is absolutely ridiculous. There are no more than a handful of psychiatrists who have testified in our criminal courts. . . ."† Indeed, as the cases assembled in this volume and other much-publicized cases show, some psychiatrists have a clear bias toward finding persons mentally ill and thus bringing about certain social consequences—just as others have an opposite bias.

Like much else that is obvious in psychiatry, this fact has been studied by a committee whose findings were then kept secret. In his testimony, Mr. McGee referred to a study by a committee of the Washington Psychiatric Society which investigated the participation of psychiatrists in criminal trials. The report of this committee, according to Mr. McGee, "has not been circularized, nor have I ever heard it referred to since they made known their conclusions to the Bar Association's Committee on Mental Health, which I had the privilege of chairing at the time. The whole tenor of their conclusions was that the institutional experts were possibly [sic] one sided in their opinions or they wouldn't be called as witnesses by the Government . . ."‡

Mr. McGee recognized that involuntary mental hospitalization is tantamount to imprisonment. He asserted that the psychiatrists at St. Elizabeths Hospital "actively see if they can't keep a person in longer. Now, it is some-

* Ibid., pp. 631–32.
† Ibid., p. 657.
‡ Ibid., p. 658.

thing that the doctors themselves will not admit, but it is a fact that it is not the illness that determines his stay at St. Elizabeths Hospital, but the seriousness of the offense that put him there."[*]

In regard to the Lynch case, Mr. McGee suggested that "The rights of a defendant 'competent to stand trial' should be identical to those of any citizen of 'sound mind,' because the two phrases should be legally synonymous. Any citizen, except in a capital offense, has the right to have his guilty plea accepted by the court, and so it should be with any person adjudged 'competent to stand trial.' Any other result can only undermine the dignity of our courts and make its officials appear ridiculous."[†] In brief, "a person who is competent to stand trial should not be commitable."[‡]

Despite the testimony presented at the Senate Hearings on the Constitutional Rights of the Mentally Ill in 1961, and despite the Supreme Court's ruling in the Lynch case in 1962, to date there has been no change in the statutes of the District of Columbia for the handling of defendants alleged to be mentally ill.

## IV

Let the Lynch case be a sober warning to those who despair of democracy and of the wisdom of letting each man be his own guide, and prefer, instead, a paternalistic type of government that helps its citizens make the "right" decisions.

The issue is not Mr. Lynch's mental health or illness; rather, it is his right, as against that of the government, to define and pursue his best interests. The facts speak for themselves: it would have been to Lynch's advantage to plead guilty, and this is what he tried to do. We usually

[*] *Ibid.*, p. 662.
[†] *Ibid.*, p. 659.
[‡] *Ibid.*, p. 666.

consider a person "mentally healthy" if he seeks, by rational and practical means, to maximize his advantages in life. Yet when Lynch showed clear appreciation that a guilty plea would serve his interests best, he was not allowed so to plead, but was forced instead to plead "not guilty by reason of insanity."

This case seems to me particularly shocking because Lynch, accused of crime, was deprived of the right to trial even though he was considered mentally competent to be tried. In practice, the tragedy of the Lynch case is what happened to Lynch; in principle, it is that such a thing could happen. The treatment accorded Lynch went one step beyond the hypocrisy of negating a defendant's right to trial by declaring him mentally unfit; Lynch had a "trial" which satisfied the *pro forma* requirements of law —but which was not an actual trial at all. Walker could claim that he was deprived of his right to a speedy trial; Lynch could not. Justice Clark specifically asserted that "here—under #24-301(d)—the accused [Lynch] has already had his trial."*

One of the questions raised by the Lynch affair is whether the defendant has the right *not* to be tried. Framed in this particular way, this question was not confronted by any of the judges or commentators who dealt with the case. They did, however, consider some closely related questions.

One is the right of the defendant and his attorney to select the defense strategy they deem best. Mr. Arens and others emphasized that Lynch was deprived of this freedom, and hence, in effect, of trial.

Another is the right of the defendant to plead guilty. In his dissent, Justice Clark noted with approval that the Criminal Rules of the Municipal Court of the District of Columbia provide that " 'the court may refuse to accept a plea of guilty.' And it further prohibits the acceptance of

* *Lynch* v. *Overholser*, p. 4374.

a guilty plea without the court's 'first determining that the plea is made voluntarily with understanding of the nature of the charge.' The opinion today acknowledges that the trial judge need not accept the plea of guilty when, as here, he had in his hands a certificate from competent doctors that the petitioner was and remains insane and in need of treatment."*

It seems to me that Justice Clark erred here on two counts. First, he ignored the evidence that Lynch understood, perhaps only too well, "the nature of the charge" against him; second, he spoke of the defendant's insanity and need for treatment, bringing in issues that were not immediately relevant—and ignored the issue of competence to stand trial, which was not contested by the government.

In contrast to the views expressed by Justice Clark, Mr. McGee maintained that "Any citizen, except in a capital offense, has the right to have his guilty plea accepted by the court . . ."† Common sense, if not legal precedent, would bear him out. I think we may further clarify this problem by formulating it in terms of the game-playing model of behavior.‡

Every person accused of crime, unless incompetent to stand trial, has the right to be tried. Charged with wrongdoing, the defendant incurs an obligation—to respond to the accusation (in a prescribed manner); and acquires a right—to be tried (unless the offense is trivial). The question arises: Is standing trial a right or an obligation? It cannot be both. Having the right to play—for example, the horses or roulette—implies having the right not to

* *Ibid.*, p. 4377.

† *Constitutional Rights of the Mentally Ill*, p. 659. This assertion is not correct. Judges have considerable latitude in denying the defendant the "right" to plead guilty in contexts other than those of capital offense and mental illness.

‡ See Thomas S. Szasz, *The Myth of Mental Illness: Foundations of a Theory of Personal Conduct* (New York: Hoeber-Harper, 1961), especially Part V.

play, or having started to play, to stop (there may be certain penalties for doing so). If playing a game is an obligation, then it cannot be a right. The two concepts are mutually exclusive.

In the case of ordinary offenses—such as a traffic violation or a minor underpayment of income taxes—the issue of trial is invariably treated as a right which the accused may elect to exercise or not. Actually, most persons charged with such wrongdoings choose not to exercise their right to trial. They prefer to plead guilty and suffer the penalties imposed by law. Were such a person forced to stand trial, he might well consider it a greater punishment than the sentence itself.

Thus it seems absurd to consider that the accuser may both bring a charge against the accused and demand a formal trial. Yet, the court's refusal of a plea of guilty (or of *nolo contendere*) produces just such a situation.

In nontechnical terms, it comes to this. The government has the privilege (indeed, the duty) to address the citizen thus: "You have driven too fast in your motorcar!" Having brought this charge against the citizen, it would be absurd if the government could also insist that the citizen could not reply, "Yes, I was driving too fast. I am sorry. I am prepared to suffer the penalty prescribed by law for this misbehavior" but, instead, that he must stand trial (and plead either "not guilty" or "not guilty by reason of insanity"). Yet this, in brief, is what the apologists of Lynch's psychiatric incarceration assert. They defend this view, perhaps, because they realize that by pleading guilty, the defendant may sometimes gain an advantage over the prosecutor (as in the bizarre context of the Lynch affair, and also, for example, by preventing public disclosure of embarrassing testimony). But here, as so often in such matters, we face a problem of values. If we value individual liberty and the right to trial, we must preserve this strategy for the defendant; we can nullify it only at the cost of nullifying trial as a right.

All this is familiar to students of games and play.* To play a game means that we may take it or leave it; when we cannot leave it but must play, then it is work. This is the basic difference, at the roulette table and the race track, between those who play and those who work.

The ordeal of Frederick Lynch teaches us the same lesson. When trial is a duty, not a right, it ceases to be the familiar "game" constructed by and for the freedom-loving men of Greece, Rome, England, and America. Though we may still call it trial, the "game," like Gregor Samsa, Kafka's hero, has metamorphosed. No longer a rational and fair contest between two spiritually equal adversaries, it is a grotesque nightmare, in which a proud and strong man (the state) crushes a tiny and repulsive insect (the accused).

* See Roger Callois, *Man, Play, and Games* (1958), translated from the French by Meyer Barash (New York: The Free Press of Glencoe, 1961).

# PART III

# 8 REVIEW AND RECOMMENDATIONS

¶ Between the forces of terror and the forces of dialogue, a great unequal battle has begun. I have nothing but reasonable illusions as to the outcome of that battle. But I believe it must be fought, and I know that certain men at least have resolved to do so. I merely fear that they will occasionally feel somewhat alone, that they are in fact alone, and that after an interval of two thousand years we may see the sacrifice of Socrates repeated several times. The program for the future is either a permanent dialogue or the solemn and significant putting to death of any who have experienced dialogue.*

## MENTAL ILLNESS AND INCOMPETENCE TO STAND TRIAL

Although mental illness is a myth, incompetence to stand trial is not. It is therefore necessary, first, to separate these two concepts and to understand clearly the meaning and import of each.

When I assert that mental illness is a myth, I mean that, because the term is a metaphor, it is easily misunderstood and misused. I do not question that the phenomena we call "mental illnesses" exist, and are in that sense "real." What I question is the wisdom of calling them either "mental" or "illnesses."

One group of psychiatric disorders consists of physical abnormalities, like syphilis of the brain and toxic psychoses (for example, acute alcoholism). These are appro-

* Albert Camus, "The Unbeliever and Christians" (1948), in *Resistance, Rebellion, Death*, pp. 73–74.

priately considered "diseases"; but they are diseases of the brain, not of the mind.

Another group consists of personal disabilities, like fears, stupidities, and discouragements. Such so-called functional psychiatric illnesses may appropriately be considered "mental" (in the sense in which we consider thinking and feeling "mental" activities); but they are diseases only in a metaphorical sense.

A third group of psychiatric disorders consists of certain antisocial acts, like homicide or homosexuality. These are social deviations, and can be considered neither "mental" nor "diseases."

For our present purposes, the chief significance of these considerations, and especially of the metaphorical character of the term *mental illness,* is this: If mental disease is the sort of thing I think it is, then fighting it with doctors and drugs is about as reasonable as fighting the War on Poverty (as President Johnson calls it) with generals and tanks. However, while no one expects generals to cure poverty, many people expect doctors to cure mental illness.

Both metaphors are misleading—and for the same reason: Both poverty and mental illness are *human problems,* complex in character, and diffuse in etiology. This does not imply that nothing can be done about them, and that we must sit back resignedly and contemplate our helplessness. On the contrary. Only correct understanding enables us to act intelligently rather than sentimentally. Let me indicate some of the things we might do about one aspect of the problem of mental illness—specifically the problem of mental incompetence to stand trial.

In contrast to "mental illness," which is either metaphor or sham—"incompetence to stand trial" is a genuine denotative concept. There *are* people who cannot and should not be tried. The questions that we must try to answer are: How do we know that they are, in fact, incompetent? And what should be done with them? I shall examine each of these problems and offer some suggestions about them.

## THE DEFENDANT'S ROLE

A crucial concept for understanding many so-called psychiatric problems, and especially for clarifying the problem of mental competence to stand trial, is social performance.

The law specifies that no person should be put on trial who cannot perform the role of defendant. No reasonable and fair system of criminal law could do otherwise. It is important to note, moreover, that what the law requires is the ability to defend oneself against a criminal charge; it does not require good health, physical or mental. Accordingly, competence to stand trial is no more a medical or psychiatric matter than is competence to be a beautician or a mortician.

The defendant must perform a certain role. If we wish to make the issue black or white—as we must, sometimes, for legal purposes—we may assert that a person either can or cannot perform this role. If he cannot, he must be judged incompetent to stand trial.

There may be several reasons for a person's inability to perform the role of defendant. Injury, such as a brain concussion, may be one; illness, such as a brain tumor, may be another; so-called mental illness, such as inability or unwillingness to confer with counsel or appear in the courtroom, may be a third. The point to remember is that in each of these instances a person is declared incompetent to stand trial, not because he is sick, but because he cannot, or will not, perform the role that society has assigned to him. Thus the man with cerebral concussion is unfit to stand trial, not because he has been injured, but because he is unconscious; the man with brain tumor, not because he has cancer, but because he is aphasic; and the man with "schizophrenia," not because he is mentally ill, but because he is unable or unwilling to play the role in which society has cast him.

For reasons that need not concern us here, the concept of incompetence to stand trial has become greatly expanded during the past few decades. Thus, commonsense judgments about competence to stand trial were abandoned, and were replaced by psychiatric pronouncements about "mental diseases." The result is a mystification of the process of establishing competence for standing trial, and an inculcation in the "public opinion" of a belief in a causal connection between "mental illness" and incompetence to stand trial. More than anything else, this linkage is responsible for the denial of the right to trial which I have detailed in this book.

What connection, if any, is there between mental illness and competence to stand trial? This question cannot be answered without specifying what is meant by "mental illness." If the category of mental illness includes behavioral deficits caused by diseases and injuries of the brain (such as cerebral hemorrhage and brain tumor), there may, of course, be a close and important connection between these two concepts. On the other hand, if the category of mental illness excludes such conditions, the connection becomes slight and insignificant.

If psychiatric diagnostic labels are used reasonably (as they rarely are), they refer either to certain complaints of the patient (for example, phobia, conversion hysteria), or to certain predominant styles of behavior which he exhibits (for example, depression, paranoia). In some ways, calling a person "phobic" or "depressed" or "paranoid" is comparable to calling him rich or poor, Catholic or Jewish, white or Negro, and so forth. Each designation tells us something about the person. The question is: Is this information *relevant* to the issue at hand—in this case, to the question of competence to stand trial?

The answer depends on our standards of competence. Suppose we wish to exclude Jews or Negroes from standing trial; describing defendants as Jewish or Christian, Negro or white will then be relevant. We know, however, that race and religion are functionally irrelevant criteria for standing trial: some Jews and Negroes can perform the task required of a defendant while others cannot; the same is true for Christians and whites.

The situation with respect to mental illness is similar. Some persons diagnosed as "schizophrenic" or "sexually deviant" may be able to perform the task of a defendant; others may not. Conversely, some persons accused of crime may not come to the attention of psychiatrists; others who do may not be diagnosed as mentally ill. In either case, persons presumed mentally healthy may or may not be capable of performing the task of defending themselves adequately (for example, because of ignorance or poverty). The point is that there is neither logical nor factual connection between mental illness and the ability to perform the task required of a defendant. Hence, describing a defendant whose competence to stand trial is in question as "mentally sick" is either irrelevant (like calling him "slightly obese"), or destructive (like calling him a "Communist swine").

If we accept the view that competence to stand trial is a question of task-performance, not of illness, the remedies for our present difficulties are at hand: We must recognize psychiatric determinations of competence to stand trial as scientistic, not scientific. Accordingly, these must be replaced by practical, commonsense determinations.

## INCOMPETENCE TO STAND TRIAL:
## FACT OR STRATEGY?

The judgment that a defendant is mentally unfit to stand trial is the final step in a long series of events. This judgment cannot be understood apart from the entire social context in which it occurs, and especially from its social consequence: the incarceration of the defendant in a psychiatric institution for an indeterminate period, often for life.

The potential outcome of a finding of mental unfitness to stand trial has a crucial effect on motivating the prosecution and the defense to request, or not request, a pre-trial psychiatric examination of the defendant. As a rule, the defendant has nothing to gain, and much to lose, from initiating such a procedure. In contrast, except in cases where the prosecution is eager to have a public trial and is confident of winning a conviction, the district attorney has much to gain and nothing to lose from initiating such a procedure: if the defendant is found fit, he will stand trial; if unfit, he will be incarcerated in a psychiatric institution. In either case, the accused is subjected to social sanctions: to trial and imprisonment if found guilty; to psychiatric "diagnosis" and detention if found incompetent.

All this makes it difficult, indeed impossible, to have an unbiased, factual determination of competence to stand trial; instead, we have a strategic determination of it. Ostensibly, we assess facts; actually, we decide on a course of action.

This problem is a common one; it is not limited to the psychiatric determination of the defendant's fitness to stand trial. The "testing" of Negro registrants to determine their fitness to vote in Mississippi is an example of a strategic maneuver: its aim is not to ascertain what such registrants can and cannot do but to exclude them from voting. In contrast, the testing of men and women in New York State to determine their fitness to drive is an example of a factual test: its aim is to establish which applicants can, and which cannot, safely operate a car, not to deny the privilege of driving to any person or group for reasons unrelated to driving. In this book I have argued that our present psychiatric methods for determining competence to stand trial resemble voter-testing in Mississippi rather than driver-testing in New York; in brief, that they are strategic, rather than factual, in character.

If one of our principal concerns is the fairness of the criminal trial, then we must guard against introducing anything into the proceedings that will give either party an unfair advantage. The pretrial psychiatric examination gives such an advantage to the prosecutor. Letting the district attorney challenge the defendant's competence to stand trial, without incurring any risk or penalty for doing so, puts the defendant at a tremendous disadvantage. (The insanity plea, where there is no automatic commitment following an acquittal on the grounds of "not guilty by reason of insanity," gives a similar advantage to the defendant.)

## ASCERTAINING COMPETENCE TO STAND TRIAL

The recommendations I propose flow logically from the point of view developed here and in my other writings on law and psychiatry. Let us be clear about our goal: to define and develop a functional—not a mentalistic—method of ascertaining competence to stand trial. Accordingly, the psychiatrist (or any other "behavioral expert," such as the psychologist) can play no part in this affair—either as decision-maker or as provider of "expert opinion." The responsibility for examining the defendant and for deciding his fitness to stand trial should be placed in the hands of one of the following persons or groups: (1) a judge or a panel of judges; (2) a lawyer or a panel of lawyers; (3) a lay jury.

## 1. The Judge as Examiner

We regard ability to stand trial as a specific skill, like dancing, driving a car, or playing chess. If we want to determine whether a person knows how to drive an automobile, we do not call in a physicist or an automotive engineer to test him; instead, we entrust the task to a policeman who knows how to drive.

Similarly, if we want to determine whether a person can defend himself against criminal charges, we need not call in a psychiatrist or a psychologist to test him; instead, we ought to entrust the task to a judge (or attorney or layman). This method is logical and simple. Why has it not been adopted? Let us consider the possible reasons.

First, the traditional role of the English and American judge: in the criminal trial, the judge plays a relatively passive role. For example, the American judge does not actively interrogate the defendant, as the Russian judge does. In the United States, the judge's role is analogous to, though not identical with, the role of umpire: he referees the game, but does not himself engage in the contest.

My recommendation does not undermine this legal tradition. When the question of the defendant's fitness to stand trial is raised, the game has not yet begun. This is the very point of the examination: the claim has been brought before the court that the principal performer—the defendant—cannot go on stage. Is it not absurd or mischievous to pretend that this examination is a part of the game itself?

If this is so, there can be no valid opposition to a judge's active participation in this determination. Would anyone object to letting the umpire decide whether or not a prospective player can enter the game or stay in it? This is an integral part of the umpire's role in sports such as boxing. He knows as much as anyone about the requirements a person must fulfill to be a player.

Still, there might be objection to this procedure based on the following argument. In the course of examining the defendant to ascertain his fitness to stand trial, the judge might gain certain information or impressions which would render him less impartial, and perhaps less judicious during the trial, than if he had had no pretrial contact with the defendant. This is undeniably true. But it would be easy to guard against this difficulty: one judge could examine the defendant before trial, and another conduct the trial. Further refinements in this basic scheme might consist in having a panel of judges, rather than an individual judge, decide on the defendant's ability to stand trial; and in providing a mechanism for appeal to a superior panel of judges should the defendant oppose the decision.

Second, judges might have avoided assuming responsibility for this task, and, instead, delegated it to psychiatrists, because of the absence of clear criteria for judging competence to stand trial; understandably, judges might feel uncertain about deciding this question. Their discomfort might be heightened because, in the absence of criteria for competence to stand trial, they would be open to criticism, however they might decide a particular case.

My response to this argument is that it is the responsibility of judges (and perhaps of legislators) to formulate such criteria; and that if there is doubt about a defendant's ability to stand trial, it should be resolved in favor of permitting him, or making him, stand trial.

Third, judges might feel mystified by so-called mental illness, and believe that anyone suspected of such a dread malady should promptly be placed in the hands of physicians. This would justify their abdicating the responsibility of determining whether or not a defendant is fit to stand trial.

In countering this argument, I would compare their doing so to their referring defendants charged with witchcraft to theologians or witch-hunters. Indeed, it is immaterial whether "mental diseases" or "witches" exist. What matters is that due process and basic human rights take precedence over psychiatric considerations. I maintain that every man is a human being first, and a "psychiatric patient" (or "witch") second. Accordingly, every man may be judged, morally and legally, by his fellow men and by agents of the legal system—regardless of his "medical" (or "theological") condition.

## 2. *The Attorney as Examiner*

Another solution to the problem of who should determine whether the defendant is fit to stand trial is to entrust the task to lawyers. Together with judges, they know best, in practical terms, what is required of a person to defend himself in court. There are several possibilities here.

First, if the defendant opposes his pretrial examination and wishes to stand trial, it would seem reasonable to let him do so, if he can retain counsel to represent him. If a defense attorney accepts a client, this implies that he believes that his client is able to stand trial. (Indeed, refusal to abide by this commonsense rule implicitly impugns the honesty of attorneys.) Of course, this practice would greatly favor the prominent and well-to-do defendant over the unknown and indigent one. This difference cannot be completely eliminated. However, the indigent defendant's position could be made to approximate that of the wealthy one by applying a modification of the same rule to him: such a defendant should have access to attorneys (for example, appointed by the court or provided by

Legal Aid societies, the American Civil Liberties Union, or similar agencies), and should be allowed to stand trial if an attorney so provided is willing to represent him.

A more impartial solution to this problem would consist of commissioning individual attorneys, or a panel, to conduct pretrial examinations of defendants suspected of being unfit to stand trial. After meeting with the defendant, they would report to the court on the possibility of preparing and conducting a defense. Who would have a better idea than an experienced lawyer? The evidence given to such a lawyer should be kept in the same confidence as the ordinary client-attorney relationship. The court would not be given any information, but only a conclusion: the defendant can or cannot manage the functional problem of assisting counsel in the preparation of his defense.

In cases where the decision is adverse to the interests of the defendant, the possibility for appeal to a superior panel of referees should be provided.

### 3. The Layman as Examiner

Finally, we might consider the commissioning of a panel composed of laymen—a kind of "jury"—to determine whether a person is fit to stand trial. This would have the advantage of defining the task of standing trial as a practical, everyday matter—like using a washing machine or driving a car; ascertaining a person's ability to stand trial would thus be a proper task for ordinary men and women.

I believe that such a panel could adequately assess, and would find fit for trial, many defendants who now oppose pretrial psychiatric examination and are found psychiatrically unfit to stand trial. Those it could not assess, or whom it found unfit, could be re-examined by panels of attorneys or judges.

## 4. The Fate of the Defendant Declared Incompetent to Stand Trial

It is futile to consider what might be the most appropriate methods of determining competence to stand trial without considering the fate of the defendant declared unfit. The reason for this is basic: a person accused of crime is immediately stigmatized as a threat to society.

Accordingly, attempts to ascertain a person's capability to drive a car or stand trial differ. In the former case, the determination is functional: if the person is found capable, he obtains the license; if not, he is denied the license. In the latter, the determination is strategic: if the person is found capable, he is tried; if incapable, he is committed to a mental institution.

If functional standards were used to determine competence to stand trial, as they are to drive a car, the alternatives would be analogous. In other words, if the defendant were found capable of standing trial, he would be tried; if incapable, his trial would be postponed (for a fixed, but brief, period, when he would be re-examined). This we refuse to do. Psychiatric determination of competence to stand trial thus serves an additional, hidden reason: it legitimizes the psychiatric incarceration of those found unfit to stand trial.

As I have argued elsewhere,* involuntary mental hospitalization is a weapon in society's battle against the individual; moreover, the use of this weapon, in contrast to traditional judicial sanctions, is not regulated by the principles of due process. I stand by my previous position that involuntary mental hospitalization, civil or criminal, has no place in a civilized, free society and must be abolished.

This would eliminate one of the major incentives for the demand for the pretrial psychiatric examination of

* See *Law, Liberty, and Psychiatry: An Inquiry into the Social Uses of Mental Health Practices* (New York: Macmillan, 1963), especially chapters 7, 12, and 18.

defendants. Indeed, were such incarceration abolished, it alone would result in the virtual disappearance of such requests by the prosecution.

What, then, should happen to the defendant found unfit to stand trial? The same as happens to persons considered unfit to drive a car, qualify for a medical license, or found medically (not psychiatrically) unfit to stand trial: they are deprived of the right to play a particular social role, but are not otherwise punished. If we sincerely wish to exempt certain persons from the burden of standing trial because of "mental" (that is, educational, emotional, and social) considerations, then we must simply exempt them, and not use their failure as justification for additional penalties.

Perhaps the simplest course would be to follow the precedent set by the disposition of persons declared unfit to stand trial because of medical illness. The defendant excused from standing trial because of high blood pressure is not penalized for his illness by involuntary confinement in a hospital or by coerced treatment of his illness. Instead, he retains his basic social role as citizen in a free society: though charged with crime, he has the same rights as other citizens similarly situated. If the charge against him allows, he can post bail; if not, he must wait, in a prison-hospital, until he is tried or the charge against him is dismissed.

I believe there should be a similar disposition of the defendant found "mentally" unfit to stand trial. If the charge against him allows, he should be able to post bail and go free. If the charge does not allow the defendant to post bail, he should be confined in prison until he is found capable of standing trial or the charge against him is dismissed. In either case, I believe the government should not have the option to coerce the defendant to undergo any experience designed to enable him to stand trial. At the same time, the defendant found incapable of standing trial and confined in prison should, if he desires, have access to the services of a psychiatrist (or other "mental healer"), just as he should, in a civilized society, to the services of other persons engaged in rehabilitation work (such as clergymen or educators). In brief, the government, through its laws, courts, and prison personnel, should neither coerce persons to submit to psychiatric activities they do not want nor deprive them of such help if they want it.

These recommendations are faithful to the principle of making the determination of competence to stand trial a functional, not a mentalistic (or psychiatric), procedure. If so considered, all justification for psychiatric incarceration evaporates. The individual who fails a test for a driver's license is not, *ipso facto,* incompetent to manage his affairs and a fit subject for psychiatric detention. Surely, there might be persons who could not stand trial but who could manage their daily lives. The case of Mr. Perroni (Chapter 4) is illustrative: assuming that he was incompetent to stand trial (which I do not believe was the case), there was no reason to assume that he could not manage his daily affairs.

It may be objected that these proposals favor the individual rather than the state. Of course they do. That is their aim. But isn't this the purpose of the Constitution and the Bill of Rights? Doesn't this distinguish a free society from a totalitarian one?

However, I do not favor creating a "loophole" for the easy escape of persons accused of crime and perhaps guilty of it. I believe that virtually everyone accused of crime should stand trial. To be sure, the scheme I have outlined would tend to benefit, rather than harm, some individuals declared incompetent to stand trial; it might, therefore, encourage the tactical use of this maneuver by certain defendants. I do not see how we can entirely prevent this.

Given the fact that prosecution and defense are antagonists in the game of criminal trial, declaring the defendant incompetent to stand trial is bound to be tactically advantageous to one contestant or the other. The prevailing rules provide an enormous tactical advantage to the prosecution. To counteract this, I have devised rules that would give some advantage to the defense. Were my suggestions adopted, the prosecution would rarely raise the issue of the defendant's fitness to stand trial. On the other hand, the defendant might do so more often than at present. However, I believe the procedures outlined would reduce the likelihood of offenders escaping trial and punishment by sustaining questionable claims of incapacity to stand trial. Additional safeguards against such abuses could easily be devised: should the defendant raise the issue of his competence to stand trial and be declared incompetent, I suggest that he be subject to mandatory re-examination at frequent intervals, and that his competent behavior outside the courtroom, while awaiting re-examination and trial, be considered presumptive evidence of his fitness to stand trial.

We are proud of our legal system of justice, committed to the moral principle that "it is better that a thousand guilty men go free than that one innocent man suffer unjustly." We should be ashamed of our psychiatric system of justice which seems committed to the moral principle that "it is better that a thousand men fit to stand trial be deprived of the right to trial and be incarcerated in psychiatric institutions, than that a single individual unfit to stand trial be submitted to the ordeal of legal justice."

# 9 SUMMARY

¶ Let us rejoice as men because a prolonged hoax has collapsed and we see clearly what threatens us.[*]

What can the community do with its members suspected of lawbreaking? The answer to this question identifies a society more accurately than any other simple statement that can be made about it. A society may have a government that is royalist or republican, aristocratic or democratic, capitalist or socialist, yet under any of these systems it may be free or despotic, depending largely on its attitude toward suspected criminals.

In general, the fewer the alternatives open to the government vis-à-vis the alleged lawbreaker, and the more precisely these alternatives are defined, the stronger the protection of individual liberties. We consider such a society free. Conversely, the more numerous the alternatives open to the government, and the more vaguely these alternatives are circumscribed, the weaker the protection of individual liberties. We consider such a society unfree.

This way of looking at society reflects, of course, the bias of individualism and personal freedom. Approaching the same problem from the point of view of group solidarity and social tranquility, we would assign different values to the government's options vis-à-vis the alleged lawbreaker. The more unhampered the moves the government can make against the individual, the more protected is the group. Such a society looks secure. Conversely, the more

[*] Albert Camus, "Create Dangerously" (1957), in *Resistance, Rebellion, Death*, p. 270.

constrained the moves the government can make against the individual, the more endangered is the group. Such a society looks insecure.

Our current attitudes toward social deviance, and especially toward lawbreaking, illustrate a conflict and confusion of moral values. On one hand, we embrace the value of personal choice and political freedom and are committed to individualism. On the other, we seek personal safety and social tranquility and become committed to collectivism.

Our love of freedom requires that the criminal law protect the citizen accused of lawbreaking, otherwise we run the risk of the government overpowering the citizen. Our love of safety requires that the criminal law protect the community, otherwise we run the risk of individuals harming each other and destroying society. This is a dilemma every modern society must face.

For some time now, but especially since the end of the second world war, our nation (though, of course, not ours alone) has retreated from the full-bodied ethic of the free society. Often we seem to prefer safety to liberty, collective irresponsibility to individual responsibility. Certainly a look at our legal-psychiatric practices will not reassure us. In placing the burden of mental illness on the citizen suspected of antisocial conduct and in punishing him with involuntary psychiatric confinement and treatment, our criminal law is becoming more like the legal systems of modern totalitarian regimes.

Like so-called martial law, the criminal law of totalitarianism is based on the premise that the integrity of the state is in jeopardy. It matters not who the enemy is or what he threatens. His presence is enough to permit the government to take certain unusual measures against offenders. But once the state is allowed to assume this posture of desperate self-defense, it acquires license to override traditional civil liberties and basic human rights.

The Stalinist dictatorship justified arbitrary actions of all kinds—arrest, deportation, torture, execution—on the ground that it was saving Communist society from its capitalist enemies. The Nazi government based its system of criminal law on its alleged need to defend itself against an international Jewish-Communist conspiracy.

Although thankfully less extreme than these examples, the dilution of our traditional criminal law with mental health practices carries our society in the same direction and for the same reasons. We are, or feel we are, threatened from many directions: by the growing economic and military power of Communist nations, by the mounting disunity between white and black Americans, and, neither last nor least, by increasing anxiety about the "mentally ill."

As a society, we do not feel secure. Our internal problems remain unaffected—may even be aggravated—by immense and costly efforts to combat collectivism abroad. We thus have the soil in which the seeds of a repressive criminal law may ripen. We must defend ourselves against the lawlessness of the Negro who wants to be an American; against the lawlessness of the white who, on the one hand, sympathizes with the oppressed Negro and, on the other, feels a burning racist hatred toward him; and finally, against the "mentally ill" whom, as a result of decades of "mental health education," we have learned to fear and despise with renewed vigor.

In response to these dangers and fears, we have "refined" our criminal law. If the accused cannot be convicted as guilty and punished as a criminal, he can be diagnosed as mentally ill and detained as one in need of involuntary psychiatric treatment. In either case, he is considered a fit subject for social control.

This may seem well-intentioned-enough policy, even if badly misconceived; its sinister aspects, however, should not be overlooked. Most of the individuals subjected to the penalties of our criminal laws and to the coerced therapies of our mental hygiene laws belong to the lower social classes. It seems probable, therefore, that those most likely to be subjected to, and least able to defend themselves against, the double jeopardy inherent in our combined criminal-psychiatric procedures will also come from this group; the evidence so far available confirms this assumption.

Combined criminal-psychiatric measures, such as the involuntary pretrial examination, may be especially oppressive for the Negro. This is because, in proportion to their numbers, Negroes commit, or are accused of committing, more offenses than whites. It is possible therefore that this type of legislation is an attempt—albeit an "unconscious" or covert attempt—to impose more rigid social controls on Negroes just as they are emerging from their centuries-old legal and psychological bondage. (Let me repeat: I do not suggest that mental health legislation is consciously intended as anti-Negro; this, however, may be its practical consequence because of the frequency of Negro crime.)

To illustrate how mental health laws may be, and indeed are, used against Negroes, and specifically to deprive them of the right to trial, I shall cite some examples of such practices reported in newspapers.

Here is one such case. "The voice from the gallery Monday hit the almost deserted Senate chamber like a rifle shot. 'How can you say you are protecting the black man when there are only five of you there?' said the voice, interrupting the Senate rules forbidding talking or demonstrations in the galleries. The young man talked on as gallery attendants, caught off guard, struggled past other spectaors to apprehend him.

" 'There are 20 million Americans who don't know what is going on here,' he continued as attendants closed in on him. 'There are 100 senators and only five of them here and only two debating,' he said."*

The man, identified as Kenneth Washington, twenty-six, of Passaic, New Jersey, was quickly apprehended. He offered no resistance to arrest. "Apparently he is mentally disturbed," said Police Captain James Powell. He was taken to D.C. General Hospital for mental observation.

Judging by the substance of his comments, Mr. Washington—how ironic his name!—was perfectly coherent. He knew the number of senators in the United States; he knew that in general people were poorly informed about the debate in the Senate concerning the Civil Rights bill. Why was this insufficient presumptive evidence for treating him as a responsible, free American? Why was he not arraigned, released on bond, and tried for his offense?

Here is another case. On July 16, 1964, Mr. Herbert Callender, chairman of the Bronx CORE chapter, went to City Hall with two chapter members, with the idea of placing the mayor under citizen's arrest. They contended that Mayor Wagner "had misappropriated public funds by assertedly allowing racial discrimination on city-sponsored construction projects."*

Mr. Callender was arrested and sent to Bellevue Hospital for psychiatric observation by Criminal Court Judge Edward D. Calizzo. He was released on July 21 after spending five days in Bellevue. "I don't think it is fair to treat a peaceful civil rights demonstrator as if he were an insane person," commented Mr. Callender.† (Is it fair to treat *any* individual accused of crime in that manner?)

Mr. Callender's psychiatric incarceration, like Mr. Walker's, was bound to provoke public criticism. It did indeed.

* Los Angeles *Times*, May 5, 1964.
* *The New York Times,* July 21, 1964.
† *Ibid.*, July 23, 1964.

The American Civil Liberties Union, for example, called it "an outrage."‡ But such "outrages" occur every day. The vicitims are the unknown men and women who populate our hospitals for the criminally insane. Like everyone else, prominent persons such as Mr. Walker or Mr. Callender need the protection of the Constitution and the support of public-spirited individuals and groups. But who has sought to protect our common citizens from that harm which causes so many groups and individuals to recoil in horror when it is committed against a well-known person?

Furthermore, involuntary pretrial psychiatric examination seems to be placidly accepted by both white and black political leaders—one of the many signs of the tight grip of the psychiatric imagery and technology on the public mind. Illustrative is a photograph and caption which shows a Negro cornered at a pier by a white policeman, the Negro's arms outstretched, his face reflecting a mixture of fear and hate. The caption reads: "Caught. Patrolman Fred Sportack holds a gun on Frank Pickney, caught as he was attacking a New York City pier watchman with a piece of lumber. Pickney was taken to Bellevue Hospital for observation."* Newspaper editors have evidently come to believe that it no longer requires explanation why a man accused of assault, and perhaps armed robbery, should be taken to a "hospital," rather than charged with the crimes he has allegedly committed.

Occurrences such as these support my contention that there is a shift in the attitude of whites toward blacks in America—the tactic of psychiatric repression replacing the tactic of racial repression; and that the involuntary pretrial psychiatric examination of defendants is one of the most important, and most effective, weapons in this battle.

‡ *Ibid.*
* *Syracuse Herald-American*, June 30, 1968.

That this weapon is not used exclusively by white against black, but is also used by white against white, does not contradict or weaken my argument; guns and tanks may also be used by one group against another, or by members of a group against fellow members.

The practices we have surveyed place the psychiatrist who considers himself a liberal—that is, one who loves liberty—in a paradoxical position. He bewails the deprivation of the Negro's right to vote in the South but applauds the deprivation of the citizen's right to stand trial in the North. But, from the subject's point of view, what difference does it make whether his right to vote is taken away because his adversaries do not like the way he looks or his right to stand trial because of the way he thinks?

INDEX
AFTERWORD

# INDEX

# AFTERWORD

It is now widely accepted, especially in the United States, that confining lawbreakers in mental hospitals as insane, without the benefit of a real trial, rather than in prisons as criminals, after a proper trial, is a recent, enlightened Western practice. Nothing could be further from the truth. The practice is neither recent, nor enlightened, nor typically Western—resembling the Oriental-despotic arbitrariness toward troublesome persons much more closely than the Occidental-legal respect toward persons accused of crimes. Many nineteenth-century cases illustrate the procedure and support my foregoing interpretation of it. The following is a typical example.

In the years before the first World War, Grigorii Rasputin —whom history knows as the "mad monk," though he was neither mad nor a monk—was, after Nicholas and Alexandra, the most powerful person in Russia. As the Empress's most trusted friend and "therapist," he exercised enormous influence over her; and she, in turn, had virtually complete control over the weak and ineffectual czar. Not surprisingly, Rasputin was widely hated and feared and was eventually assassinated in 1916. However, there was a previous, failed attempt to kill him. In 1914, a woman named Chionya Gusyeva, dressed as a beggar, approached Rasputin in his home town of Pokrovskoe and, when Rasputin reached for his money, stabbed him in the lower abdomen. Rasputin survived. As for Gusyeva, she was treated much like countless Americans have been and continue to be:

Gusyeva was arrested. . . . She announced that she had tried to kill Rasputin for abusing his so-called sainthood, for his heresies, and for raping a nun. The authorities felt it would be a mistake to put her on trial. After a short imprisonment she was conveniently declared insane and put in an asylum in Tomsk. Her relatives made repeated attempts to get her out, on the grounds that she had "got better," but the doctor in charge insisted that she continued to display symptoms of "psychological disturbance and exalted religiosity." She did not get out until after the February Revolution . . .*

This procedure has all the earmarks of traditional Oriental despotism: it is arbitrary; it is unilateral, the defendant's "betters" deciding how best to deal with her; it is devoid of any mechanism for appealing the punishment; and, while defined as compassionate and humane (even medical and therapeutic), the charade simply serves the convenience of the defendant's adversaries.† Long ago, this paternalistic procedure for dealing with persons who disrupt the social order was grafted to the tree of the American legal system. By pushing unwanted persons out on this limb, we ensure that they fall to their psychiatric deaths, while we bask in the glory of our therapeutic rationalizations.‡

In *Psychiatric Justice* I have addressed one of psychiatry's most characteristic and most important social practices—namely, the setting aside of the criminal trial and its replacement with psychiatric methods of punishing persons accused of crimes. Why do I consider this to be an especially important issue? Because I value individual liberty and believe that a fair trial, conducted in public, is one

---

* Alex de Jonge, *The Life and Times of Grigorii Rasputin* (New York: Coward, McCann and Geoghegan, 1982), p. 238.

† See, for example, Karl A. Wittfogel, *Oriental Despotism: A Comparative Study of Total Power* (New Haven: Yale University Press 1957), and Tibor Szamuely, *The Russian Tradition*, ed. Robert Conquest (New York: McGraw-Hill, 1974).

‡ See, generally, Thomas S. Szasz, *Insanity: The Idea and Its Consequences* (New York: Wiley, 1987), especially chapters 9, 10, and 11.

of our most powerful safeguards against political tyranny, regardless of the tyrant's motives—to enslave and exploit his victims or protect and treat them.

There are, of course, many methods for determining guilt and punishing lawbreaking other than the criminal trial as practiced in contemporary English and American courts. Indeed, figuratively speaking, the phenomenon of rule-following/rule-breaking begins at the simplest, impersonal-organismic level—namely, the transgression of biological rules and its consequences: to survive as *organisms*, we must eat and drink what is nutritious or at least safe, and avoid eating and drinking what is non-nutritious or poisonous. On a higher, interpersonal level, we observe or violate social rules: to survive as *persons*, we must obey certain rules or be punished for disobeying them. The important difference between these two phenomena is that the deleterious consequences of violating biological rules are automatic—that is, they do not require the intervention of human agents; whereas the deleterious consequences of violating social rules are not automatic, but require the intervention of human agents. Furthermore, because the crux of social life is obeying and disobeying rules, all of us, at all times, are both potential rule followers and rule breakers. As modern sociologists have noted, in an important sense it is only the violation of rules and their punishment that define what the rules *really* are. This raises two simple but all-important questions: How do we know or ascertain that a rule has been broken? And, having ascertained it, by whom and by what means is the rule breaker punished? A brief glance at history gives us all the answers we need for our present purposes.

In the Judeo-Christian world view, history begins with a crime and a punishment. The Fall was the crime, and our life-and-death its punishment. To be sure, Adam and Eve never received a trial—much less a fair one. There was no need for it: God, the Perfect Autocrat, knew when they were good and when they were bad. Accordingly, God needed no one else and nothing else to mete out justice: His perception, judgment, and punishment—all of which were just, by definition—were enough. When monarchs ruled by divine decree, emperors, kings, czars decided, in a similarly autocratic-despotic style, who was to be punished and how—and the punishment was always, by definition, just.

But unlike gods, human beings are not omniscient. It long ago occurred to them that a person might be accused falsely and punished unjustly. To determine whether rule violation has, in fact, occurred, more than accusation is needed; the accusation must be true. To punish justly, more than superior power is needed: the punishment must be fair and fitting. Out of such sentiments arose various mechanisms for adjudicating offenses, among them our Anglo-American concept of due process.

In one form or another, trial is an ancient and virtually universal institution. Let us remember in this connection that Socrates and Jesus, Servetus and Galileo, witches and heretics, even Stalin's alleged enemies were all tried. To be sure, by our standards, these trials were not fair. But they were, morally and politically, better than no trial at all—better than people being massacred in the middle of the night by unknown executioners; better than people disappearing, without a trace, into concentration camps or the Gulag; better than people being dispatched, with a mockery of due process, to prisons called mental hospitals.

To appreciate what is bad, from a libertarian point of view, about despotic law enforcement, whether of the Oriental or psychiatric kind, we must be clear about what is good about the modern Anglo-American idea of a fair trial. As I see it, nearly all that is bad about the former and good about the latter can be put in one word for each

—namely, *unilateral* and *adversary*. When God punishes the Israelites in the Bible, He weighs the evidence, He decides, He metes out the penalty—and that's that. And so it has been through the ages. Against this religious-despotic-paternalistic-therapeutic model of administering justice, there stands—often assailed, frequently feeble, but always beloved by the accused and all who treasure personal liberty and responsibility—the adversarial model. Although not as old as the despotic method, the adversarial procedure is also of ancient origin.

However, the history of social controls does not concern us here. What does concern us is that the modern Anglo-American concept of a fair trial can be reduced to three basic elements, namely: prosecution, defense, and judge/jury. In effect, the trial is a contest: the contestants—prosecutor and defense attorney—engage in an argument or debate whose outcome they themselves cannot decide; the decision-maker or umpire (judge/jury) cannot join the contest but must, instead, conduct it according to certain rules and must decide who wins and who loses (or whether the contest is a draw).

As a people, we could decide that we do not like this system of adjudicating criminal responsibility; that we no longer believe that some persons charged with crimes are guilty and others innocent; and that those not proved guilty are entitled to remain free and unmolested by the government. But we cannot, it seems to me, continue to regard more and more lawbreakers as not-bad-but-mad and hope to preserve our hard-won political liberties.

In the East, where the right to property was never a fundamental value, the right to personal liberty never developed. In the West, where the two rights developed in tandem, both rights remain fragile and endangered—by Communist subversion and aggression from without and, perhaps more importantly, by psychiatric-therapeutic erosion from within. This erosion, beginning at about the time of the French Revolution, gathered momentum all through the twentieth century, reaching a critical level today. Now, in our typical psychiatrized non-trial, the prosecution does not prosecute, the defense does not defend, and the judge does not preside over a trial; instead, all three parties join in pretending to protect the defendant while, in fact, they are destroying him. The result is a regression to an ancient, religio-despotic criminal procedure where the guilt of the defendant was assumed from the outset and the "trial" was merely the ceremonial purging of evil from the community. This turning away from the heavy existential demands of the adversarial criminal trial is evident already in many nineteenth-century insanity trials, including the classic so-called trial of Daniel McNaughton. I say so-called because, as I intend to show, McNaughton was never *really* tried: his trial was a charade, a mere formality.

The facts of the case are briefly as follows. On January 20, 1843, Daniel McNaughton shot and killed Edward Drummond, Sir Robert Peel's private secretary. Believing himself victimized by the Tories, McNaughton wanted to shoot Peel but mistook Drummond for the Home Secretary. For reasons that need not concern us here—but principally because of the mounting aversion against the death penalty in Victorian England—counsels for both defense and prosecution, as well as the judges, all agreed that McNaughton was insane and should not be found guilty.*

The proceedings against McNaughton began on February 2, 1843, when he was asked to plead: "How say you, prisoner, are you guilty or not guilty?" After a pause, McNaughton answered: "I am guilty of firing." Lord Abinger (Lord Chief Justice of England) then asked: "By

---

* *The Queen Against Daniel McNaughton*, 1843, Central Criminal Court, Old Bailey, in Donald J. West and Alexander Walk, eds., *Daniel McNaughton: His Trial and the Aftermath* (London: Gaskell, 1977), pp. 12–73.

that, do you mean to say you are not guilty of the remainder of the charge; that is, of intending to murder Mr. Drummond?" "Yes," replied McNaughton.* Lord Abinger did not ask whether McNaughton intended to murder Sir Robert Peel; instead, a plea of "not guilty" was entered on his behalf. A fairly lengthy trial ensued at which much lay testimony was given in support of the interpretation that McNaughton knew perfectly well what he was doing, that he intended to kill Peel, but merely shot the wrong man. For example, Benjamin Weston, an "office porter" who happened to be on the scene, testified that "The prisoner drew the pistol very deliberately, but at the same time very quickly. As far as I can judge, it was a very cool, deliberate act."† Others, among them a surgeon named James Douglas, testified similarly.

I am a surgeon, residing at Glasgow. I am in the habit of giving lectures on anatomy. I recognise the prisoner as having been a student of mine last summer. I had the opportunities of speaking to him almost every day; I merely spoke to him on the subject of anatomy. He seemed to understand it. . . . I never observed anything to lead me to suppose his mind was disordered.‡

Nine "medical gentlemen" led by Dr. E. T. Monro, one of the most prominent alienists of the day, then testified, "all emphasizing that his delusions of persecution meant that 'his moral liberty was destroyed.' The Crown presented no medical evidence to rebut this, even though McNaughton had obtained firearms, had watched his victim for several days, and had waited till his victim's back was turned."§ At the conclusion of all the testimony, the

* *Ibid.*, pp. 12–13.
† *Ibid.*, p. 22.
‡ *Ibid.*, p. 29.
§ Roger Smith, *Trial by Medicine: Insanity and Responsibility in Victorian Trials* (Edinburgh: Edinburgh University Press, 1981), p. 103.

chief prosecutor addressed the jury and asked it to find the defendant not guilty by reason of insanity:

SOLICITOR GENERAL: Gentlemen of the jury, after the intimation I have received from the Bench I feel that I should not be properly discharging my duties to the Crown and to the public if I asked you to give your verdict in this case *against* the prisoner. . . . This unfortunate man, at the time he committed the act was labouring under insanity; and, of course, if he were so, he would be entitled to his acquittal (emphasis added).*

I emphasize the word *against* to indicate that the prosecutor considered the decision to execute McNaughton as being against him, and the decision to imprison him for life as being *not against* him. But McNaughton never asked for this. Clearly, it was the lawyers and judges, not McNaughton, who were disturbed by the prospect of his being put to death. And so, in the end, the chief judge, C. J. Tindal, instructed the jury to bring in a verdict of not guilty by reason of insanity, leading to this colloquy:

TINDAL, C. J.: . . . If you think you ought to hear the evidence more fully, in that case I will state it to you, and leave the case in your hands. Probably, however, sufficient [evidence] has now been laid before you, and you will say whether you want further information.

FOREMAN OF THE JURY: We require no more, my Lord.

TINDALL, C. J.: If you find the prisoner not guilty, say on the ground of insanity, in which case proper care will be taken of him.

FOREMAN: We find the prisoner not guilty, on the grounds of insanity.†

* West and Walk, *Daniel McNaughton*, p. 72.
† *Ibid.*, p. 73.

It is a shameful travesty of justice that, ever since 1843, historians and scholars, psychiatrists and lawyers, have spoken and written about the "McNaughton trial," inasmuch as there never was a McNaughton *trial*. Calling what happened in court to McNaughton a criminal trial—formally designating it as "The Queen Against Daniel McNaughton"—is an Orwellian untruth. The Queen did not proceed *against* McNaughton, she proceeded *for* him, so that, as the judge himself phrased it, "proper care will be taken of him."

Actually, English and American law is familiar with circumstances where judicial authorities do not seek to prosecute and punish a person but, on the contrary, endeavor to protect him (from himself and those who might take advantage of his helplessness). Called an *ex parte* proceeding, such an action is defined as follows:

On one side only; . . . done for, in behalf of, on the application of, one party only. . . . A judicial proceeding, order, injunction, etc. is said to be *ex parte* when it is taken for granted at the instance and for the benefit of one party only, and without notice to, or contestation by, any person adversely interested.*

This is exactly how McNaughton was treated: The judicial authorities did not solicit his consent for treating him as a madman who, like a helpless child, cannot care for himself. Instead, assuming the duties of *parens patriae*, counsels for both the prosecution and the defense as well as the judges all relinquished their customary roles and assumed instead the duties of guardianship. The legal proceeding responsible for McNaughton's fate after 1843 should have been called *Ex parte the Queen, in the matter of the mad Daniel McNaughton*. Ironically, Queen Victoria, like

* Henry C. Black, *Black's Law Dictionary* (St. Paul, Minn.: West, 1968), pp. 661–62.

Daniel McNaughton, was a party to this proceeding in name only. Actually, she was very angry with the conduct of the trial, maintaining that it is absurd to suggest that a British subject who deliberately sets out to assassinate one of her ministers is not guilty of a crime. Her displeasure with the (non)trial generated the historic hearing before the House of Lords that led to the adoption of what we now call "the McNaughton rule."

Did McNaughton's self-appointed guardians help their ward? Yes, if we equate helping McNaughton with saving him from the gallows, whether or not he wanted to be saved. No, if we believe there are fates worse than death. *De jure*, McNaughton was treated as if he had been insane when he shot Drummond. *De facto*, he was treated as if he had been, was, and would always remain insane. McNaughton was confined as a madman for the remaining twenty-one years of his life, dying in Broadmoor in 1864.

By the time McNaughton came to trial, this method of disposing of capital cases was not at all unusual. "In practice," comments Roger Smith in his definitive study of Victorian insanity trials, "a warrant of removal to a criminal asylum usually meant a permanent removal. It was extremely difficult to attribute 'recovery' to someone who had shown potential for violence."* It was, indeed, because there was no desire ever to set malefactors free. Everyone, including the alienists, knew perfectly well that imprisonment for life in an insane asylum without the possibility of parole was a terrible punishment. For example, Dr. Forbes Winslow, a leading Victorian alienist and the proprietor of two private insane asylums, actually promoted the insanity defense by touting the terrors of psychiatric confinement:

To talk of a person escaping the extreme penalty of the law on the plea of Insanity, as one being subjected to no kind or

* Roger Smith, *Trial by Medicine*, p. 23.

degree of *punishment*, is a perfect mockery of truth and perversion of language. Suffer no punishment! He is exposed to the severest pain and torture of body and mind that can be inflicted upon a human creature short of being publicly strangled upon the gallows. If the fact be doubted, let a visit be paid to that dreadful *den* at Bethlehem Hospital . . . where the criminal portion of the establishment are confined like wild beasts in an iron cage!*

Thus, already in 1858 psychiatrists had hit upon this clever formula for advertising the asylum: for the non-criminal, the insane asylum is a *hospital*—the ideal place for treating mental illness; for the criminal ("where the criminal portion of the establishment are confined"), the asylum is a *prison*—the ideal place for storing "wild beasts," secure equally from escape by the hard-hearted criminal and release by the soft-hearted judge. Psychiatrists still use the same tactic to promote and justify involuntary mental hospitalization.

Surveying the fate of insanity acquittees serving life sentences in insane asylums, Smith wryly observes that "medical superintendents accepted their custodial role."† That, I think, is putting it mildly. Actually, "medical men" in Victorian England vied for the privilege of being the executioners of such brutal punishments, and ever since psychiatrists throughout the world have eagerly emulated them. These sobering facts alone should suffice to lay to rest, once and for all, the absurd canard that psychiatric institutions are hospitals, not prisons; that institutional psychiatrists dispense treatments, not tortures; and that the inmates of mental institutions are patients, not prisoners.

Let me now return to the slightly different subject of *Psychiatric Justice*—namely, unfitness to stand trial be-

* *Ibid.*, p. 31.
† *Ibid.*, p. 23.

cause of mental illness. From the legal point of view, insanity at the time of the crime is not the same as insanity at the time of trial: the former renders the accused not guilty by reason of insanity; the latter renders him (temporarily, in theory) unfit to stand trial. In either case, the result is about the same—the authorities denying an accused person a trial, or at least a speedy trial, without the participation or agreement of the defendant; and incarcerating him, as insane, in a psychiatric institution.

What has happened with respect to the particular procedure—the pretrial psychiatric diagnosis and disposition of defendants—described in this book since its publication in 1965? *De jure*, a good deal; *de facto*, very little. This is not the place for a review of the voluminous legal and psychiatric literature on incompetence to stand trial. A brief summary of one landmark case, and a few additional remarks, should suffice.

In May 1968, Theon Jackson, a twenty-seven-year-old mentally defective deaf-mute, was arrested for snatching the handbags of two women. The total value of his loot was nine dollars. Brought before an Indiana court, the judge ordered Jackson to submit to a pretrial psychiatric examination. Jackson was examined by two state-appointed psychiatrists, who diagnosed him as mentally unfit to stand trial. The trial court thereupon committed Jackson to the care of the Indiana Department of Mental Health until such time as he could be certified as fit to stand trial. The facility in which Jackson was confined had no staff person who knew sign language, and there was not even so much as a bureaucratic pretense at "treating" him or doing anything else to render him mentally competent to stand trial. Jackson's lawyer filed a motion for a new trial, which was denied. The State Supreme Court affirmed the denial, whereupon the case was appealed to the U.S. Supreme Court, which agreed to hear the case and rendered a decision on June 7, 1972.

Because the Court ruled against Indiana's indefinite quasi-criminal commitment statute, *Jackson v. Indiana* is, in legal circles, considered a very important case. In fact, however, the petition on behalf of Jackson, as well as the Court's ruling, were based on extremely narrow criteria. Concerning the former, the record states that,

Petitioner's counsel . . . contend[ed] that his commitment was tantamount to a "life sentence" without his having been convicted of a crime . . . absent the criminal charges against him, the State would have had to proceed under other statutory procedures for the feeble-minded or those for the mentally ill . . .*

In summary, the Court decided that Indiana's indefinite commitment of a criminal defendant solely on account of his incapacity to stand trial violates due process. Such a defendant cannot be held more than the reasonable period of time necessary to determine whether there is a substantial probability that he will attain competency in the foreseeable future. If it is determined that he will not, the state must either institute civil proceedings applicable to indefinite commitment of those not charged with crime, or release the defendant.† In effect, the Court ruled that persons accused of crimes deemed unfit to stand trial ought to be committed "civilly" rather than "criminally." In practice, the decision has meant that defendants who, before *Jackson*, might have been confined indefinitely as mentally unfit to stand trial, would, after *Jackson*, be confined indefinitely following "acquittal" by reason of insanity. (The poet Ezra Pound was incarcerated from 1946 to 1958 in St. Elizabeths Hospital, in Washington, D.C., as psychiatrically unfit to stand trial;‡ John W. Hinckley,

---

* *Jackson v. Indiana*, 406 U.S. 715 (1972), p. 715.

† *Ibid.*, p. 716.

‡ See, Thomas S. Szasz, *Law, Liberty, and Psychiatry: An Inquiry into the Social Uses of Mental Health Practices* (New York: Macmillan, 1963), pp. 199–211; and, "The Martyrdom of Ezra Pound," in Thomas S. Szasz,

Jr., who attempted to assassinate President Ronald Reagan in 1981, is incarcerated in the same psychiatric prison after having been acquitted as not guilty by reason of insanity.*)

Writing for a unanimous Court in *Jackson v. Indiana*, Justice Blackmun offered a revealing comment on the broader issue of involuntary mental hospitalization: "The States have traditionally exercised broad power to commit persons found to be mentally ill. Considering the number of cases affected, it is perhaps remarkable that the substantive constitutional limitations on this power have not been more frequently litigated."† And, in a footnote to this passage, he added:

In 1961, it was estimated that 90% of the approximately 800,000 patients in mental hospitals in this country had been involuntarily committed. . . . Although later U.S. Census Bureau data for 1969 shows a resident patient population almost 50% lower, other data from U.S. Department of Health, Education, and Welfare estimate annual admissions to institutions to be almost equal to the patient population at any one time, about 380,000 persons per annum.‡

As I write this, the total number of patients in mental hospitals is somewhat smaller still, but the significance of psychiatric power to commit is not a whit less. Moreover, popular opinion—that is the sentiment prevailing among lawyers, psychiatrists, journalists, and the general public—is swinging back toward reembracing prolonged, even permanent, involuntary psychiatric incarceration as the

*The Therapeutic State: Psychiatry in the Mirror of Current Events* (Buffalo: Prometheus Books, 1984), pp. 158–65.

* See Thomas S. Szasz, "Reagan's Diagnosing Hinckley," "The Case of John Hinckley," and "On Hinckley's 'Innocence by Insanity,'" in *The Therapeutic State*, pp. 147–56; and Thomas S. Szasz, *Insanity*, 255–71.

† West and Walk, *Daniel McNaughton*, p. 737.

‡ *Ibid.*

proper remedy for social ills—especially homelessness and crime.*

The criminals "saved" by psychiatry in the nineteenth century stayed incarcerated until they died, sometimes for as long as forty-three years. John W. Hinckley, Jr., currently the most famous American insanity acquittee, has already spent more than seven years in confinement, and his "cure" does not seem imminent. Compare this with what happens to *convicted criminals*: "Those released from prison [in the 1980s] for murder and nonnegligent manslaughter served a median of 78 months in confinement."†
Thus, with capital punishment virtually abolished and prison-time served for murder shorter than ever, "psychiatric justice" is now even more punitive and more unjust than it was in the nineteenth century.

The particular psychiatric practice I examined and criticized in this book—namely, the pretrial psychiatric examination of defendants, the legal-medical judgment that they are mentally unfit to stand trial, and their subsequent psychiatric incarceration—hinges on, and is an integral part of, the psychiatrist's power to "hospitalize" persons against their will. Psychiatrists have always had, and continue to have, a veritable love affair with practicing coercion, which they equate with and then peddle as compassion; reciprocally, legislators, lawyers, and lay persons have had a love affair with submission to psychiatric coercion, which they equate with and then peddle as care. So long as this mutuality prevails, so long as virtually everyone believes that psychiatrists are entitled to exercise

* See, for example, E. Fuller Torrey, "Homelessness and Mental Illness," *USA Today*, March 1988, pp. 26–27.
† Stephanie Minor-Harper and Christopher A. Innes, "Time served in prison and on parole, 1984." Bureau of Justice Statistics Special Report, December 1987 (Washington, D.C.: U.S. Bureau of Justice), pp. 1–12.

power over persons labeled "mental patients," psychiatrists will gladly exercise such power and people will gullibly submit to it. Accordingly, it is both naive and foolish, albeit no doubt self-satisfying, for politicians, physicians, and the press to indulge in periodic outbursts of indignation at psychiatric "abuses."* It is the very legitimacy of the psychiatrist's power—his moral and legal right to intimidate, much less coerce or imprison—that requires our scrutiny—and, in my opinion, our condemnation and rejection.

THOMAS SZASZ

Syracuse, New York
June 1988

* See, for example, "Notes and news: Human rights abuse in mental hospitals," *The Lancet*, April 23, 1988, pp. 953–54.